Patterns of Vengeance:
Crosscultural Homicide in the
North American Fur Trade

Patterns of Vengeance

CROSSCULTURAL HOMICIDE IN THE NORTH AMERICAN FUR TRADE

John Phillip Reid

Ninth Judicial Circuit Historical Society

Library of Congress Cataloging-in-Publication Data

Reid, John Phillip

Patterns of vengeance : crosscultural homicide in the North American fur trade / John Phillip Reid.

p. cm.

Includes bibliographical references and index.

ISBN 0-9635086-1-X (alk. paper)

1. Fur trade—Social aspects—Northwest, Pacific—History—19th century. 2. Northwest, Pacific—Ethnic relations. 3. Hudson's Bay Company—History—19th century. 4. Homicide—Northwest, Pacific—History—19th century. 5. Revenge—History—19th century. 6. Indians of North America—Legal status, laws, etc.—Northwest, Pacific—History—19th century. 7. Indians of North America—Northwest, Pacific—Government relations. 8. British—Northwest, Pacific—History—19th century. I. Title.

F880.R45 1999
975.5'03—dc21

99-052258

For the memory of
Samuel I. Golieb

and the Samuel I. Golieb Fellows
New York University School of Law

Laura Kalman
John Wertheimer
Amy B. Stanley
George Chauncey, Jr.
Sarah Harrison
Joseph Biancalana
Judith Gilbert
David Langum
Reva Siegel
William Cuddihy
Sybil Lipschultz
John Hughes
Felicia Kornbluh
I. Scott Messinger
Liam O'Melinn
James Baird
Louis Anthes
J. R. Pole
Mark Weiner
Laura Benton
Daniel J. Hulsebosch

Thomas C. Mackey
Cornelia Dayton
William Forbath
Julia Rudolph
Reuel E. Schiller
Annette Igra
Barry Cushman
Susanna Blumenthal
Philip Uninsky
Victoria List
James A. Wooten
Catherine McCauliff
Harvey Rishikoff
Michael Millender
Carl J. Meyer
Charles F. Pazdernik
Steven Wilf
Paul Brand
David Meerse
Dalia Tsuk
Matthew C. Mirow

Contents

Foreword

MOST HISTORIANS THINK of western legal history in terms of the law as it pertains to water, land, mining, or the environment. This is often the law of cases, trials, litigants, legislation, and advocacy. John Phillip Reid's current study is different. He is not concerned with who was right or wrong or just or unjust, or cases and trials in the traditional sense. He is more concerned with how peoples behaved toward each other, how they settled disputes over homicides, and how they understood or misunderstood each other's legal practices. He is concerned with both the patterns and the norms of behavior.

He examines how Indian ideas, words, theories, and behavior relating to vengeance for homicide were borrowed, integrated, and even assimilated, consciously or unconsciously, by whites, who adapted, accommodated, used, and misused them. Thus he offers historians of the frontier an unusual opportunity not only to further their knowledge of Indian-white relations, but also to see how looking at a particular issue—vengeance for homicide—through the eyes of a legal historian can revise their thinking.

Reid is not interested here in the traditional, chronological historical narrative, although his knowledge of the narrative is obvious and his familiarity with the sources impressive, and many of the incidents he discusses are well known to specialists. Instead, his approach is topical and analytical. He demonstrates that, if Indian and white ideas, language, and behaviors are properly juxtaposed, the results add greater subtlety to the traditional frontier narrative. This is not forensic history. If he is making a case for anything, it is that frontier historians have frequently oversimplified, if not distorted, a complex idea when they have used the word "vengeance."

Readers should not be perplexed by Reid's methodology in his discussions of vengeance. Many of the Native Americans he deals with lived in small groups, and it is possible to extrapolate only from their behavior and by analogy with similar groups—some of them much larger and geographically separate—what their values were and what their words meant. Different societies—whether matrilineal, patrilineal, or bilineal—often attached different meanings to the same word, frequently contributing to confusion among whites. Reid explains what the written sources do not expressly disclose. His explication of a specific Indian group's values and legal system centers on the behavior of that group, on others like it for whom suitable evidence exists, and on the power of logical inference on which all historians depend.

Nor should readers be perplexed because Reid, ignoring a chronological narrative, utilizes some materials from the colonial Southern frontier while writing a virtual case study of homicide and vengeance among the trappers, traders, and mountain men—both British and American—of the Far Northwest. He reviews the actions and words of the leaders of the great fur companies in confronting Native Americans on the questions of homicide, vengeance, and satisfaction. These are words that had quite different meanings for white and Indian groups, both within each society and between them. For example, as he points out, colonial governors could be wholly confused by the limitations of the power of Indian headmen who could not deliver up or punish manslayers and yet could negotiate for material satisfaction on behalf of their groups for homicides committed by whites. Moreover, a fur company's Indian policy, such as that of the Hudson's Bay Company, hinged on viewing every Indian manslayer as an individual to be punished before there could be peace, while Native Americans thought of white manslayers not necessarily as individuals to be punished, but often as members of a group that had committed an injury (a tort?) for which only satisfaction in property or blood would brighten the path to peace between two groups. As Reid makes clear, not all homicides are murder in white society and in certain circumstances there are no penalties. Native American societies differed, and there was always a need to provide satisfaction to cover the eyes of the deceased. Moreover, the question of who had the "legitimate" authority to punish or to take vengeance against a manslayer was equally important in both societies. Otherwise, in Native American society blood vengeance may be seen as a separate act of manslaying and one calling for retribution.

Reid's work is, in part, a renewed plea for scholars to realize that the application of white words for Indian actions—vengeance, for example—without careful thought to the context in which they are used is at best imprecise and at worst a distortion of events. As such, it is an inadequate descriptive term with which to explicate Indian and white patterns of behavior regarding homicides.

Each of Reid's chapters is an analysis of a particular aspect of vengeance resulting from a homicide or a case study of the circumstances involving its application. Vengeance took many different forms in white and Indian societies. The restatement of facts, incidents, and policies in several chapters is neither redundancy nor emphasis, but part of Reid's nuanced depiction—or a more exact legal reading—of a specific aspect of manslaying and how vengeance was construed by the peoples involved.

In his first chapter, Reid establishes a benchmark for vengeance by what he calls "payback vengeance," which is simply undifferentiated revenge—capricious, unstructured, and unprincipled, unlike the examples of vengeance in the chapters that follow. In the second of these, "Vagaries of Vengeance," he deals with the difficulties of the application of crosscultural norms of jurisprudence in cases of homicide. Examples indicate that the patterns varied between whites and Native Americans as well as within the groups themselves. For example, whites were mystified, but had to be satisfied—that is, to accept an Indian practice—when a Chickasaw male committed suicide in the place of his nephew, who had killed an Englishman. The English wanted the actual culprit punished, but for the Chickasaw, blood was required for blood spilled, and the uncle's blood was enough. This made sense in the Chickasaw matrilineal clan system. Indians with a patrilineal clan system would have been confused by the act, but for reasons quite different from those of the whites.

In chapter 3, "Crosscultural Vengeance," Reid explains that the quest for mutual understanding in a crosscultural world proved impossible for generations in part because the British doubted that Indians even had laws: "Therefore when they encountered Indian legal ways they did not always recognize them as law or, when applying Indian law, they did not realize that they did so. Conduct they condemned when practiced by Indians they themselves might adopt, without giving its legality or its morality a second thought." Governor James Glen of South Carolina, for example, blended British and

Indian law when he was willing to accept blood for blood as material satisfaction from the Creeks as the punishment of Creek manslayers of Cherokees, something quite traditional with the Indians, but wholly unacceptable in English or Scottish law.

Reid continues his delineation of kinds of vengeance in chapter 4, "Principled Vengeance," with an example from English fur traders, in which the punishment for homicide had other purposes than rude payback vengeance. The fur traders' response to manslaying was often associated with other social purposes, ranging from making the Indians more respectful of whites or demonstrating white military power. For Reid, the use of the word "principled" in this context may destigmatize vengeance, but he finds precision especially valuable in explaining why fur traders pursued certain policies that went beyond English or Scottish law.

In chapter 5, "Causation of Vengeance," Reid examines the causation of vengeance between whites and Indians and often among Indians themselves. Common-law concepts like personal responsibility, accident, self-defense, intent, or malice were usually unimportant to Indians, although there were exceptions; what counted was liability and cause. For Indians, and often for whites, liability was fixed not on an individual but collectively on the family, town, clan, band, or nation of the manslayer. Reid makes clear that, although fur men had a wide view of causation, it did not extend to Indians in general. Vengeance required a focus within a structure. Indians, however, were hard pressed to differentiate between English and Americans, and some Indians held the view that collective causation rested with any white. These distinctions are important because they explain why the fur men more than the Indians, except when they dealt with other Native Americans, employed targeted rather than indiscriminate vengeance.

Chapter 6, "Mechanics of Vengeance," explains the differences between whites, who easily adopted a culture of vengeance as personal revenge outside the law, and Indians, who viewed vengeance for homicide as part of a legal process. For whites, "Kill my dog; I will kill yours." For Indians, the responsibility for assuming the task of securing vengeance for homicide depended on many factors. It could be a different family member, depending on a matrilineal or patrilineal group or a band or even a nation. Moveover, homicide in domestic violence—that is, manslaying within a group—required different responses. The issues were not as complex among whites; the Hudson's Bay Company officers sometimes felt little responsibility to respond to a homicide unless it touched their personnel. The mechanisms by which vengeance was applied go a long way in explaining aspects of western history that appear to be unique in the historical narrative.

Reid continues this discussion in chapter 7, "Compensation Vengeance," by taking up such questions as who was entitled to take vengeance for a homicide, whether vengeance was to be taken at all, and, if blood vengeance was not sought, who would determine the proper payment compensation to the victim's family or group. He examines the circumstances that provided legitimacy to the avenger and those conditions in which, for a variety of reasons, blood vengeance was not taken. These ranged from avoiding a blood feud within a small group that could ill afford to lose men to preventing wars between whole nations. As he points out, allies needed each other and tried to resolve homicides without additional bloodshed. Some groups developed cultures in which blood vengeance deviated from the social norm. In some instances, when blood vengeance occurred, the avenger was privileged—that is, no action was taken against him. The fur men, Reid concludes, may never have really understood the theory of payment compensation for manslaying, but they effectively manipulated it to their own advantage. They were culturally predisposed to reject payment in lieu of vengeance for the death of their people, but when an Indian was killed by a white they were perfectly willing to give satisfaction for vengeance, if Indians sought it, to escape blood vengeance. Payment compensation for manslaying may have been an almost universal practice among Native Americans, but Reid argues that without understanding such key questions as why it was accepted, who fixed the compensation, and how it was used, the historian may well misread the past.

Chapter 8, "Company Vengeance," is a case study that successfully challenges the assertions of Frederick Merk and many Canadian historians that the British fur men created a West for Indians that was peaceable, orderly, and governed by law, while the Americans were brutal, lawless, and genocidal. Looking beyond the parliamentary acts of 1803 and 1821, which were never applied to native peoples, Reid finds that the Hudson's Bay Company's policy was to rule the Indians with a rod of iron. The company functioned with almost sovereign power, and "company law," not common law, was the prevalent rule. Not only was the policy blood for blood—virtual payback vengeance—but also in some instances the decision to execute was summary. Rarely did company officers in London question such actions, even when the execution was based on the decision of a single official. Company men took blood vengeance for homicides as well as for the theft of horses or other company property. Perhaps Reid's most telling indictment of the company is in his use of the correspondence of Dr. John McLoughlin, its chief factor on the Columbia, which discloses his willingness to kill off an entire nation if it did not kill a manslayer. In a sense, chapter 9, "Efficiency of Vengeance," continues the discussion, but emphasizes that the issue is not the brutality or cruelty of the Hudson's Bay Company's treatment of the Indians as contrasted with Americans or how it treated its own servants, but, rather, the certainty of the company's application of vengeance and its efficiency.

Chapter 10, "Restraining Vengeance," and Chapter 11, "Controlling Vengeance," are essentially two case studies. The first, demonstrating how vengeance could be restrained, analyzes an episode in which the North West Fur Company was called upon to respond to an attack on one of its brigades in which two hostile Indian chiefs were killed and the brigade lost all of its supplies but suffered no fatalities. Examining the advice given to the retaliatory party by other Indians, the arguments of the Indians who attacked the brigade, and the decision reached by the company officer, Reid shows how he reflected on Indian intergroup animosity, Indians' legal logic, company economic considerations, and why payment compensation rather than blood vengeance proved the best solution. In the second case study, the attack on Jedediah Strong Smith's party in Oregon, Reid demonstrates how vengeance was controlled. Although homicides were involved, he finds that British fur-trade officials had so assimilated Indian legal practice that they could justify the retrieving of converted property rather than a blood-for-blood solution. They provided a rationale for homicides that would have been totally unacceptable in English or Scottish law at the time. Both chapters indicate the complexities the British fur companies faced in dealing with Native Americans when their goals were profit and long-term safety, not warfare, although they did not shrink from risks—even if it meant hanging Indians whose kin might seek blood vengeance.

In chapter 12, "Theory of Vengeance," Reid asks why did the whites take vengeance, how did they explain their actions, what did they think they were doing, and why did they think they had little choice. The answers to these questions indicate not only how far the fur men, both British and American, had deviated from the Anglo-American tradition of the law but also how much of Indian practice they seem to have assimilated as well as misunderstood or ignored.

Reid's examination of vengeance is not a treatise with a closed end. He admits that he has looked closely only at the white side of a double-edged experience. He concedes, too, that with the limitations of evidence there is much that may remain shrouded in the past, much that historians may never be able to learn. Historians should be wary of reading into the past the current social climate regarding violence, revenge, and vengeance. In a way, Reid has opened a Pandora's box regarding the British and American responses to Native American homicide. In the end, he asks his readers to ponder the following question: Whose world, the Native American's or the white's, was based on a morality of vengeance?

Martin Ridge

Preface

THIS IS A STUDY of issues, not a history of events. It asks why things happened, not what happened or what were the consequences. It is concerned with a single, particular, and very unusual action, retaliation for homicide committed in a crosscultural environment. *Patterns* of vengeance are studied, not the "historical" question of how vengeance for homicide evolved from its imposition by the first fur trappers or Hudson's Bay Company's traders, acting in a legal wilderness, to the implementation of state-imposed law. The objective is to study principles of law as they were applied at a particular stage in multicultural history.

There are aspects of legal-history methodology that should be kept distinct. One is the difference between legal history and forensic history. Professional historians sometimes confuse forensic history with the lawyers' technique of finding answers through analogy or precedent. Forensic history, also called "law-office history" or "lawyers' history," is the use of isolated evidence from the past to argue a case either before an appellate court, an administrative board, or a legislative committee. It consists of rummaging through history and picking out bits and pieces to sustain an argument about current law. It is good law or, at least, good advocacy, but it is not history. Contrary evidence is ignored; only supporting material is used. There is no effort to reconstruct the past, or to make an impartial evaluation of how things happened or why developments progressed as they did.

Quite different is the legal-history methodology of examining historical analogies to discover how principles and rules of law might be applied in fact situations. Although exploration by analogy has been a standard practice among anthropologists studying the western Indian nations,[1] it seems less familiar to historians of the transboundary North American West, and may be misunderstood much as forensic history has been misunderstood.

The author of this book employed the technique of analogy in an earlier work, *A Better Kind of Hatchet*. He was faced with the question of whether eighteenth-century British officials in North America, by employing English concepts, misunderstood and incorrectly described family relationships among Indians of the South. The Creek and Cherokee peoples, for example, had a law of maternal clan relationships in which both men and women belonged to the clan of their mother and were not related, or legally close, to members of their fathers' clans. The British did not understand this arrangement, and when they encountered the avuncular relationship of maternal uncles as teachers, guardians, avengers of blood, and closest kin to their sisters' sons, they assumed that uncles and nephews were fathers and sons, and called them that. There was no evidence from Cherokee material of familial relationship between individual Cherokees, and so the author turned to the more fully documented Creek evidence, not to prove something about either Cherokee law or Cherokee history, but to illustrate matrilineal-clan relationships.

The Creek headman, Malatchi, was known to the British as "Brims' Son" because the British believed him to have been the son of "Emperor" Brims, headman of the Lower Creek town of Coweta during the 1710s. They assumed he was Brims's son because he was close to Brims, much as a son was to a father in European society, and because he "succeeded" to Brims's position of influence among the Creeks. But Brims and Malatchi were both members of the Wind clan of the Creek nation, a fact that has been accepted even by historians who say they were father and son. If Malatchi had been Brims's offspring he could not have belonged to the same clan as Brims. Since Malatchi was a Wind, under the rules of the Creeks'

1. For example, the use of evidence concerning the Iroquois during the 1680s to illustrate the effects of terrain, as well as the choice of weapons on military tactics among the Sioux. Secoy, *Changing Military Patterns*, pp. 68-69. The analogy was considered relevant because "[t]he Post-gun–pre-horse military technique pattern of the Sioux appears to have been essentially the same as that of the tribes of the Northeastern Woodlands area with respect to the size of the fighting force, their arms, means of transportation, and method of battle." *Ibid.*, pp. 67-68.

matrilineal clan system, his mother must also have been a Wind. As a Wind, she would not have borne the child of Brims, who was also a Wind, for by the laws of incest a father and mother had to be members of different clans. It cannot be doubted that, in fact, Malatchi's mother was Brims's sister. This conclusion is substantiated by considering Malatchi's "sister," Mary Bosomworth. Malatchi called her "sister," and the British assumed they were children of the same woman. That was not necessarily the Creek meaning. Mary, in a deposition, boasted that she was "descended by the maternal Line from the Sister of the Old Emperor of the Creek Nation of the same Blood as the present Mico's, or chiefs." The "Old Emperor" was Brims, and by the "present chiefs" she meant Malatchi and a brother of Brims, a man who was Malatchi's uncle and her uncle. That was why Malatchi called her "sister": they were children of sisters, two of Brims's female siblings, and all of them—Brims, his male and female siblings, Malatchi and Mary—belonged to the same clan and were the closest of close clan kin. The purpose of drawing this analogy was to use Creek evidence—evidence of a particularity not available from Cherokee sources—to unravel how the eighteenth-century British had used English kin terms to anamorphose southeastern Indians into their world, imposing their nuclear-family, lineal-descent kin relationships upon the matrilineal clan-kin terms of the southeastern native peoples. The point was not that Creek law can fill gaps in our knowledge of Cherokee law, but that Creek law can fill gaps in our knowledge of the matrilineal clan system and matrilineal clan-kin terms.

The same technique informs this book. Chapter 2 discusses the difficulty of crosscultural applications of principles in a multicultural legal world. For this particular aspect of patterns of vengeance, evidence from the fur trade in the transboundary North American West is sparse. To flesh out the picture so that principles can be clarified, the author has turned to instances of French difficulties with cross-cultural application of law when dealing with the Chippewas, and British difficulties dealing with the southeastern nations. A document from South Carolina, never before published or discussed, is quoted to illustrate misunderstandings encountered by a government in which law was sovereign command when making a demand for blood vengeance upon a nation in which law was custom unenforceable by coercive sanctions. The purpose is not to use the history of the Chippewas or of the Cherokees to learn something about the history of the transboundary western fur country. The purpose is to get a clearer understanding of certain problems of carrying out blood vengeance in a crosscultural situation.

It is not suggested that the world of French Canada or of colonial South Carolina was like that of mid-nineteenth-century Oregon or British New Caledonia. What legal historians do suggest is that when analogies are appropriately strong, similar legal issues can be used to illustrate the law—not the society—in a different epoch or a different jurisdiction. Indeed, if the questions were not about crosscultural application of the principles of vengeance, but about the mechanisms and issues of paying compensation in lieu of vengeance in kind, the analogies most useful for illustrating possible issues of the law of the Chinook, the Clatsop, or the Wasco-Wishram might well be found in the codes of Anglo-Saxon England or of ancient Gaul.

It may be thought farfetched to use Anglo-Saxon codes to illustrate legal principles that may or may not have been applied by the native nations along the Columbia River, but if the purpose is to pose historical issues rather than relate historical narrative, Anglo-Saxon law provides the best material we have for learning what questions to ask about the law of compensation among Columbia River nations. The idea is to raise questions, not to answer them.

Most historians of the customs of the Indians of the Columbia take notice of the fact that all the nations along the river knew of, and accepted, some form of compensation for settling certain liabilities that arose from what they, the historians, call "murder." That word, "murder," delineates the failure of many scholars to consider the issues discussed in this book. Labeling all killings as "murder" is a key reason they have treated all deaths as if of equal culpability, never asking whether the Indians weighed degrees of liability—that is, whether Indians of certain nations distinguished between a deliberate slaying committed with an evil mind, on the one hand, and mitigation of liability on the other, as when the killing was accidental or the homicide was committed in defense of one's own life or family, or death resulted from a misfired hunting weapon or was caused by bad advice, carelessness, or gross negligence. Was it likely that compensation would have been the same for homicide *per infortunium* of a friend while shooting at targets or engaged in ball play as for premeditated killing with malice and intent? In the historical literature of the transboundary North American West, such issues are not even raised, let alone answered.

A related issue is who had the authority to compose a homicide by accepting compensation in lieu of vengeance in kind, and who determined the amount that would be paid. Some of the few studies that mention legal composition in the transboundary Northwest say it was the "chiefs," leaving the impression either that families of victims were not a factor or that the writer did not think of the possibility. Is it likely that the brother of the homicide victim had no role in the decision? That possibility is less likely in the case of a domestic homicide than in the case of international homicide, where public opinion and the general welfare of the nation may have been more determinative. But even this question is not addressed. Few scholars who mention compensation as an instrument of national policy heed the distinction between domestic and international homicide.

This study is concerned with the legal folkways adopted by fur traders and trappers taking vengeance against Indians for homicide. It does not deal with cases of Indians taking vengeance for homicide, either domestically or internationally, whether against other Indians or against fur traders and trappers. The Indian law of homicide cannot be ignored, however, since a main thesis of the book is that the mountain men of the transboundary North American West acted primarily on Indian legal principles rather than applying principles of European or common law. Largely, they followed international law, but domestic law was occasionally a consideration and cannot be overlooked. In the following chapters it will be noted that there are questions that cannot be answered because not enough of the domestic law of the nation being discussed is known. It is not simply that the law of some nations is completely unknown,[2] but that what is known for other nations does not answer the questions that need to be answered if the law of vengeance for homicide is to be understood.

Most of the Indian nations in contact with the fur traders and trappers in the transboundary West were not governed by matrilineal or patrilineal rules of kin relationship and kin obligations. They lived, rather, in bands, families, households, or other groups that were as important to them as were the clans among the Choctaws or Creeks, but were less structured along descent lines and less definitive of kin relationships. What we know about the legal obligations of kinship are at best generalities,[3] not rules for liability or procedures

2. For example, the Kettle Falls Indians: "Information on marriage rules and kin obligations of the Sxoielpi is almost nonexistent from any period, including this century." Chance, *Influences of HBC*, p. 22.

3. For a typical example of a discussion of kinship obligations in the region, *see* Steward, "Shoshonean," pp. 254-56.

for evening the score of homicide. For example, a male member of a nation might take up a lifelong relationship with a female of the nation and, for social or demographic reasons, reside with her band, leaving the neighborhood or band of the household in which he had grown up. What if he spends the remainder of his years with his wife's band? He could become very close to the man we would consider his brother-in-law. Suppose that vengeance was legal and was practiced in that nation. If the brother-in-law were killed, accidentally or otherwise, by a fellow member of the band, would the man have anything to say about whether vengeance should be taken? About whether compensation was acceptable? About the amount? If compensation were paid, would he share in it? What if it were the man himself, not the brother-in-law, who was killed? He had left the band of his youth and had not been in regular contact with his male siblings for years; his closest social ties were with his wife's brother. Would the members of the band, especially his wife's brother, have more to say than his own male siblings about how the homicide was resolved? It seems unlikely that legal duties and legal rights created by marriage and social arrangement could become stronger and take precedence over legal duties and legal rights created by birth, but it is possible. We just do not know the answers to these questions for most of the Indian nations of the fur-trapping area of the transboundary North American West. We do not know because such questions have not interested historians and anthropologists, but until they are answered we will not know all we need to know of the domestic law of homicide.[4]

The fact that we cannot answer every question should not preclude us from looking for patterns of vengeance. One purpose of an issues book, after all, is to raise such questions, so that future historians will seek some answers. At the least, one hopes that historians of the transboundary North American Indians will cease assuming

4. Such questions are not answered, even in those obvious books where we would expect to find answers, *e.g.*, Sidney L. Harring, *Crow Dog's Case: American Indian Sovereignty, Tribal Law, and United States Law in the Nineteenth Century* (New York: Cambridge University Press, 1994); E. Adamson Hoebel, *The Law of Primitive Man: A Study in Comparative Legal Dynamics* (Cambridge: Harvard University Press, 1954); K. N. Llewellyn and E. Adamson Hoebel, *The Cheyenne Way: Conflict and Case Law in Primitive Jurisprudence* (Norman: University of Oklahoma Press, 1941); Jane Richardson, *Law and Status Among the Kiowa Indians*, American Ethnological Society, Monograph no. 1 (New York, 1940).

that the Indian nations had no law. Scholars should no longer say such things as that the Hudson's Bay Company "made use of the only concept of justice the native could understand: the primitive law of revenge," because "[t]o the Indians, legal procedures were incomprehensible,"[5] or argue that "formal legal relations did not really exist among Indians," because "there were no Indian states."[6]

5. Johansen, "McLoughlin and the Indians," p. 18.
6. White, "What Chigabe Knew," p. 155.

Introduction

In reacting to homicides or to attempted homicides perpetrated upon them by a member or members of an Indian nation, fur traders and trappers of the North American West often employed words derived less from English, Scottish, French, or American ways of expressing thought about legal responsibility than from a pan-Indian legal vocabulary. They spoke of "covering the dead," of "drying the tears" with "compensation," of being "owed blood," and of "vengeance." Always and everywhere, they spoke of vengeance.[1]

We must give close heed to Indian ways of speaking, for they are a key to much of what we want to know. At the same time we must be wary of English words, of what is familiar and of what we may too easily assume we understand. Expressions used by the trappers and traders who wrote about their experiences in the western fur trade and—what is much worse—words employed by many recent historians of the North American West may lead us astray. Even the most fastidious of scholars can be careless about the nuances of legal meaning that lie beneath the surface of everyday vocabulary. Consider the best study ever written of the crosscultural conflicts causing friction between native American traditions and European ways of conducting government and business. "Perhaps the most perplexing intercultural concern of the French and Algonquians," the author explains, "was how to settle and limit the num-

1. Admittedly, "covering the dead," or "covering," had several meanings, some of which were unrelated to liability for homicide or compensation in satisfaction of homicide. Grinnell, *Blackfoot Lodge Tales*, pp. 253-54.

ber of murders arising from the trade, where there was no authority in the West capable of creating a monopoly on violence and establishing order." And, on the next page, he continues: "Most murders in the West left no trace in the documents, but an examination of those that are recorded can be rewarding."[2] We read these sentences and we have no difficulty understanding them. But can we be certain that the author conveyed what he intended when we recall that the word "murder," as defined in most dictionaries, does not mean the killing of a human being, that is, a homicide? Rather, it means the *unlawful* killing of a human being, an *unlawful* homicide.

When a historian notes that a fur trapper was "murdered" by Blackfoot within the territorial limits of the Blackfoot nation or by a Mandan within one of the Mandan villages, does that historian mean that the killing was unlawful by Blackfoot or Mandan law? We may guess that the historian has not even thought about lawfulness, and, knowing the attitudes of the "new" historians of the West, who are less interested in discovering the past than in indicting the present, we may doubt whether many would care. But when we say that an Indian who killed a fur trapper was a "murderer" rather than a "manslayer," and that the act was "murder" rather than "homicide," we are dealing with more than meaning and the risk of misunderstanding. We are concerned with judgments passed upon actions.

Historians may protest that they were not judging, and they would probably be right. But they should acknowledge that to use the words "murder" and "murderer" to describe nineteenth-century killings of white people by Crees, Assiniboins, Sioux, or Blackfoot runs the risk of applying the norms of a single legal culture—and the historian's legal culture at that—and may not take into account the law of the Cree, the Assiniboin, the Sioux, or the Blackfoot.

The point may be made more clearly by asking how best to characterize the conversion by Indians of property possessed by American or British people. Historians generally describe the action by using the verb "to steal." Perhaps no other subject so well delineates the problems of understanding crosscultural conflicts between Native Americans and the English-speaking frontiersmen of North America than that of Indians "stealing" property possessed by the so-called mountain men, the fur trappers of the transboundary montane West. Of the many obstacles to be overcome, one of them is vocabulary. We have English words that explain British and Ameri-

2. White, *Middle Ground*, pp. 76, 77.

can concepts regarding the appropriation of property rightfully possessed by another person, but those concepts—and, therefore, the words that explain them—may not be neutral concepts or neutral words in a crosscultural moral or legal context.

There is no problem with the term "steal" if we are describing the thoughts of persons from whom property was taken. We understand an American mountain man or a Hudson's Bay Company employee who, in his journal, says that Indians "stole" horses from his fur brigade. Even a lawyer traveling with a trapping expedition made sense when he wrote that the Blackfoot had "stolen a dozen of our best horses."[3] It is possible that no one reading those words has ever wondered whether the lawyer heeded his concepts. Obviously that lawyer, writing in his diary by the light of the camp fire, did not think about crosscultural technicalities. He simply used the same word, "stolen," that was being used by the mountain men with whom he was traveling.

Describing the taking of their horses, the fur trapper and the lawyer used the same word, "steal," in its popular sense. That they were also describing something that Indians had done—that they were saying that Indians had "stolen" their horses—was understood, but incidental to the fact that their property had been "stolen." There are problems, however, if a historian or a twentieth-century lawyer describes the same event with the same word. Yet historians invariably do. When recording that William H. Ashley had about eighty horses appropriated by Bannock Indians, a historian wrote that Ashley's horses were "stolen by a marauding band of Bannock Indians."[4] Again, we have no trouble understanding what is meant from Ashley's point of view. But does "stolen" tell us what the Bannocks did from the Bannock perspective? Perhaps to say that Ashley's horses were "stolen" does not make us think of burglary, armed robbery, or grand larceny, but does have connotations of criminality, wrongfulness, and unjust enrichment. What our historians seldom ask is whether those implications describe the actions of the Bannock Indians from the Bannock cultural perspective. What if taking horses from non-Bannocks was not a crime in Bannock law? What if it was not even wrong in Bannock morality? What if Bannocks thought taking horses from aliens and adding them to the Bannock nation's stockpile was a national good? Does the use of the word "steal" in the

3. Ball, "Across the Continent," p. 90 (entry for 2 July 1832).
4. Dale, *Ashley-Smith Expeditions*, p. 166.

crosscultural taking of Ashley's horses by the "marauding band of Bannocks" misdescribe what occurred?

The point is not the familiar argument that historians misrepresent Indian-white activities when they say "Indian uprising" rather than "Indian war," "Indian conspiracy" rather than "Indian nationalism," "massacre" rather than "battle," or "kidnap" rather than "take prisoner." The point is that twentieth-century scholars—even those intending to write politically correct history from the Indian point of view and to judge Indian actions by Indian values—when discussing or describing Indian actions with our legal vocabulary tend to impose our legal values upon Indian actions and to judge those actions by non-Indian values. To say that the Bannocks stole Ashley's horses may preclude scholars asking about Bannock social and legal values.

Even when the problem is recognized, it seems difficult to escape the vocabulary, or so it appears if we consider what James P. Ronda wrote in his splendid study, *Astoria and Empire*:

> Fur trade captains . . . knew that unguarded goods . . . might soon vanish into native hands. Virtually every European who spent any time along the Northwest coast complained about theft and the seemingly unrepentant thieves. From the Indians' perspective, this unabashed pilfering wore a very different, noncriminal face. . . . [T]he Chinookans believed those who had large numbers of axes or other valuable goods should be willing to share with those having only a few. What the furious partners saw as a theft, Indians viewed as a sensible redistribution of surplus goods.[5]

It all depends on what Ronda means by "theft" and "seemingly unrepentant thieves." Was he repeating the trade captains' complaint, or describing an occurrence?

Perhaps there is no solution. The Native American legal perspective requires a crosscultural application of law that defies our comprehension. The challenge is not that aspects of the Indian legal perspective will forever remain beyond our knowledge; that is obvious. There is no reason to be troubled that there is much about Indian law, or about the law of particular nations, that we will never understand or even suspect. The challenges, rather, are those concepts that we can understand, but, because of our legal, moral, and social assumptions, we tend not to ask about. We can comprehend,

5. Ronda, *Astoria*, p. 229.

even if we cannot prove, that there may have been Indians who would not have thought that helping themselves to property possessed by fur trappers was either legally criminal or morally wrong. But what if those Indians had said that the fur trappers stole from them when they shot antelope on their traditional hunting grounds, or that they stole from them when, in the treeless plains, they burnt the scarce wood to cook the antelope meat?

The day before "discovering" the Sink of the Humboldt River, some members of the Hudson's Bay Company's Snake country trapping expedition led by Peter Skene Ogden had difficulties with the Paiute Indians. "One of the trappers while in the rear of the camp in the act of visiting his traps had his horse stolen," Ogden recorded in his journal. "Add to this daring exploit is another which also happened to another trapper who had been down to the lower part of the river to set his traps, and was on his return when four Indians came up to him and not being on his guard managed to deprive him of his gun and would have also his horn and life had he not been very active and made his escape."[6]

To understand the crosscultural aspect of what occurred on the Humboldt, the peculiarities of Paiute society are relevant. Those Indians were the most economically backward Ogden had encountered. They had not mastered agriculture, could not domesticate horses, and lacked the materials for making effective hunting weapons. Their country was a harsh, barren desert, capable of sustaining little life, yielding them slight alimentation except small game, berries, roots, and some fish. The horse that they "stole" from the Hudson's Bay Company trapper would provide a feast that they might think incredible.

We need not quarrel with Ogden for saying that the trapper's horse was "stolen." But we should ask whether the word has as much meaning as Ogden supposed when it is applied to only one side of the crosscultural equation. What of applying it to the non-Indian or the fur-trapper side? While the Paiutes were skulking about Ogden's camp, shooting arrows at the horses in the hope that their carcasses would be left behind, the Hudson's Bay people were trapping the beaver upon which the Paiutes partly depended for survival. Although we cannot be sure, as Ogden did not mention such matters, it is quite possible that the fur men were catching fish in the river, killing frogs along the banks, or picking the scarce berries from the

6. Entry for 26 May 1829, Ogden, *Fourth Snake Journal*, p. 152.

bushes. Ogden and all other mountain men would have considered it absurd if they had been told that Indians considered that they were "stealing" the Paiutes' food. In their legal culture, beaver were wild animals belonging to no one and the berries were there for the picking. But what if the Paiutes made the legal argument that the horse was as much game as was the beaver, or the moral argument that the trapper wanted only to have the pelt of the beaver or to ride the horse, while they could not survive without the meat from at least one of them? What if the Indians said that the mountain men, who, because they had horses to eat, were obviously not in need, when appropriating berries and frogs along the Humboldt were "stealing" from people they, the mountain men, knew were always in want and were seldom able to satisfy that want?[7]

Answers to these questions are not as important as asking them, for the questions can warn us that applying the law of one culture to a different legal culture may sow the seeds of misunderstanding. When we employ the word "steal" to describe the conversion of a fur trapper's horse by an Indian but not to the killing of beaver by that trapper, our meaning may be clear, but only because the law we apply is our law, the law of a single culture in what was a multicultural legal world.[8]

The lesson is even stronger for the words "murder" and "murderer." The consequences flowing from the judgment implied by these words might be more imperative and more deadly, yet "murder" was the word men of the fur trade always used when characterizing international homicide. During the first decade of trapping expeditions on the Pacific side of the Rocky Mountains, a party belonging to Montreal's North West Company was attacked by unidentified Indians at the Cascades portage of the Columbia River. One of North West's partners was badly wounded and the attackers seized all the company's property being transported to new posts inland. "The disaster set the whole North-West machinery at Fort George in motion," Alexander Ross, an officer of the North West Company who was there, later recalled. "Revenge for the insult, and a heavy retribution on the heads of the whole Cath-la-yach-e-yach

7. There were also questions of trespass and of the right of Indians to payment for taking beaver and other animals; to make fur trappers pay for appropriating "property." Ronda, *Astoria*, p. 229.

8. These issues are raised in a somewhat different context and with more discussion in *Law for the Elephant*, pp. 325-34.

nation, was decreed in a full council." The idea, he explained, was to destroy "the vile banditti of the cascades, root and branch."[9]

Nine years after that, in 1823, William H. Ashley's fur company's expedition to the headwaters of the Missouri River was attacked and driven back downstream by Arikara gunmen. Colonel Henry Leavenworth, United States Army, was ordered by the secretary of war to reopen the Missouri. "[A]lways bear in mind that it is not only an individual but the whole A'rickara nation that owes us blood," Indian Agent Benjamin O'Fallon admonished Leavenworth, "and I am in hopes that no true American will tamely stand by and witness the reception or even recognize a white flag, so long as the brow of an A'rickara is decorated with the scalp of our people."[10]

At Fort Kamloops, a fur post on the North Thompson River in New Caledonia, Samuel Black, a chief factor for the Hudson's Bay Company, had what appeared to be an inconsequential argument with Le Tranquille, a Shuswap headman. The Indian had twice demanded that Black give him a gun that he claimed the owner, a North River Indian, had made over to him. Black said he needed more authorization than Le Tranquille's word, and apparently threats were exchanged in anger. Five days later the Shuswap was dead.[11] In less than a week Black was shot to death by a young Shuswap, generally identified as Le Tranquille's nephew,[12] avenging his uncle's death by killing Black, the man whom he believed had been the "cause" of the death. Officers of the Hudson's Bay Company called the slaying of Samuel Black an "atrocious deed,"[13] generally inexplicable except that it was a "savage" act committed by a person they thought of as a "savage," an act that had to be avenged. When vengeance had been exacted, that is, when the Shuswap manslayer himself was killed "by a sort of compound execution" (he was shot while attempting to swim a river and died from drowning as well as from bullet wounds), Hudson's Bay Company employees

9. Ross, *Adventures*, p. 267. The vengeance taken is described in ch. 10 *infra*.
10. Morgan, *Jedediah Smith*, p. 61.
11. John McLoughlin to George Simpson, 20 March 1841, in *Letters of McLoughlin Second Series*, p. 247; Patterson, "Introduction of Journal," p. xcii.
12. John McLoughlin to the Governor and Committee of Hudson's Bay Company, 24 May 1841, *Letters of McLoughlin Second Series*, p. 33; Morice, *History*, p. 181 n. 1; Watson, "Hudson's Bay Explorers," p. 11.
13. George Simpson to the Governor and Committee of Hudson's Bay Company, 20 June 1841, *Simpson's London Letters*, p. 30; John McLoughlin to Simpson, 20 March 1841, in *Letters of McLoughlin Second Series*, p. 33.

termed the execution "almost too good a fate for such a cold blooded villain,"[14] and said the officer of the company who had directed the manhunt was "deserving of the highest commendation."[15] Hudson's Bay people referred to the killing of Black as "murder" and called his manslayer (or, to use a possible Indian concept, his avenger of blood) a "murderer." They did not refer to the killing of the Shuswap avenger as "murder" or to those who executed him as "murderers."

We do not know what the Shuswaps called the killing of Black, but we may be reasonably certain they did not use the words "murder" or "murderer." They were more likely to have used the word Ross had used when writing of the North West Company on the Columbia River—"revenge"—or to have said, as O'Fallon had said to Leavenworth, that "blood" was "owed." Behind each word—"revenge," "blood," "owed"—and many others, such as "pay," "satisfaction," and "compensation," lay not only the maxims of the law of homicide for dozens of western Indian nations, but also the seeds of crosscultural misunderstanding and conflict.

14. Donald Ross to James Hargrave, 17 April 1842, in *Hargrave Correspondence*, p. 393.

15. Donald Manson to George Simpson, 6 December 1841, in Black, *Journal of a Voyage*, p. 232.

ONE

Payback Vengeance

WE ARE INTERESTED in patterns of behavior and norms of action: of rules, and principles, and of possible borrowing by one legal culture from an alien legal culture. But first it is necessary that one point be clearly understood. There were occasions when fur traders and fur trappers took vengeance against Indians for a homicide, or when Indians retaliated against fur men, and, no matter how closely we examine the circumstances, we will find no apparent guiding restraints that look like rules of behavior—no maxims governing conduct or principles controlling actions. Consider four examples:

1. In 1677 a young Potawatomi living in the area of Green Bay was killed by a bear. The bear tore "off his scalp, disembowled him, and dismembered his entire body." "[B]y way of avenging . . . this death," the kinsmen and friends of the dead man killed more than five hundred bears. "God," the Potawatomi explained, "delivered the bears into their hands as satisfaction for the death of the Young man who had been so cruelly treated by one of their nation."[1]

2. In 1833 a party of fur trappers led by Nathaniel Wyeth was traveling up the Columbia River when a capot and two blankets belonging to a member of the group were appropriated by some Indians. The trappers, Wyeth wrote, "went to the village just below our camp to recover them." The natives "acknowledged the theft but the thieves had run off." For some reason, the trappers "took two canoes to our camp." Later, before the party continued its jour-

1. White, *Middle Ground*, p. 10 (quoting a Jesuit missionary who received some of the bear meat and robes).

ney, "the man who had lost the articles took an ax and broke the worst canoe," leaving the other canoe for the Indians.[2]

3. At the rendezvous of 1837, members of Jim Bridger's trapping brigade, including Kit Carson, David Crow, and a dozen Delawares, took revenge on some Indians of the Bannock nation who had killed a trapper. They did so by swimming to an island where the Bannocks had left their horses and appropriating the entire herd.[3]

4. During April 1829, Peter Skene Ogden was leading the Snake country expedition of the Hudson's Bay Company along the Humboldt River "when one of the trappers arrived and informed us that the Indians had stolen three of his traps. Although I was fully aware it would be of no avail, I sent men with him to see if they could discover any Indians with orders to shoot them."[4] They found none of the Paiutes, but had they done so there might well have been bloodshed. George Frederick Ruxton, a Briton, recalled another time when Indians whom he identified as "Diggers," quite likely also Paiutes, took two horses belonging to a party of trappers. The mountain men got revenge by invading the Digger camp, killing and scalping all the Indians they could ride down. Ruxton called the action a "slaughter," yet seems to have approved, for he described it as "a case of mountain law, and the practical effects of the '*lex talionis*' of the Far West."[5]

"Revenge" and "satisfaction" are the normative words, linking these four cases with the more morphotic, behavioristic, and rule-controlled instances of vengeance that will be discussed in subsequent chapters. The governing principle, however, is "payback." The avenging parties were responding less to a particular fact situation and shaping their actions to how they would have responded to analogous fact situations than "paying back" a person or a group that injured them. It was a reaction that motivated some of the more excessive practices of Indian warfare. "If a Blackfoot," for example, "had a relation killed by a member of another tribe, and afterwards killed one of this tribe, he was likely to cut him all to pieces 'to get even,' that is, to gratify his spite—to obtain revenge."[6]

Not too much should be made of payback vengeance. It was

2. Entry for 8 February 1833, Wyeth, *Correspondence and Journals*, p. 182.
3. Lecompte, "David Crow," p. 140.
4. Entry for 16 April 1829, Ogden, *Fourth Snake Journal*, p. 142.
5. Ruxton, *Life in West*, pp. 82-83.
6. Grinnell, *Blackfoot Lodge Tales*, p. 254.

revenge, pure and simple, an evening of the "score," making a perpetrator of an injury "pay" for that injury, and feeling satisfied that an enemy had suffered and that aggression had been answered in kind. Its chief interest to us is not its quality or how it was exacted, but the contrast it provides to the more structured, principled instances of vengeance that occurred in a majority of the known situations when fur trappers and traders took vengeance for homicide against Indians in the North American West. That it existed and occurred is a fact not to be overlooked, but it is as a contrast that payback vengeance helps define and delineate the more principled vengeance generally practiced by mountain men. It need not, therefore, be analyzed in detail, but can be summarized by considering some of the incidents of vengeance recorded by one American mountain man, James Ohio Pattie, who trapped beaver in the Southwest during the 1820s.

In 1824 the trapping party of which Pattie was a member was traveling on the Sante Fe Trail when

> we came upon the dead bodies of two men, so much mangled, and disfigured by the wild beasts, that we could only discover that they were white men. . . . Our feelings may be imagined at seeing the mangled bodies of people of our own race in these remote and unpeopled prairies. We consoled ourselves with believing that they died like brave men. . . . We collected the remains of the two whites, and buried them. We then ascended the stream for a few miles, and encamped.[7]

Here they found "signs of Indians," signs indicating these Indians could have been the slayers of the two white men, as they had "left the spot but a few hours before." Pattie's brigade sent out a party to locate the Indian camp, and, after it had been found, selected sixty men to attack it.

> About midnight we came in sight of their fires, and before three o'clock were posted all around them, without having betrayed ourselves. We were commanded not to fire a gun, until the word was given. . . . Twilight at length came, and the Indians began to arise. They soon discovered two of our men, and instantly raising the war shout, came upon us with great fury. Our men stood firm, until they received the order

7. *Personal Narrative of Pattie*, p. 26.

> which was soon given. A well directed and destructive fire now opened on them, which they received, and returned with some firmness. But when we closed in on them they fled in confusion and dismay. The action lasted fifteen minutes. Thirty of their dead were left on the field, and we took ten prisoners, whom we compelled to bury the dead.[8]

Questioned, the prisoners admitted that their people had killed the men after the two, who may not have been trappers and quite likely not even Americans, refused to surrender half their powder and balls.

> Their bows and arrows were then given them, and they were told, that we never killed defenceless prisoners, but that they must tell their brothers of us, and that we should not have killed any of their nation, had they not killed our white brothers; and if they do so in the future, we should kill all we found of them, as we did not fear any number, they could bring against us. They were then allowed to go free, which delighted them, as they probably expected that we should kill them, it being their custom to put all their prisoners to death by the most shocking and cruel tortures.[9]

Because much will be made later in this book of crosscultural borrowings of Indian ways and law by the fur trappers, it is well to note that nothing Pattie described was borrowed. Not every Indian group would have killed its prisoners, as he claims, but Indians would not have refrained from killing because the prisoners were "defenceless." Also, the payback was motivated by racial factors. The two victims avenged had been "white men." That fact was stressed by Pattie. Race would not have held much interest for Indians. They paid back homicides committed against members of their own nation, and, on occasion, against members of allied nations. Indians were generally unconcerned when fur trappers killed Indians with whom they were neither related nor connected. Indeed, in most cases Indians of one nation cared little or nothing about the welfare of Indians of another nation.

Some months after avenging the deaths of the two "white men," Pattie joined a brigade of French trappers led by Michael Rebates.

8. *Ibid.*, p. 27.
9. *Ibid.*, pp. 28-29.

Due to Rebates's carelessness, the party was nearly wiped out by Papagoes, Pattie and one Frenchman alone escaping, to be joined later by the badly wounded Rebates, who had witnessed most of the killings. "I had not the heart to hear him relate what became of the rest of his comrades," Pattie recalled, knowing they had been hacked to pieces. "Feelings of deep and burning revenge arose in my bosom, and I longed for nothing so much as to meet with these monsters on any thing like terms of equality."[10]

He soon had his chance. Later that same day, he stumbled upon a party of American trappers led by Ewing Young and including several destined to become famous in later years—Milton Sublette, Thomas Peg-Leg Smith, and George Yount. "At hearing my sad story," Pattie wrote, "they expressed the hearty sorrow of good and true men, and joined us in purposes of vengeance against the Indians."[11]

> We were now thirty-two in all . . . under a genuine American leader, who could be entirely relied upon. . . . In the morning of the 31st, we examined all our arms, and twenty-six of us started to attack the village. . . . Two of our men were then ordered to show themselves on the top of the bank. They were immediately discovered by the Indians, who considered them, I imagine, a couple of the Frenchmen that they had failed to kill. They raised the yell, and ran towards the two persons, who instantly dropped down under the bank. In order to prevent the escape of the two men, they spread into a kind of circle to surround them. This brought the whole body abreast of us. We allowed them to approach within twenty yards, when we gave them our fire. They commenced a precipitate retreat, we loading and firing as fast as was in our power. They made no pause in their village, but ran off, men, women and children, towards a mountain distant 700 yards from their village. . . .
>
> We appropriated to our own use whatever we found in the village that we judged would be of any service to us. We then set fire to their wigwams, and returned to our camp.[12]

Pattie then emphasized the payback aspect of the vengeance when boasting that the Papagoes "paid a bloody price for their treachery,

10. *Ibid.*, p. 135.
11. *Ibid.*, p. 136; Carter, "Ewing Young," pp. 382-83.
12. *Personal Narrative of Pattie*, pp. 137-38.

for 110 of them were slain." He had no regrets; certainly none after gathering up the remains of the dead Frenchmen. "A sight more horrible to behold, I have never seen," he wrote. "They were literally cut in pieces, and fragments of their bodies scattered in every direction, round which the monsters had danced, and yelled."[13]

It is worth noting another fact distinguishing the fur-trapper payback vengeance from the vengeance practiced by most Indians. When Pattie's people entered the Papago village, the place "was so completely evacuated, that not a human being was to be found, save one poor old blind and deaf Indian" who apparently did not realize he was in danger. "We did not molest him," Pattie noted. He would have been killed had the attackers been Indians of an enemy nation.[14]

There is a touch of unreality to Pattie's story. It is too bloody. As he and the various trapping brigades he joined slowly worked their way westward, eventually getting to California, he had an astonishing number of deadly encounters with Native Americans. Once, in the desert, he and the group he was with took off after a band of Mohaves who had attacked them: "We put spurs to our horses, and overtook them just as they were entering a thicket. Having every advantage, we killed a greater part of them, it being a division of the band that had attacked us. We suspended those that we had killed upon the trees, and left their bodies to dangle in terror to the rest, and as a proof, how we retaliated aggression."[15]

It has been suggested that vengeance fed on vengeance and payback fed on payback. "The date of this brush with the Mohaves is in doubt," Ann W. Hafen has noted. "Pattie places it early in March, 1826. It could well have been several months later. This would place

13. *Ibid.*, pp. 137-39.

14. *Ibid.*, p. 138. Over three years later, also in the area of the Gila River, Pattie was with a trapping party that had all its horses run off by Indians. They attacked the village of those Indians:

> [W]hen we arrived at it, we found it to contain not a single living being, except one miserable, blind, deaf, and decrepit old man, not unlike one that I described in a hostile former visit to an Indian village. Our exasperation of despair inclined us to kill even him. My father forbade. He apparently heard nothing and cared nothing, as he saw nothing . . . , and his eyes appeared to have been gouged out. . . . We then set fire to the village, burning every hut but that which contained the old man.

Ibid., p. 223.

15. *Ibid.*, p. 147.

it between Jedediah Smith's summer visits of 1826 and 1827, and would explain the unexpected hostility Smith experienced when returning to the Mohaves in 1827."[16] Smith had lost several men when the Mohaves attacked him that summer, and Hafen is saying that maybe the Mohaves were paying Smith back for the bodies Pattie and his fellow trappers left dangling from the trees. Even more interesting is the fact that many months later the Hudson's Bay Company's Snake country expedition, wandering down the Colorado River far south of the Snake River, crossed the hunting grounds of the Mohave nation. There the brigade encountered Indians who, its members suspected, had killed Smith's trappers. "My men were eager to revenge the massacre upon them," Peter Skene Ogden later recalled, "but as I had no proof that these were the guilty persons, I withheld my consent to their entreaties."[17] The British fur men of Hudson's Bay Company wanted to pay back the Mohaves for killing Americans, persons not only of a different nationality than they but whom their employer thought of as serious commercial competitors. As will be discussed below, Ogden probably restrained his men not because he was uncertain these Indians were the individuals who had attacked Smith, but because he was not certain they belonged to the same nation as the manslayers.[18]

For reasons that will be explained, it did not always matter to fur trappers like Ogden if some of the Indians against whom they "paid back" had not been a party to the original injury. They did, however, want them to have been responsible in some way. The purpose of most fur trappers when taking vengeance was not simply to damage Indians. Pattie himself expressed this thought when writing of December 1829, when, once again, his party had all its horses appropriated by Indians. The men had to make canoes, and were floating down a branch of the Gila River when they spotted "two Indians perched in a tree near the river bank, with their bows and arrows in readiness." Before the Indians could get shots off at them, the trappers killed both. Pattie went to inspect the bodies.

> We discovered that they were of the number that had stolen our horses, by the fact, that they were bound round the waist with some of the hemp ropes with which our horses had been tied. We hung the bodies of the thieves from a tree,

16. Hafen, "James Ohio Pattie," p. 240 n. 9.
17. [Ogden,] *Traits of Indian Life*, p. 9.
18. *See* ch.4 *infra*.

> with the product of their own thefts. Our thoughts were much relieved by the discovery of this fact, for though none of us felt any particular forbearance towards Indians under any circumstances, it certainly would have pained us to have killed Indians that had never disturbed us. But there could be no compunction for having slain these two thieves, precisely at the moment that they were exulting in the hope of getting a good shot at us.[19]

There is no need to follow Pattie further. One more instance is all that is required to wrap up this outline of payback vengeance. On 16 April 1825, when trapping the Colorado River, Pattie's brigade met a large party of Shoshones.

> [T]hey had muskets, which we knew they must have taken from the white people. We demanded of them to give up the fire arms, which they refused. On this we gave them our fire, and they fled to the mountains, leaving their women and children in our power. We had no disposition to molest them. We learned from these women, that they had recently destroyed a company of French hunters on the head waters of the Platte. We found six of their yet fresh scalps, which so exasperated us, that we hardly refrained from killing the women.[20]

Unable to wreak vengeance on the Shoshone men who had fled beyond their reach, the trappers turned their anger on the Shoshone women. "We had killed eight of their men, and we mortified the women excessively, by compelling them to exchange the scalps of the unfortunate Frenchmen for those of their own people."[21] That was the payback. We may not think it vengeance at all. But the women had to watch their men being scalped and to accept the still-dripping scalps.

19. *Personal Narrative of Pattie*, pp. 227-28.
20. *Ibid.*, p. 152.
21. *Ibid.*

TWO

Vagaries of Vengeance

JOHN MCLOUGHLIN, known to history as "the father of Oregon," was for many years the superintendent of all the operations of the Hudson's Bay Company west of the Rocky Mountains. During July 1830 he sent a letter to William Connolly, the company's chief factor in New Caledonia, instructing him to reprimand William Kittson, one of Connolly's subordinate officers in the company. "I was informed," McLoughlin told Connolly, "that Mr Kittson had offered two Horses to get an Indian Killed [LaSauris?] will you have the Goodness to state to Mr William Kittson that the Company will not allow such proceedings and that it must not be done—It is only when Indians have murdered any of the Companys Servants or any person belonging to the Establishment that we can have a Right to Kill the Murderer or get him Killed."[1]

The twentieth-century reader may think the important point made by McLoughlin was that Hudson's Bay Company employees were not to kill Indians except when avenging homicide. What probably caught Connolly's attention was the claim that Hudson's Bay officers had "a Right to Kill" a "Murderer or get him Killed." Left unsaid but surely understood by Connolly was the implication that officers like Kittson were not only the judge and the jury in deciding whether an Indian was a "murderer," but also the legislators in promulgating what types of homicide constituted "murder," and what elements of a killing were required to make a manslayer a "murderer." As an organization, Hudson's Bay Company had enacted no

1. John McLoughlin to William Connolley [*sic*], 2 July 1830, *Letters of John McLoughlin*, p. 109.

rules, not even guidelines. The company's officers were given no instructions except that they should act "lawfully." But what law should they apply, and to whom? Had London thought about the matter it might have assumed it was common law, but that was not what McLoughlin wrote to Connolly.

Historians of the North American West usually do not consider Indian law, and there are times when their readers should wonder whether twentieth-century historians have realized that Indians had law. Yet, despite what both nineteenth-century mountain men and twentieth-century scholars might think, Indians had law—at least two kinds. One was international law, the law by which the nations regulated their conduct toward one another. The second was domestic law, the law of the Blackfoot, of the Flatheads, of the Crees, and of all the Indian nations.

Indian law has to be taken into account. It was forever intruding upon events, especially on the most elementary level: the individual Indian's understanding of personal accountability and the Indians' expectations concerning the consequences of events. The internalization of legal principles shaped those expectations, and those expectations determined how Indians reacted to fact situations. A case in point was recorded by Alexander Ross, the chronicler of the early fur trade on the Pacific Coast who went to the Columbia River as a clerk in John Jacob Astor's Pacific Fur Company and remained to serve both the North West Company and the Hudson's Bay Company. Ross was a colleague of John Clarke, who ran the Spokane post for the Pacific Fur Company. One day Clarke discovered that a silver goblet, his prize possession, had been appropriated by a native. Calling together the local headmen, and swearing that he would have revenge on the culprit, Clarke demanded the return of his property.

> [T]he whole tribe was called together, the council sat, and soon afterwards they returned in a body, like messengers of peace, bringing the glad tidings to Mr. Clarke that the silver goblet was found; at the same time the chief, stepping forward and spreading out his robe, laid the precious vessel before him. "Where is the thief?" vociferated Mr. Clarke. The chief then pointed to a fellow sitting in the ring as the criminal. "I swore," said Mr. Clarke, "that the thief should die, and white men never break their word." The fellow was told his fate: but he kept smiling, thinking himself, according to Indian custom, perfectly safe; for the moment the stolen

article is returned to the rightful owner, according to the maxims of Indian law, the culprit is exonerated.[2]

Ross's terms are too sweeping. He spoke of "Indian law," when it would have been more accurate to have said Spokane law, or Nez Percé law, or, possibly, Columbia River region law. He was, however, correct about the point he was making. The Indian who was singled out as the "thief" was not expecting to be judged by English law or Scots law but by the only law with which he was familiar, the law of his own society. By hanging him, Clarke applied no law except the drumhead law of the jungle, but when the dead man's kin and tribesmen struck back and killed employees of the Pacific Fur Company,[3] they were applying a principle of vengeance so universal throughout the Native American nations that it can accurately be termed "Indian law."

It may be claimed that what is here termed "Indian law" cannot be "law," and, at best, is something less than law. For there to be law there must be a sovereign capable of ordering obedience and of coercing compliance with the mailed fist of monopolized power. But that definition is too narrow for the transboundary North American West. There, during the first half of the nineteenth century, law was more than coercive command. It was the custom of the country, the expectations of the people, the way an individual reacted to a set of facts and circumstances, in part because he or she knew others would react the same way. Similar expectations were determinative of Indian international law. In international law, a nation, tribe, or band of Indians reacted to a set of facts and occurrences, in part, because its headmen knew that other nations, tribes, or bands would react the same way. There may have been far fewer rules than in a European society, and what rules there were quite often were much more ambiguous in definition and much less precise in application, for there was no sovereign to legislate the norms of behavior before an injury occurred or to pass judgment afterward.

Clarke had violated the legal expectations of that young Indian on the banks of the Palouse River, not only by hanging him. Perhaps as surprising and discomfiting to the natives was to be asked to identify the culprit. In most Indian cultures, as Ross correctly stated, the crisis would have been over once the goblet was recovered. The orig-

2. Ross, *First Settlers*, pp. 213-14.

3. Barrett, "McKenzie, McDonald, Ross," p. 16.

inal taking became "a thing done in the dark," not only to be left forever uninvestigated, but never again to be mentioned. The taught values of legal behaviorism conditioned members of those face-to-face societies not to resent insults and to sense discomfiture when the fires of social conflict were being stirred. By raising the matter of the goblet, and then by making the unheard-of demand to know who had converted it, Clarke had made every Indian present uneasy.

We are not concerned with precise legal rules here, but with the difficulty of the crosscultural application of principles. Still, two norms of jurisprudence can be mentioned to illustrate the intricacies of crosscultural behavior. One was somewhat vague and flexible, subject to negotiation and to the whims or strengths of the individuals involved. The other was one of the most rigid maxims of North American Indian law, changing from nation to nation only in the identity of which individual kin or clan member might be liable under its tenets.

The first is the doctrine that liability for homicide might be mitigated under certain circumstances and between specific sets of people if sufficient "compensation" were offered by the party liable for the homicide and accepted by the party possessing the right to exact vengeance. The principles involved were outlined by Richard White, in explaining the crosscultural failure of compensation when the Indians of North America's first "West" sought to impose the practice of compensation on the French of New France. When homicides

> occurred between Algonquians and Frenchmen, each side brought quite different cultural formulas to bear on the situation. For northeastern Indians, both Algonquians and Iroquoians, those people killed by allies could be compensated for with gifts or by slaves or, failing these, by the killing of another member of the offending group. The decision about how to proceed was made by the dead person's kin, but extensive social pressure was usually exerted to accept compensation short of blood revenge, since killing a person of the offending group often only invited future retaliation. Among the French the matter was simpler. Society at large took the responsibility for punishing murder. Punishment was not left to the kin of the victim but rather to the state.[4]

4. White, *Middle Ground*, p. 76.

The only acceptable "compensation" under French law, White concludes, was the death of the slayer.[5]

In the laws of both medieval Gaul and Anglo-Saxon England, not only was compensation the practice, but at times its rate was fixed by law and, under certain circumstances, its payment was mandatory. If they had been told this of their ancestors, the French and the British of eighteenth- and nineteenth-century North America might not have believed it. For them, compensation was for savages who did not value human life, not for civilized Europeans. In a typical case, two Frenchmen were killed by Chippewas acting with hostile intent. The Chippewas, in White's words, "offered the French the calumet—the standard ceremony for establishing peace and amity—and then they offered slaves to resurrect the dead Frenchmen and end the matter." The official who negotiated on behalf of the French rejected the very notion of compensation, denying "the legitimacy of such cultural equivalence," telling the Chippewas "that a hundred slaves and a hundred packages of beaver could not make him traffic in the blood of his brothers."[6]

The French officer was caught in a crossing of legal cultures he did not comprehend. The Chippewas were not asking him to "traffic" in blood, but the opposite. They wanted him to avoid further bloodshed. Compounding the French misunderstanding, they were also applying norms of Chippewa legal behavior that assumed that the French would respect the wishes of anyone with whom they were bonded in a national, familial, or symbolic relationship. By the obligations of reciprocity linking their "father" the king of France to his "children" the Chippewas, the French should have allowed the Chippewas, by paying compensation, to "wipe away the tears of the dead," and they, the French, in their turn, would have "whitened the path of peace" by accepting it.

The French officer probably had no idea that his decision seemed amazingly harsh to most Indians. Neither did the British or American fur men, who time and again said the same thing when Indians asked them to accept compensation in lieu of blood when one of their people had been killed.[7] It would be wrong, however, to conclude that the crosscultural void was absolute in every respect or for every area of potential conflict. Despite their cultural imperative

5. *Ibid.*
6. *Ibid.*, p. 78.
7. *See* text at ch. 7, nn. 32, 33, 34, 35, 36 *infra*.

that "murderers" must be "punished," Europeans could understand the pragmatism and function of compensation. They might claim that it was devoid of any morality, but at least when one of them paid compensation to escape vengeance in kind, they could appreciate its possibilities for maintaining peace and restoring social harmony.

By contrast, there would be situations where the crosscultural gulf was absolute. Few eighteenth- and nineteenth-century people coming from a European legal culture were able to comprehend the Indian doctrine that liability for homicide was fixed by one principle and one principle only—causation. We cannot be certain about the role of causation in the domestic laws of most North American Indian nations, but for Indian international law the doctrine was both universal and simplistic. Should a member of one nation kill a member of another nation, no matter the circumstances, the nation of the victim understood that it had what we might call a "right" to retaliate against the nation of the manslayer. Whether the victim's nation actually took revenge might depend on unrelated circumstances, as for example, that the two nations were traditional allies in war, had extensive trade with one another, or one was much larger and militarily superior to the other. But the existence of the "right" was not determined or affected by such considerations.

An objection could be made that the concept of "right" is too strong. The manslayer's nation seldom acknowledged that the victim's nation was privileged to exact retaliation, that is, that it had a "right." But universally, after a member of a nation committed an international homicide, the leaders of that nation anticipated retaliation. More to the point, especially in the transboundary area of northwestern North American, Indian leaders might act on that anticipation by offering compensation to the victim's nation in lieu of vengeance in kind. It is in the fact that all nations anticipated possible retaliation, and in the second fact that many both offered and accepted compensation in lieu of vengeance in kind in situations of international homicide, that we have implicit recognition of the "right" to retaliate. The rule is found in the expectation. The process is in the choice between physical vengeance and compensation for the death. But the principle was causation. Just the fact that a member of one nation had been the cause of the death of a member of another nation, gave rise to both the rule and the process. Except for negotiating the acceptance and the amount of compensation, there was no known mechanism in international law for evaluating the nature or quality of causation. That is why causation seems to us both absolute and simplistic. To prove the act of homicide was to prove liability, no matter the circumstances.

It was just said that we can be less certain about the doctrine of causation in the domestic laws of most North American Indian nations than about the doctrine in their international law. Again the reason is that scholars pay it no heed. Questions such as liability for acts done in "heat of passion," or liability for deaths caused by pure accident committed without known fault, simply do not occur to anthropologists who label every homicide as "murder." In those Indian nations whose law of homicide is known, however, a male manslayer or his kin group was liable because he and they "caused" the death. Facts, circumstances, and defenses that would in European law mitigate a homicide, such as that the killing was an accident, done in self-defense, committed without intent or malice aforethought, or not "designedly," were immaterial in any of the Indian laws that are known. Causation was the single probative factor. If that doctrine appears too simplistic to have been universal among most Indian communities, then it is for historians to stop equating homicide with murder and uncover the process by which mitigating circumstances such as accident, intent, or self defense could be weighed. That these and similar factors might be considerations in negotiations for compensation in lieu of vengeance in kind, does not affect the rule that causation was the only probative fact. The payment or amount of compensation was irrelevant to the doctrine that causation alone determined liability.

Alexander Henry the Younger has left us a striking instance of crosscultural incomprehension when discussing a homicide that occurred at his factory, the Pembina River post of the North West Company, in the Red River area of today's Minnesota. A drunken Chippewa, imagining he was in pursuit of Sioux, picked up a gun while inside the fur fort and shot one of Henry's employees. "The Indian although very drunk on seeing the mischief he had done fell a crying and lamenting, and assureing the bystanders, that he did not do it intentionally and if they were of a different opinion . . . [t]hey were welcome to kill him, he was ready to die, they might strike as he knew he was deserving of death."[8] The Chippewa was speaking what we may reasonably guess was pure Chippewa law, the law of absolute liability for a homicide. He was the cause, and he expected to die. Henry, who had been upstairs and did not witness

8. Entry for 30 October 1805, Henry, *Journal One*, p. 180.

the shooting, came down and, instead of killing the Chippewa as all the Indians at Pembina expected, did something incomprehensible to them. He undertook an investigation—not into the cause but into the circumstances of the killing: "On mature deliberation I could not punish the fellow with death. It appearing very plainly to me that it was an intire accident, and not designedly, for had he been maliciously inclined he actually would have prefer[r]ed making use of his own Gun that stood near him and was well loaded with Ball and primed. . . . From the direction the shot had taken it was plain to discover that the Gun must have gone off in an awkward position, and not with any premeditated aim of doing mischief."[9]

By then, Henry and the Chippewa, had they conversed, would have found each other incomprehensible. They were thinking of diametrically opposed legal concepts. The Chippewa knew he was the cause of the homicide, that as the cause he was liable, and that he was about to be executed. Henry understood causation, but did not accept the Chippewa's rule that causation was the only relevant fact to be considered. Instead, and somewhat surprisingly, he weighed two of the elements that were controlling in the common law of homicide, which he identified as premeditation and maliciousness.

> The Indian remained always seated upon the hearth, intirely naked with his head between his legs, every moment expecting to have his brains knocked out, but I could not find one single trifling circumstance that might induce me to suppose him guilty of premeditated murder . . . , and I could not bear the idea of having him dispatched without sufficient provocation and justice on my side. The next morning he was perfectly sober, but affraid to see me. He sent me word before he went away, that he should always remember me and be thankful to me for the charity I had done him in giving him his life. He sincerely laments the unfortunate affair and assures me it was not done designedly.[10]

It would hardly be possible to find a more crosscultural fact situation than this case at Pembina, crossing Chippewa absolute liability against European excusable homicide. The Chippewa, knowing he was the cause of the fur trader's death, waited patiently to be executed, fully expecting not only that the blow would fall but probably

9. *Ibid.*, pp. 180-81.
10. *Ibid.*, p. 181.

convinced that it was "right" that the blow be struck by someone in the North West Company. Henry also knew that the Chippewa was the cause of his employee's death but, for him, causation was only one element to take into account. He may not have been able to explain all his values, but the legal culture he had internalized led him to investigate whether the Chippewa, as he put it, was "guilty of premeditated murder." He then asked if the Chippewa acted with intent or "maliciously," or "designedly." Finding none of these elements, he astonished not only the manslayer but probably every other Indian in the area by telling him he would not take his life.

The Chippewa's legal culture told him that it was Henry's right, maybe his duty, to kill him. Henry's experience in Indian country taught him that he might execute the manslayer, but his legal culture convinced him he did not have the right. Henry did not reach that decision from fear that if he killed the Indian other Chippewas would retaliate and kill him. As we shall see below, his training as a fur trader would have persuaded him that not to revenge a killing done "designedly" was to invite Indians to kill again. Henry did not act as the natives expected him to because his law was in conflict with their law. Legal cultures were crossed.

There is much more to the dimensions of crosscultural vengeance than the serious predicament of diametrically opposed legal principles. There is also the apparently almost insolvable challenge faced by eighteenth- and nineteenth-century Europeans of not being able—or willing—to understand that the North American Indian nations had systems of domestic law. We shall see instances of this difficulty in the remainder of this study, but to delineate it now it would be best to look at two examples from the North American Southeast in the eighteenth century, not because they are more typical or more revealing, but because they are more extensively documented and, therefore, open to deeper analysis. These two examples concern the legal concept that seems to have provided Europeans with their greatest difficulties—aside from the rules of kinship and the notion of shared yet private ownership—in understanding Native American law: the concept of collective liability for homicide.

For a summary of the concept, it might be best to turn to a description by a nonlawyer. Again, it is provided by Richard White, contrasting the French with the Indians of the first North American West. "In the French scheme of things, exactly who committed the murder was of supreme importance, since the individual killer was held responsible for the crime," he explained, employing the words "murder" and "crime" as if discussing events in the context of a single legal culture. "For the Indians, identifying the murderer was not as important as establishing the identity of the group to which the murderer belonged, for it was the group—family, kin, village, or nation—that was held responsible for the act."[11]

There is no need to go into the complicated ramifications of this law—who were the kin sharing liability and what did liability entail. It is enough to understand that when an Indian committed a homicide, even if acting alone and in defiance of all the people he knew, liability did not attach to him as the individual responsible agent as guilt attached to a murderer under European law. If the homicide were committed against a member of his nation, liability attached not only to him but to certain persons of a definable kinship to him. If the homicide were international—if the victim and the manslayer belonged to different nations—liability attached to all members of the manslayer's nation.

For an illustration of these principles in operation, both in international law and national law, it is best to turn to a nation whose domestic law of liability is better known than are the domestic laws of the Indian nations of the transboundary West. In the early 1750s a number of Chickasaws, perhaps seeking a respite from the extensive French-Chickasaw wars, had taken refuge in the Creek nation in what is today Georgia or Alabama. One of these Chickasaws, a young man, killed a British subject. The colonial government in Charles Town, South Carolina, sent an agent to the Creeks demanding the manslayer's life in retaliation. Under the international law of the Southeast, a host nation was liable for the actions of alien guests, and the Creeks acknowledged their responsibility. It was, they told the agent, "just and reasonable that Blood for Blood should be given."[12] The problem the British faced, though they did not appreciate it, was that no one in either the Creek or the Chickasaw nation was legally privileged to execute the vengeance. If a Creek killed the Chickasaw manslayer there was likely to be a Creek-Chickasaw war. If a Chickasaw killed the young man his clan was probably obliged to retaliate, and there was no machinery by which a member of a manslayer's clan could legally take vengeance against a manslayer.

The British would not have considered assigning one of their people as an avenger of blood even if they had been asked, and

11. White, *Middle Ground*, pp. 76-77.
12. *Law of Blood*, pp. 80-81.

assured by the Chickasaws they would not take retaliatory revenge. They did not understand the limitations of Creek or Chickasaw law, and saw no reason why Creek or Chickasaw headmen should not be expected to face up to an obvious duty. The agent was told to demand that someone in authority in either of the nations execute the slayer. In other words, in this crosscultural situation, the British expected the Creek and Chickasaw headmen to act as if they were European government officials, not Creeks or Chickasaws.

The situation might have remained at an impasse had not the Creeks exercised their influence. They threatened to expel a sizable number of Chickasaw refugees in the nation if the British were not given satisfaction. Reacting to the Creek demands, the manslayer's uncle reminded him of his duty. "I have heard all your Talks and find you are mad," he told his nephew, referring to the nephew's arguments of why he would not kill himself. "The Blood of a white man is spilt and by your own Laws Blood ought to be in Satisfaction. In Case you throw away the English, you, your Women, and Children must become miserable or be made Slaves to the French."[13]

If the manslayer did not have a brother or an older uncle living among the Creeks, the uncle scolding him would have been his closest male relative. Chickasaw kinship was by matrilineal clans, which meant that the uncle was the young man's mother's brother. The young man's father's brother would have been a "father," not an uncle. Thus, when the uncle sent word to the British agent that if his nephew were unwilling to die, he, the uncle, would take his place, the Creeks and the Chickasaws thought that the crisis was resolved. A close-clan kin, one of the relatives who shared legal liability with a manslayer for a homicide, would pay the blood price. In their law, the blood debt would have been satisfied. They were puzzled when the British agent objected. The young man, he told them, must die and no one else would do, and the reason was that the manslayer alone was "guilty." We may be reasonably certain that no Creek or Chickasaw understood what was meant. One Chickasaw headman thought it was the British agent who did not understand, for he assured the agent that satisfaction would be paid: either the manslayer or his uncle "would be the Attonement." The agent replied that the British demanded the application of individual guilt and would not accept collective liability, which, as his words indicate, he made no attempt to comprehend. "I then informed him that it was not our

13. *Ibid.*, p. 81.

Laws that the Innocent should suffer for the guilty," the agent reported to Charles Town, "to which he replyed that by the Laws of their Nation one of the same Blood was equally satisfactory."[14]

The crosscultural misunderstanding was complete. The crisis might not have been resolved had the uncle not been a man of decision, willing to act not only upon his understanding of the law, but on the expectation that everyone else, including the British, understood and accepted that law, and would follow it. While the agent and the Chickasaw headman were conferring, the uncle

> retired to a Conferrence with his Nephew and told him that the Day was come, that one of them must dye. He asked him the Question if he was willing to suffer Death, to which the Nephew made no Answer. Without further Hesitation the Uncle replyed, I see you are affraid to dye, therefore I must dye for you. Upon which he immediately repaired to his own House to seek for his Gun which his Wife had hid from him, but finding a long French Knife, with that in one Hand and Paint in the other with which he besmearhed himself, came out into the open Street and made a publick Declaration that as one of his Family had spilt the Blood of a white man and was affrayed to dye for it, he was now going to pay the Debt for him for the Good of his People and for Satisfaction to the English, and with the greatest Undauntedness stuck the Knife into the Gullet and immediately dyed of the Wound.[15]

The British were mystified. About all they understood was that they had to accept the uncle's death in satisfaction of the blood debt owed them by the Chickasaws. That was why the crisis ended. "We must be satisfied with what has been done since that is your Way," the Governor of South Carolina told the Creeks, but in the future, he warned, the British did not want the blood of "innocent" people substituted to pay the vengeance debt owed by the "guilty."[16] The message was read to the Creeks, but, we may assume, they understood even less than did the British.

14. *Ibid.*, p. 80.
15. *Ibid.*, pp. 81-82.
16. *Ibid.*, p. 82.

THREE

Crosscultural Vengeance

IT IS WELL to recapitulate what has been said. The point made is not that Europeans were incapable of understanding Indian law. They understood it when they had to, and often incorporated it into their policy and even into their practices when dealing with Native Americans. The point, rather, is that the Europeans, or at least the British, did not think the Indians had law, and therefore when they encountered Indian legal ways they did not always recognize them as law, or, when applying Indian law, they did not realize that they did so. Conduct that they condemned when practiced by Indians they might themselves adopt, without giving thought either to its legality or its morality.

Two quotations from Hudson's Bay Company officers reveal how fur traders could understand actions taken by Indians yet not comprehend the legal nature, content, or quality of those actions. "I am also informed that Sesewappew's son is grieved for the loss of his father, & is going to war to revenge his death," Matthew Cocking wrote of an Indian while traveling along the Saskatchewan River. "Such is the superstition & wild notions of the natives," he added with apparent distaste, perhaps even disapproval.[1] Decades later another Hudson's Bay Company officer stationed in what is today the state of Washington wrote to a colleague in today's Manitoba, "You have of course heard of the murder of poor McKay at Pillar Rock last Summer—Speedy vengeance was however taken on the murderers who were taken and hung up."[2] Both fur traders knew

1. Entry for 12 August 1772, Cocking, "Journal," p. 102.
2. Dugald Mactavish to James Hargrave, 10 April 1841, *Hargrave Correspondence*, p. 343.

what was going on: vengeance for homicide. But they interpreted the nature and quality of the actions by the nationality of those taking vengeance. What was superstition and wild Indian notions to one was accepted, expected, and perhaps even Europeanized behavior to the other.

The French—at least French officials—seem to have had a greater awareness than did the British of crosscultural problems when dealing with Indians. In the late seventeenth century, for example, two Frenchmen were killed by Indians belonging to a number of nations. French authorities seized the manslayers and, after a hearing at which the defendants confessed their liability, decided to execute them. Some French traders and hunters living in the nations to which the condemned men belonged protested. If these Indians were killed, they argued, vengeance would be taken against them. The French commander realized they might be right, and sought a middle ground between French law and Indian law. Noting that two Frenchmen had been killed, he ruled that two blood debts were owed and, therefore, only two Indians needed to die. "[B]y killing man for man," he announced, "the savages would have nothing to say, since that is their own practice."[3]

The French official was probably correct. That principle was not only the general custom in Indian international law, it was the rule in the domestic law of many Indian nations, and most likely was the law in the nations to which the men condemned to death belonged. Whether he was applying the principle accurately is another matter. Indians generally took one life because in domestic law, if not international law, the blood price was usually exacted by a private kin group, not the state. In most cases the kin group was owed but one debt, and hence was satisfied with one death. The French official was acting for a sovereign state, not a private kin group, and his premises should have been different. The significant point, however, is that he realized that the Indians had law, and justified his decision on Indian legal principles. By contrast, British colonial officials seldom, if ever, inquired about Indian law, and did not recognize its legal nature even when applying it.

It may not seem credible that people could apply legal principles alien to their own culture without appreciating what they were doing, but that is what eastern colonial governors and western mountain men did all the time. Take one more example, from the records

3. White, *Middle Ground*, p. 79.

of colonial South Carolina. In 1752 a Creek headman, the Acorn Whistler, led a party of thirty-seven other Creeks from the Creek nation to Charles Town, probably for purposes of trade. Next day twelve Cherokees also arrived. As the two nations were then at war, the British became alarmed. The Cherokees were significantly outnumbered, and under the international law of the southeastern nations South Carolina was accountable for the safety of all visitors.

The colony's governor, James Glen, warned the Acorn Whistler to keep away from the Cherokees. The Acorn Whistler promised good behavior, but in 1752 it was a rare Creek who could resist the lure of Cherokee scalps. One night the Creeks slipped over to the Cherokee camp, killed as many as they could find, and fled home to their nation.

Fearful of trouble with the Cherokees, and also hoping to arrange a Cherokee-Creek peace, the governor dispatched an agent to the Creeks demanding that they execute the Acorn Whistler as blood atonement to the Cherokees. What happened next was explained by Glen in a remarkable "talk" he sent the Cherokees. The talk is striking for the way he blended Indian law with English common law or Scots law.[4] There is every indication that he did not realize he was doing so. To highlight the shifting of principles, his discussion of common law is in regular type. When he switches to Indian law—or his version of southeastern Indian international law—the text is in italics.

> In [the] Summer Last a noted Head man of the Creek Nation Came to Charles Town accompanyed with Eleven of the upper and twenty Six of the Lower Creeks and the Day after 12 of your People happened to arrive here also and being apprehensive that the Creeks might take that opportunity of Falling upon their Enemies I sent for them to the Town house and in [the] Presence of my beloved men I acquainted them that the Cherokees were our Friends and under our Protection and therefore tho they were at war with them I cautioned them not to hurt any of them while in our Settlements which they faithfully promised to observe notwithstanding of which the next day they took an opportunity and Killed some of them and then made their escape. The headman, and some others however Stayed behind and

4. Glen's training was in Scots law. On the issues in the Acorn Whistler case, there was no difference between the two laws.

> protested that They were Innocent and Ignorant of that Base Transaction, and as the English never punish the Innocent for the Guilty we permitted him and the others to return to their own Country; however I soon after Sent an agent to that nation *to demand Satisfaction for that offence acquainting them that Nothing but the Blood* of some of the most guilty *would Satisfy us for the Blood of our Friends the Cherokees. This Occasioned Several meetings of the Headmen in the Nation who* upon enquiry into the matter found the Acorn Whistler the Leader of that gang *had been the sole Contriver and Director of all the mischief* and tho he was one of the greatest men in the nation *and had many Relations both in the upper and Lower Creeks* and many Warriors at his Command Which might render it Difficult to take his Life yet they Determined *he should Die as a Satisfaction to the English* which they accordingly Executed a few Days after which has been publickly approved by the Whole nation. . . . but there is one thing which I must not omit mentioning. There were two of our People killed two months ago on the Road going to the Chickasaws near the Coosaws in the upper Creek Nation and it is reported that Some of the Cherokees murdered them and brought in their Scalps and a Bridle and Powder horn belonging to them. *This can not possibly be passed over or put off.* What I hope therefore that you will immediately make the most Strict and Dilegent Enquiry into it and without Hesitation *put to Death two of the Persons that Shall be found* **most guilty**.[5]

This talk is a splendid and typical example of the British applying law to the American Indians, although it is more extreme than fur traders' and trappers' later actions in the transboundary North American West. The case of the Acorn Whistler is discussed to illustrate analogous principles of law, not analogous application of law. Its value to us is to illustrate the problems of crosscultural vengeance, not to indicate what would be happening in the fur country of the Rocky Mountains eighty years later. Glen's idea was that he was applying European legal doctrines, modified by equitable principles to serve the needs of "savages," to be sure, but still "civilized" law. After all, he

5. Talk by Governor James Glen to the Cherokee Indians, 15 November 1752, *South Carolina Council Journal*.

more or less had to impose either English or Scots law, since to him neither the Creeks nor the Cherokees had law of their own. As we can see by reading those parts of the talk that are in italics, he was not applying pure common law or Scots law, and we can doubt whether he or anyone else in a comparable situation ever could.

After stating a few carefully selected facts, Glen asserted that "the English never punish the Innocent for the Guilty," an argument he would soon repeat to the Creeks when scolding them for letting the Chickasaw uncle die in the place of his nephew. We can be certain that the Cherokees did not understand what he was talking about. The trader who translated Glen's talk to them may have rendered Glen's word "Guilty" to match their concept of "liable," but there was no way the Cherokees could think of any Creeks as "Innocent" of these homicides. All Creeks were collectively liable.

From the European concept of "guilt," the governor switched to a demand for "satisfaction," a southeastern Indian legal doctrine. Now it was Glen who probably did not understand. He said that he demanded blood to satisfy the Cherokees because "Nothing but the Blood of Some of the most guilty" would do. There was a conceptual as well as a functional inconsistency between the British notion of "guilty" and the southern Indian notion of "satisfaction." The two should have conflicted, for, when used with the concept of "satisfaction," the concept of "guilt" implied collective liability, not absence of "innocence," yet Glen combined them in the same sentence.

That Glen used the word "satisfaction" at all is striking evidence of how he had internalized southeastern Indian legal vocabulary. He did not realize the full jurisprudential meaning of the word, or even that it had peculiar legal connotations. If asked, we may suspect he would have said it was a word used in talking to Catawbas, Choctaws, Pee Dees, or other Indians in diplomatic contact with South Carolina; a word much like those used in talking to children. He would not have employed it when writing to other British subjects or officials about the criminal liability of a non-Indian, or of the need to punish a white person who had violated the law. It was, however, more than a way of communication with Indians. It was an indication of how much Indian ways and Indian norms helped to determine the manner in which non-Indians dealt with Indians, even though they did not realize they were invoking Indian legal concepts.

Whether the Cherokees followed Glen's meaning up to this point is doubtful, but they probably understood better than he did what had actually happened in the Creek nation when he said his demand for blood "Occasioned Several meetings" of Creek headmen. Glen thought that the headmen—or, at least, some headmen in the nation—could have ordered the arrest and execution of the Acorn Whistler. The Cherokees would not have had that idea. They were totally unfamiliar with a person, institution, legislature, or tribunal possessing coercive power. Certainly they would have had great difficulty in contemplating a state or sovereign authority to execute. They might not even have comprehended the power to arrest.

Perhaps the most revealing statement in the talk is when the governor told the Cherokees that after inquiry the Creek headmen had determined that the Acorn Whistler *"had been the sole Contriver and Director of all the mischief,"* and, therefore, it was decided that it was he who would pay the satisfaction. Although he did not realize it, Glen was here adopting southeastern Indian law. He applied the Indian legal principle of causation without a reservation. In common or Scots law, all of the Creeks who joined actively in the killing of the Cherokees, not just the leader, would have been charged with murder. In an English or Scottish court, that the Acorn Whistler had been "the contriver," "director," or "cause" of the massacre could have been evidence of motivation, or evidence to establish the sequence of events. It would not have limited guilt to the Acorn Whistler. Here, however, Glen unconsciously slipped into Indian legal thought and told the Cherokees that because the Acorn Whistler was *"the sole Contriver and Director"* of the homicide he was the cause, and liability should be limited to him alone. Again, it may be suspected that the Cherokees accepted the implications of what Glen was saying more completely than he did. The text now changes to regular type because the governor, misunderstanding why the Creeks could not execute the Acorn Whistler, explained it by his own British assumptions. He was, Glen said, "one of the greatest men in the nation" and *"had many Relations both in the upper and Lower Creeks* and many Warriors at his Command." Glen was correct to emphasize that the Acorn Whistler had relatives in the nation. More particular was the fact that he was a member of a Creek clan with close-clan kin certain to avenge his death.[6] Glen was incorrect, however, to state that the Acorn Whistler was "one of the greatest men in the nation." The Cherokees would have known that rank was immaterial. It hardly mattered whether the man was "great." As the

6. A brief account of Creek clan relationships is in *Better Kind of Hatchet*, pp. 19-22.

Cherokees well knew, no headman would dare execute even the most nondescript Creek wrongdoer, male or female. He would have run too great a risk. The vengeance of that person's close-clan kin was certain to follow.

It was also incorrect to say that the Acorn Whistler had "many Warriors at his Command." The first mistake was the word "command." The European sense in which Glen meant the word was meaningless to either the Creeks or the Cherokees. Only those warriors who happened to have been members of the Acorn Whistler's clan would have had a legal interest in avenging his death. Indeed, had he been killed and had he "many Warriors," as Glen said, it is virtually certain that some of them would have been members of the same clans as the headmen who had *caused* the Acorn Whistler to be killed, and, as clan members, would have shared liability for the homicide, the more so if they were close-clan kin.

The Acorn Whistler did die—or at least Glen was told that he was killed—and the governor correctly states that he died as "a Satisfaction." The word "executed," however, has the wrong connotations. It implies punishment by the sovereign, not satisfaction by vengeance. Glen probably said the execution "has been publickly approved by the Whole nation" to impress the Cherokees with the Creeks' sincerity and their desire for peace. In fact, the Cherokees must either have been astonished to hear this news or—and this is more likely—have had no idea what Glen meant. If the Acorn Whistler was really killed by the Creek headmen, very few Creeks would have known about it, and none would have "publickly approved" it. When Glen's agent demanded that they act, the headmen had been at a loss. The law made any public action impossible. A leading warrior named Chiggilli told two other headmen, Estepaichi and the Ollassee King, that they could kill the Acorn Whistler without fear of retaliation. "You are his own Flesh and Blood," Chiggilli argued, though it must be understood that the expression "flesh and blood" is a very loose translation into idiomatic English of a discussion of Creek clan relationship that the governor's agent did not comprehend. "Either of you or any of his own Relations may kill him and who has any Thing to say to it?" That both Estepaichi and the Ollassee King insisted that Chiggilli was wrong, and that their own lives would be in danger if they killed the Acorn Whistler, is persuasive evidence that the Creek law of intraclan homicide was ill-defined. This is not unimportant when we realize that the law governing Creek clan kinship was more structured and more precisely defined than the laws of many of the Indian nations with whom the fur traders and trappers would be dealing in the North American West. That Estepaichi and the Ollassee King anticipated vengeance meant that they feared it from members of their own clan, undoubtedly from the Acorn Whistler's close-clan kin. The matter was resolved by persuading the Acorn Whistler's nephew to kill him. Unless the Acorn Whistler had brothers living, a nephew—the son of a sister—would have been his closest male clan kin. But even the nephew would not act without a pledge of secrecy, and we may well be suspicious that he acted at all. The British do not seem to have been too particular about proof.[7]

Finally, the last three sentences of Glen's talk raise the point that two Carolinians had recently been killed by Cherokees. Although the governor said that they had been "murdered," he did not ask that the "murderers" be "punished," as he would have if he had been applying either English or Scots law, but that the Cherokee nation pay satisfaction. It is remarkable, but even when he was applying inconsistent principles, Glen was inconsistent. He had wanted and had expected as just law that the Cherokees accept the death of the Acorn Whistler in satisfaction for a number of Cherokee deaths, perhaps as many as twelve. His legal theory had been that as the Acorn Whistler had been the principal cause, his death should satisfy any blood debt owed by the Creeks. However, when two Carolinians had been killed, he demanded two deaths in satisfaction. Whether or not they spotted the inconsistency, the demand made sense to the Cherokees, as it was good Cherokee law. Two Carolinians had died and so two blood prices were owed. Glen himself may not have considered that this was not common or Scots law as he had so internalized this aspect of the Indian law of homicide. Under those laws—or the law of any European country—all the Cherokees who were party to the killings should have been equally guilty. The number of victims was immaterial. Instead, Glen asked for only two blood debts, and although he used a European concept—"guilt"—he probably meant "liable" in the southeastern Indian context of collective liability. For this reason, the two final words are here in a third type, as they could belong to either legal culture.[8]

7. *Law of Blood*, p. 87.

8. Glen also adopted the southeastern Indian principle that the killings "*can not possibly be passed over or put off*." It was a principle that would often be restated in the transboundary fur country of the North American West.

We have considered Glen's talk to the Cherokees, not because it bears on the topic of this study, but to show how an educated person could borrow principles from a preliterate legal culture and blend them with principles of his own legal culture without realizing what he was doing. There was also an important difference between the governor and the traders and trappers of the transboundary montane North American West who are our main interest. When he sought to "punish" a homicide committed by an Indian against a British subject, Glen intended to apply law, and believed that he was following a loose form of European, or what might be called "civilized," law. The fur men of the transboundary mountain West generally had no illusions. They intended to take vengeance, and they said so. If asked, many might have said they practiced payback vengeance, nothing more. But when we look at how they actually behaved we see that in most situations they were acting with greater legal sophistication. Like Alexander Henry the Younger, who, before exacting the blood debt, investigated whether the Chippewa manslayer had acted "designedly," most of the fur traders and trappers applied rules and principles, some of which were *sui generis* to the western mountains, some of which we can recognize as common, Scots, American, or European law, and some of which they borrowed from Indian customary law. There was a persistent mixing of the concept of individual personal guilt from the European or Christian, Anglo-Saxon tradition, with the concept of collective liability basic to most North American Indian law. Before discussing the rules and principles that the mountain men adopted, we can end this examination of crosscultural borrowing by looking at an instance of crosscultural thinking in the western mountains. It was laid out in an order promulgated by John Work when he was in command of the Hudson's Bay Company's annual fur-trapping brigade known as the Snake country expedition.

Originating at Fort Vancouver on the north side of the Columbia River, the Snake country expedition of 1832–33 was looking for new beaver fields. For the first time the Hudson's Bay Company was not sending the expedition east across the mountains to the trapped-out beaver streams of the Snake River Valley, but to the largely unexplored rivers of central California. During the trip up the Columbia to Fort Nez Percés,[9] where his men would be outfitted for the overland journey south to the Mexican territories, Work was told that

9. A Hudson's Bay trading post near the mouth of the Walla Walla River, later known as Fort Walla Walla.

one of his trappers from the year before had been killed. "The Indians at the Dalls & Chutes," he recorded in his journal, "inform us that our man Soteaux whom we lost on the 8th July was murdered by two Mountain Snakes who lay in wait for him as he passed a thicket and shot him with arrows but little reliance can be placed on the account."[10] By "Snakes," Work meant members of a branch of the Northern Shoshones, a people whom the British and American fur men, as well as most other Indians, called "Snakes," presumably because they used painted snakes on sticks as war symbols.

Soteaux or Satoux, whose first name is not recorded in Work's journals, had been a member of the expedition Work had led through the Blackfoot country during the fall, winter, and spring of 1831–32. Because of the Blackfoot, it had been the most dangerous trip that Hudson's Bay people had undertaken to the Snake country, and Soteaux had been one of Work's most reliable subordinates, often riding ahead of the brigade, bringing back word of danger.[11] On John Day's River in today's Oregon he had disappeared, and, although Work sent men out looking for him, even inquiring among the Snake Indians, he was never found.[12]

The story told at The Dalles seems to have been the first Work heard of Soteaux since he vanished, although, as with most tales related by Indians, he did not put much stock in it. About three weeks later, however, he changed his mind. Two of his men "fell in with some Caiouse [Cayuse] Indians on [John] Day's river, from whom they learned that Soteaux was killed by three Snake Indians who laid in wait for him as he was passing a rock, laid hold of him & stabbed him with a knife before he had time to fire upon them."[13] Work believed this version, though he does not say why. He might have remained suspicious because the manslayers were identified as Snakes by Cayuses, who were their enemies. There may have been other persuasive proof that Work does not mention. In any event, once convinced the manslayers were Snakes, it was the Snakes to whom he began looking to take vengeance.

Had the expedition of 1832–33 been going to the Snake country, as had previous expeditions, Work might have met hundreds of Snakes, and vengeance could have been a possibility. Going south

10. Entry for 22 August 1832, Work, *California Journal*, p. 2.
11. As when he spotted Blackfoot. Entries for 3 and 9 December 1831, *Journal of John Work*, pp. 110-11.
12. Entries for 12, 14, 16 July 1832, *ibid.*, pp. 172-73.
13. Entry for 14 September 1832, Work, *California Journal*, p. 5.

out of Fort Nez Percés, however, he did not expect to meet many Snakes. The bulk of the nation was on the eastern side of the mountains, and he would be skirting their most western bands, people he called "the mountain Snakes," whom he preferred to avoid, as they "are notorious thieves and would no doubt steal our horses should they find a chance."[14] That was apparently why Soteaux had been killed, to get his property. Work wanted to take vengeance, but doubted that he would ever confront the killers.

> It was three individuals, a father & two sons, of these people on the east side of the mountains on the head of burnt river who murdered our man Soteaux in July last, and it being deemed absolutely necessary to punish the murderers if possible but at the same time not just to punish the innocent for the guilty, it is arranged that should any article belonging to the deceased be recognized the Indians in whose possession it may be are to be punished instantly. These villains live in detached families & seldom assemble except during the salmon season when a few of them sometimes collect together to make fishing wears [weirs]. Did we even know the family who committed the murder we might almost as well go after elk or deer as pursue them into the mountains.[15]

We should be struck by the fusion of multilegal elements in Work's reasoning. He wanted his men "not to punish the innocent for the guilty," probably the one concept he applied that he knew contrasted with Indian law. It was a British, European, or Christian value but he was not using it as he would have in British, European, or Christian society. When he told his men not "to punish the innocent for the guilty," he meant that they were not to kill just any Snakes in satisfaction. That would have been satisfaction in Indian international law. Had Soteaux been a Flathead, for example, and had he been killed by three Snakes, the Flatheads would have killed one Snake in retaliation, and that would have ended the affair—unless the kin of the slain Snake retaliated by killing a second Flathead.[16]

14. Entry for 21 September 1832, *ibid.*, p. 6.
15. Entry for 21 September 1832, *ibid.*
16. Or if the Snakes as a whole or a band of the Snakes took vengeance. For (as discussed in the next paragraph) international vengeance was not privileged, and the right to take vengeance was not limited to certain kin but might be taken by any Snake.

Work was crossing legal cultures in two ways. He was using the British concept of "innocent," not known in most Indian law, but applying it according to Indian principles. He was not defining innocence as it was defined by common law, in which guilt for an action is assigned to the actor and everyone else is "innocent." By "innocent," he meant third-party Snakes: Snakes other than the three manslayers or members of their "family." In the domestic law of most Indian nations, unlike their international law, when a member of a nation killed another member of the same nation, liability did not attach to every other member of that nation. If that was Snake law, for example, then if one Snake killed a second Snake, it would not have been legal for the kin of the second Snake to have killed any third Snake in satisfaction. Liability attached to the manslayer and to his kin group that shared responsibility for his acts. The kin group, that is, that would have taken satisfaction had he been the person killed, or who would have shared any compensation paid in lieu of vengeance in kind. Work was using the British concept "innocent" in this Indian sense.

There may be doubts as to whether Work said that he would exact Indian liability rather than common-law guilt. Admittedly, his words are not as clear as one would like. Yet we can be reasonably certain what he meant. On the basis of what he said and how he acted on other occasions, it is evident that when he wrote that "[d]id we even know the family who committed the murder we might almost as well go after elk or deer as pursue them into the mountains," he meant that it was as difficult to track the "family" as it would be to hunt particular elk or deer. In other words, were the Hudson's Bay trappers able to identify the manslayers and, therefore, their "family," Work and his men would have obtained satisfaction by killing any three of them, though, given their cultural values, we may guess they would have killed only males and spared females.

Particular attention should be paid to the striking way Work phrased the sentence just quoted. It shows how much he had absorbed Indian ways of thinking. He said that "the family who committed the murder" was not known. He would not have used those words—"the family who committed the murder"—unless he had been conditioned to think in some degree of Indian collective liability, as well as Christian individual responsibility. After all, people in London, Montreal, or Boston thought of the particular individuals who killed as "committing murder." They did not think or say that the family of a manslayer was guilty of "committing murder," even when saying that the manslayer was. For Work to have said the family "committed" the "murder" meant he had internalized either Indian ways of speaking or Indian principles. That is, although he was not conscious of it, during his years of dealing with Indians his concepts regarding criminal responsibility had made a leap from the concept of individual guilt to include collective liability.

There is an evident inconsistency. Work had only internalized his acceptance of collective liability unconsciously. Consciously he rejected it. Indeed, he had done so explicitly two sentences before writing that "the family" had "committed the murder." In stating that one of his objectives was "not just to punish the innocent for the guilty," he intended that his men kill only Snakes who would have been "guilty" by common-law concepts. That much is clear. Less clear is who was not to be "punished." What did he mean by "the innocent"? Had he been asked, we may suppose he would have said he meant all Snakes who had not been party to the killing of Soteaux, including members of the manslayers' kin group who were liable under the Indians' doctrine of collective kin responsibility, if that doctrine was part of Mountain Snake law. Because of the way he mixed legal concepts, he and his men were prepared to kill three of the manslayers' kin if the manslayers were not found. When legal cultures were crossed in the mountains of the transboundary North American West, those who did the crossing could be led down paths they, intellectually, did not want to travel to places they were, in practice, perfectly willing to go.

There was nothing unique about the way Work mixed legal principles. Most fur traders did. After all, with the first decision usually made—to take "vengeance" against the "guilty"—legal concepts were crossed. In this case, Work mixed concepts or principles from three sources, drawing some from common law, or what we might call European legal values, some from American Indian law, and at least one method of proof from the *sui generis* practices of the western fur trappers.

Work was clearly thinking in common-law terms when he contemplated holding the three Snakes liable for the death of his trapper. Under the domestic law of some Indian nations and the international law of the Indians in general, only one life would have been taken in satisfaction because only one person had been killed. Vengeance would have been obtained by killing one of the manslayers, by killing one member of the close kin who shared their liability, or, applying international law, by killing one Snake.[17] Work, however, expected that if the manslayers were identified and apprehended, the three would be killed, or, if they were identified but not apprehended, that three members of what he called their "family" would be killed. By assuming that vengeance would be taken against three individuals, he was thinking of common-law guilt rather than Indian-law liability. We may assume that he preferred attaching responsibility for the killing on the *individuals* who, with deliberate intention, participated in the killing, rather than liability on the social unit, the "family," whose members, in Shoshonean jurisprudence, shared liability because their kin had "caused" the death.

John Work deserves our respect. He was much more astute than we might think. True, when he said "family" he probably was thinking of the European extended family or, perhaps, the European household, not of an Indian or a Snake family. Even so, he was remarkably accurate in fixing liability upon the Shoshonean "family" as the legal unit or kin group bearing collective responsibility for a homicide committed by a member. The Shoshone people, including those Work called the Mountain Snakes, had neither matrilineal clans nor patrilineal clans—the kin groups upon which collective liability was fixed in some Indian nations such as the Creeks, Chickasaws, Omahas, Crows, and Cherokees. The Northern Shoshone, rather, have been described as "both bilateral and bilocal."[18] Among the Shoshonean bands the "most important kinship groupings" "were families and family clusters." The nuclear family was the basic *social* unit of society: "Groups of families that came together for certain activities, ceremonies, and recreational events were not based on any principle of fixed membership, and they shifted in their composition from year to year."[19]

In domestic law, as opposed to international law, that social unit, the nuclear family, was also the responsible unit of society. It was the kinship group that both exacted vengeance and fixed liability for homicides and, perhaps, other injuries. According to one expert, "Disputes and hostilities arising from such matters as murder, theft,

17. It is possible, but not likely, that a nation with a domestic law making only one person liable might, in its international law, attach liability to as many persons as were party to the killing. Thus in this case—an intentional killing in which three Snakes killed one Canadian—three Snakes were liable for three blood debts.

18. Murphy, "Northern Shoshone," 2: 292.

19. Shapiro, "Kinship," in *ibid.*, p. 620.

wife-stealing, and other violations of custom were settled between families. None of these was a 'crime' against the community, for the community did not exist in any corporate or legal sense."[20]

Like Governor Glen before him, Work was inconsistent in applying legal principles crossculturally. He assessed the individual guilt of common law only when contemplating vengeance against the three manslayers. He abandoned common-law principles and adopted Indian law in part when he suggested that in lieu of the three manslayers his men might kill three members of the manslayers' "family." That is, he turned from the common-law concept of individual guilt to the collective liability of North American Indian law. Of course, he was still mixing laws. Had he followed Indian principles exclusively, he would have taken only one life from the family.

Finally Work adopted a method of proof other mountain men are known to have applied in similar situations. Any Snakes found with property that was in the possession of the dead trapper when he was killed would have been summarily executed. At first glance this looks like an effort to modify absolute liability by introducing a rational element, the Europeanization of the Indian custom of vengeance, by formulating rules of evidence for the determination of "guilt." But, in truth, it was the same nonrational liability for homicide that was the hallmark of most North American Indian nations' laws of homicide, with only a thin veneer of evidentiary protection, more a procedural gloss than corrective substance. Not only was a Snake found with the trapper's property subject to the same summary execution as before, but, under Work's rule, judgment could have been more summary than it would have been without the rule. Mere possession with nothing else would have been conclusive, and the Indian in possession was to be "instantly" killed.

David L. Brown would have approved Work's burden of proof. Attending the American fur trappers' rendezvous of 1837, he justified, on grounds of circumstantial evidence, the killing of Pawnark Indians by mountain men. "[T]hese Indians were never known as friendly to whites," he reasoned, "and were moreover vehemently suspected of having secretly murdered many of the trappers, whose mangled bodies had been frequently found in the vicinity of their haunts, and whose deaths could in nowise be accounted for, but by supposing *them* to be the guilty authors."[21]

20. Steward, "Shoshonean," p. 254.
21. Brown, *Three Years*, p. 17.

Johnson Gardner, an American fur trapper, also resolved liability on circumstantial evidence. He burnt two Arikara males after catching them with "a rifle, knife, powder horn, and other items known to belong to [Hugh] Glass," another American trapper, whose exploits were legendary in the mountains. According to John Sanford, who told the Indian agent in St. Louis, William Clark, of the killings, the Arikaras were scalped and burned alive when unable to explain why they were "possessing the worldly goods of a white trapper."[22] At common law, exclusive and unexplained possession of recently stolen goods shifted the burden of proof from the prosecution and placed it on the defendant being tried in criminal court for stealing those goods. In the mountains of the nineteenth-century North American West, it would seem, unexplained possession was all the evidence the accuser needed. Mere unexplained possession meant conviction.

Work's choice of words may make the rule appear harsher than it probably was. He wrote that "Indians" possessing an article that had belonged to the deceased should be "punished instantly," but most likely he did not mean just any Indians. The manslayers had been identified as Snakes, so Work would probably have limited "instant punishment" to Snakes, and not killed non-Snakes who might have possession of the property. If the possessor were a Flathead, it could be presumed that he had bought the property from the Snake manslayers, and he would be asked where he had purchased it, and from whom. If he were a Blackfoot, he or another Blackfoot had undoubtedly taken it in a raid and had killed the Snake who possessed it.

22. Haines, "Johnson Gardiner," p. 159. *See also* Haines, "Hugh Glass," pp. 168-69.

FOUR

Principled Vengeance

THERE IS NO NEED to make a fuss over words. The narrow definitions and artificial distinctions that anthropologists spend pages in formulating are of little interest either to law or to history. There may be some limited usefulness in insisting that vengeance can be labeled a "blood feud" only when it occurs between groups that are related, such as between clans of the Crows, bands of the Blackfoot, or families of the Snakes, and that vengeance occurring between nonrelated groups, such as between the Sioux and the Chippewas, is not "blood feud."[1] The idea is to distinguish feuds or vengeance from war or total vengeance—to say, for example, that "[w]hereas feuds can occur only within a politically organized whole, war occurs beyond such an organization and always involves two groups that are politically unrelated,"[2] or that "if a man of one tribe kills a man of another tribe, retribution can only take the form of intertribal warfare."[3]

Although neither history nor law need be so confining, it would be useful to borrow an anthropological technique and fasten a label onto the type of actions being discussed. The result may only be to distinguish the vengeance practiced in the fur country of western North America from payback vengeance, but there should be other benefits. Merely to draw the distinction serves to emphasize what was going on. The claim that fur-trade vengeance differed from sim-

1. Leopold Pospisil, "Feud," *International Encyclopedia of Social Sciences* 5 (1968): 389-90.
2. *Ibid.*, p. 391.
3. Evans-Pritchard, "Nuer," p. 278 (writing of "tribes" within the Nuer).

ple, unadulterated payback vengeance is based on several factors. One of these is that fur-trade vengeance followed, to a rather surprising extent, certain rules and principles, some of which came from law, whether common law, Scots law, or Native American international law.

Another difference between fur-trade vengeance and payback vengeance is that fur-trade vengeance was executed for more purposes than merely to pay back a manslayer. If we look carefully at most cases of fur-trade vengeance, we can see that, as a general rule, vengeance for a homicide was also taken for some other purpose than simply to "pay back." It could be for a social purpose, as when seeking to deter further homicides; for a military purpose, as when it was intended to convince Indians of the superiority of European technology; or for a legal purpose, as when trying to make Indians of a particular nation more respectful of the "rights" of other people. It can be useful to use the terms "purposeful vengeance" or "principled vengeance."

Among the Indians of North America vengeance was used for an assortment of purposes, including the avoidance of further homicides or vengeance in kind, and even the avoidance of warfare. In the Southeast, for example, any killing of a member of one nation by a member of another could be a declaration of war. This was true even of a killing in retaliation for homicide—a payback killing—because in international law a retaliatory killing was never privileged. That is, a retaliatory killing was not lawful in international law even if the vengeance were taken against the actual, confessed manslayer whose "guilt" was both admitted and condemned by every member of his nation. Following an international homicide, however, there were various ways to avoid war. One, of course, was diplomatic negotiations. Another was the doctrine of the "set-off," under which a homicide committed by a member of one nation upon a member of a second nation could be set off against a blood debt the second nation owed to the first. Because the score or the debt was even—or, as some Indians would say, was "balanced"—each side was "satisfied," at least in theory, and each side, if it wished, could avoid war by declaring it had obtained satisfaction.

In 1750, for example, the Upper Creeks sent as their ambassadors to the Overhill Cherokees a party of Shawnees instructed to acknowledge Creek responsibility for an attack on an Overhill hunting camp, during which four Cherokee men had been killed, seven women taken prisoner, and several horses run off. Later, the Cherokees and their allies killed or captured eight Upper Creeks. This, the Upper Creeks argued, amounted to a set-off, putting the two nations "much upon a Ballance" and providing both with grounds for saying that a state of war did not exist.[4]

Even British officials in the colonial era acknowledged the "legality" or legitimacy of the international set-off, sometimes carrying it to extremes, as in 1772 when John Stuart, the superintendent of Indian affairs for the southern colonies, demanded satisfaction from the Upper Creeks for killing three colonists. The Creeks claimed that one of their men had been beaten to death in August the year before. Stuart insisted the Creek had died accidentally by falling from a canoe while drunk, but he was willing to set off his death against the death of one of the three colonists. In addition, a Creek had been killed by Georgians while running off horses. Although the Creeks had been warned they would be pursued if they "stole," Stuart agreed to set off this death also. Stuart concluded that there was "one Murther unattoned for," permitting the Creeks to keep peace with the British by paying only one blood debt.[5]

When southeastern Indians were killed by British subjects, the colonial authorities, much like the fur men of the western mountains in the next century, expected the nations to accept commutation in place of specific performance. Sometimes, in their most arrogant moments, they even tried to treat compensation paid by them as mandatory for the Indians. Yet when Virginia promised compensation for the death of a number of Cherokees during 1765, and the Cherokees (after waiting three years in vain for payment) killed five Virginians in retaliation, the killings were excused as justified, countersatisfaction was not demanded in return, and war was avoided. The Cherokee killers, Stuart explained to Virginia officials, "were authorized by the custom of their country to act as they did, and their plea of never having received any satisfaction was undeniable."[6]

The premises upon which Stuart acted would not be law by some definitions, such as the claim that law can exist only within societies with a sovereign empowered to command obedience. They were, however, law to Stuart. He argued Cherokee custom that justified Cherokee behavior within Cherokee society to exculpate that same behavior in international affairs. By this criterion the tests of law are

4. *Law of Blood*, pp. 169-70.
5. *Ibid.*, p. 170.
6. *Ibid.*, p. 172.

not just the certainty of punishment or the force of command. There is also the test of social harmony preserved and social peace maintained. To be law, the customary procedures from which Stuart borrowed did not have to be capable of adjusting every claim the people might have, of settling every conflict in society, nor need it adhere to rigid, precise rules. Predictability is a more important criterion, and that predictability need not be the predictability of how a tribunal or official will rule under a specific set of circumstances. Just as legitmating is the predictability of how one party to a dispute will act under familiar circumstances and how the other party will respond. There is also the prediction of how one party to a homicide will argue and whether the other party—accepting the argument or not—responds to the argument in a way that acknowledges that it could have a bearing on the resolution of the dispute and could provide the basis for mitigation, settlement, forgiveness, termination, or avoiding vengeance in kind. That is why every vengeance in kind exacted for an international, interracial, or crosscultural homicide should not be dismissed as simple payback vengeance. The exacting of vengeance on the southeastern frontier, as John Stuart showed, was not an arbitrary process, nor would it always be in the transboundary western frontier of the North American fur trade. It was too often carried out according to certain rules and undertaken only when supported by the family, community, or nation of which both the victim and the avenger of blood were members. Alexander Henry the Younger's decision not to execute the Chippewa manslayer is a case in point.

Critical in determining the nature of vengeance, aside from the predictability of how it would be seen, is its contribution to the maintenance of social order, whether within a single society, across international divisions, or between diverse cultures. Unlike simple payback vengeance, the more structured, practiced vengeance of the western fur trappers and traders was thought of, intended to be, and generally carried out as a sanction. There were at least two purposes: to strike back at or "punish" a transgression, and to deter similar transgressions in the future. Alexander Henry the Younger emphasized the punishment element when he released the Chippewa after determining that the man had not been culpable as he had not acted "designedly," "maliciously," or with premeditation.

The most frequently stated purpose was to deter. Thus principled fur-trade vengeance, in contrast to payback vengeance, was not arbitrary or ad hoc. For vengeance to deter others, the vengeance had to be known to those who might commit the same transgression. It also had to be regular in incidence and certain in application, indicating it would be executed again against anyone repeating the same transgression.

To illustrate the distinction, consider two killings perpetrated by fur traders out of Montreal in the general area of the Saskatchewan River during the late 1790s. These traders were generally referred to as "Canadians" to distinguish them from Hudson's Bay Company people, who were termed "English." They were also called "Frenchmen," at least by officers of Hudson's Bay, even though most of them were British, not French, citizens. One day, at their post at Setting River, "a party of Canadians caught three Stone [Assiniboin] Indians who they supposed were come to steal Horses & brought them prisoners to their House." Three nights later, one of the Assiniboins broke out and disappeared. The escape "so enraged the Canadians that they immediately butchered the remaining two & tossed their Bodies in the River." Whatever the Canadians thought they were paying back, these killings were not confused with principled vengeance by anyone at the time, at least not by the fur traders. "What may be the consequences of so rash an action time only can determine," the officer in charge of the Hudson's Bay Company's post on Setting River lamented, "but I am afraid it will occasion the loss of lives of some poor Men, if ever they should be met by the Indians, from the Houses."[7] He meant that the Assiniboins might take vengeance against any fur traders caught away from either of the Setting River posts—Hudson's Bay Company's as well as the Canadians'.

By contrast, no lament was expressed by a second Hudson's Bay Company officer describing the killing of two other Indians by Canadian traders. Nor did he seem to worry about retaliation. He was Peter Fidler, and the killings occurred at Cumberland House, where the Canadians had built a post right next to one maintained by the Hudson's Bay Company. On the first of June 1796, thirteen canoes carrying Canadian traders stopped at Cumberland. Their arrival alarmed Indians who were trading at both houses. "[A]ll the Indians run away in the night except one man," Fidler reported. The reason, he noted, was that "they are frightened that the Frenchmen will kill them as they [the Canadians] had one American man murdered by those Indians this winter near to Isle à la Crosse."[8] In other words,

7. Johnson, "Introduction to Edmonton," p. 168 n. 1.
8. Entry for 1 June 1796, Fidler, *Cumberland Journal*.

these Indians, knowing that some members of their nation had killed an employee of one of the Canadian traders, anticipated that the Canadians might take vengeance against some of them.

If the Canadians were looking for vengeance—and no doubt they were—they got satisfaction soon enough. Next morning two Indians arrived with meat to sell to the Hudson's Bay house.

> [T]hese two men was known to be the principals in the murder of one of their men this last winter at Ile a la Crosse. Just as one had stepped out of his Canoe (ie Charles's Brother alias Beardy) he was immediately seized by the Canadians that was ready to take him when he landed and they hauled him into their house. The other cal[l]ed the Little Gut had not disembarked when the other man was seized, and he immediately pushed his Canoe from the shore and pad[d]led with all the haste he could to get out of the Canadians way. They immediately manned one of their Canoes with seven men besides Mr. W[illiam] McKay and pursued him, also sending several men a long shoar armed to prevent his landing. They overtook him near the old houses [abandoned Hudson's Bay Company buildings] where they fired and shot him dead thro the head.[9]

The Canadians carried Little Gut's body back to their house, laid it on a platform in the yard, and began questioning Charles's Brother about the homicide at Ile à la Crosse. Fidler, the Hudson's Bay Company factor at Cumberland House, who seems to have been present, implies that the Indian told them nothing, saying he lay "foaming at the mouth and appeared quite insensible." The Canadians then took him outside and laid him beside Little Gut "but he seemed not to take the least notice." So they decided to hang him. "[W]hen they had carried him without the gates he began to sing very loud and continued till he came to the Tree where he was to be hung; they then made him confess every thing with the rope about his neck which he did, and informed of every one who was accomplices with him. [H]e said that he was the sole cause of the Death of the Canadian and seemed perfectly satisfied that he deserved this ignominious Death."[10]

Before hanging Charles's Brother, the Canadian trappers ob-

9. Entry for 2 June 1796, *ibid.*
10. *Ibid.*

served a few formalities, perhaps to emphasize the solemnity of the affair.

> [T]hey desired him if he had any thing to say concerning his wife a[nd] Children. [H]e said he had nothing to say on that head but recommend[e]d his eldest son to the protection of Mr. [George] Sutherland [of the Hudson's Bay Company, not a Canadian] which was the only request he made. They then hauled him up about 5 feet from the ground. [H]e had not hung 3 minutes when he gave a great struggle and the rope broke that he was suspended by, but he never afterwards moved. [B]ut they hung him up again as soon as the rope could be adjusted and let him hang one hour afterwards before they cut him down. They then took both him that was shot and him that was hung and hauled them a little way from their house and let them lay.[11]

The Canadians went to the trouble of suspending the body a second time and letting it hang for an hour because they were doing more than paying back Charles's Brother for the homicide at Ile à la Crosse. They wanted to insult him so much that every Indian for miles around would hear about it. It was a way of letting Indians know what happened to the manslayers of fur traders. They had the same thing in mind when dumping the bodies outside the stockades to be clawed apart by wolves and other animals. They expected that Indians coming to trade at Cumberland House would point out the spot to one another. That was why William McKay became furious on learning that, after he and the other Canadians had left Cumberland House, Fidler had ordered the bodies to be buried. He not only accused Fidler of "Committing an action beneath an Officer" of the fur trade, but said he had done so "purposely to show the savages" that he supported them in killing Canadians.[12] The degree of McKay's anger gives us a clue as to the Canadians' expectations that the sight or memory of the violated bodies really would deter other Indians.

McKay was wrong in one respect. Fidler agreed that Little Gut and Charles's Brother should have been killed. More importantly, he thought that the Canadians had succeeded in teaching the Indians the intended lesson. "There was only one Indian man present at the

11. *Ibid.*
12. Johnson, "Introduction to Edmonton," p. 40-41 n. 4.

execution and a boy," he noted, "and they appeared very much terrified and shocked never seeing or hearing of the like before." In fact, they were so shaken that he gave them "some Liquor to drown away melancholy." Other Indians, he was sure, would learn what had happened and would think twice before killing another fur trader. The hanging, Fidler concluded, "will be a means of deterring the Indians in future and prevent them from ill using or killing any [fur traders] this while to come."[13] We might say that this was wishful thinking, but Fidler was a Hudson's Bay Company fur trader and, like most fur traders, he understood that swift, brutal vengeance was the only way to deter Indian homicides.

13. Entry for 2 June 1796, Fidler, *Cumberland Journal*.

FIVE

Causation of Vengeance

IF THERE WAS one rule of vengeance for homicide that was universally applied in the western fur trade, it was that liability attached to a person or to a group for causation. Common-law notions like "guilt," personal responsibility, accident, self-defense, intent, malice, or *mens rea* were of no account in the law of vengeance. Liability and causation were what mattered, little else. Of course, it was of interest that a certain known, identified person had perpetrated the homicide being avenged, but that fact did not determine upon whom vengeance would be taken, and sometimes was not of much importance. However, this does not mean that mountain men were unconcerned about whom they killed. It mattered to them. There is no reason to doubt James Ohio Pattie's satisfaction in finding that the two Indians he and his companions shot out of the tree in the Gila River country had been the very men who had run off their horses.[1] Most mountain men who have left us their thoughts wanted to pay back in person anyone who did them an injury, at least for a homicide, but, as Pattie made clear when describing all the other acts of vengeance to which he was a party, personal guilt was of only secondary importance. What mattered was liability for cause.

There were few exceptions to the rule of causation. Alexander Henry the Younger gave us one when he did not take vengeance against the Chippewa who killed "undesignedly." Henry was thinking of common-law "guilt" and Christian responsibility, knowing that neither was the rule among the Indian nations or even among fur traders. A few years later, on the Saskatchewan, Henry investigated

1. *See* text at n. 19, ch. 1 *supra*.

a report that his hunter at Rocky Mountain House "intended to watch [for] and murder a Peagan at the House." If it were carried out, he realized, the plot "would be attended with serious consequences to us here, and indeed to the River in general."[2] He was saying that even if the Piegans were convinced that the hunter alone had killed one of their people, they would have held liable everyone connected with Rocky Mountain House and even, perhaps, everyone in the fur trade on the Saskatchewan, whether employed by Henry's North West Company or the Hudson's Bay Company.

In a letter to his commanding officer, Major General Winfield Scott, in 1824, Brigadier General Henry Atkinson indicated how far the concept of "causation" could reach. He reported that, all winter, news had been coming in of killings of American fur traders and trappers by Arikara Indians. "Taking then the Indian character into view, is it not reasonable to suppose they would seek every opportunity to revenge the death of those of their tribe who fell in the conflict in August by our troops?" he asked. "Certainly," he answered, and he did not mean that the Arikaras would limit vengeance to the fur company that had inflicted the first homicides or to the troops that had gone to the aid of the those the Arikaras had been fighting. Americans had caused the deaths of the Arikaras and it was Americans who were liable—any Americans. Vengeance had fallen on fur traders and trappers only because the Arikaras found them near at hand. "I now think," Atkinson concluded, "that the Missouri is shut against our traders, from the Great Bend up."[3] He meant that Arikaras were killing Americans.

Fur traders often knew when they were liable for vengeance, and generally they knew why. After John Clarke hanged the Indian for taking his prized silver goblet,[4] he left the Palouse River and joined other members of the Pacific Fur Company at the Walla Walla. Alexander Ross described what happened:

> [W]e were at a loss to account for the unusual movement and stir among the Indians, who seemed to be assembling from all quarters in great haste. The mystery was, however, soon cleared up when Mr. Clarke joined us, and related the affair of the silver goblet at the Catatouch camp. What did [Clarke's superior officers] Stuart and M'Kenzie say? What

2. Entry of 24 January 1811, Henry, *Journal Two*, pp. 594-95.
3. Henry Atkinson to Winfield Scott, 30 March 1824, *West of Ashley*, p. 76.
4. *See* text at n. 2, ch. 2 *supra*.

> could any man say? The reckless deed had been committed, and Clarke's countenance fell when the general voice of disapprobation was raised against him. The Indians all along kept flying to and fro, whooping and yelling in wild commotion. At this time, Tummeatapam came riding up to our camp at full speed. "What have you done, my friends?" called the old and agitated chief. "You have spilt blood on our lands!" Then pointing to a cloud of dust raised by the Indians, who were coming down upon us in wild confusion—"There, my friends, do you see them? What can I do?" The chief did not dismount, but wheeling round his horse again, off he went like a shot, leaving us to draw a salutary inference from the words "What can I do?"—meaning, no doubt, that we had better be off immediately. Taking the hint, we lost no time. Tents were struck; some had breakfasted, some not—kettles and dishes were all huddled together and bundled into the canoe, and, embarking pell-mell, we pushed with all haste for the inauspicious shore.[5]

Indeed, they kept moving for fifteen days, "passing the falls, the narrows, and the cascades, without the least interruption," until they reached the safety of their stockades near the mouth of the Columbia River.[6] Only one of them was "guilty" of hanging the Indian; the other officers had not been with Clarke and would have stopped him if they had been, yet all were liable, and it may be that some of them paid the blood price.[7]

Two ingredients propelled the doctrine of causation. One was the cultural urge many Indians felt to avenge an injury. It may be too extreme to say that vengeance was a conditioned reflex, a social necessity, but certainly, for some people under certain circumstances, it was a legal duty. The second ingredient was collective responsibility. Liability was seldom individual, but almost always fixed collectively upon the family, town, clan, band, or nation of the manslayer, not just upon the manslayer alone.

A story told by John Tanner demonstrates these two ingredients. An American who had been kidnapped and adopted by Indians as a

5. Ross, *First Settlers*, pp. 221-22.

6. *Ibid.*, p. 222.

7. At least Gabriel Franchère, another officer in the company, thought that was why John Reed and his companions would be killed. Barrett, "McKenzie, McDonald, Ross," p. 16.

boy, Tanner lived for many years as a member of both the Ottawa and Chippewa nations. He once joined a war party of Chippewas, Crees, Assiniboins, and Ottawas seeking vengeance against Sioux for a raid on the Chippewas near Pembina on the Red River. When the party started from the Red River it had four hundred members. During the first day of the campaign, one hundred Chippewas dropped out.

> In the following night, the Assinneboins left in considerable numbers, having stolen many horses, and, among others, four belonging to me and Wa-me-gon-e-biew [Tanner's friend]. I had taken but seven pairs of moccasins, having intended to make the whole journey on horse back, and it was now a great misfortune for me to lose my horses. I went to Pe-shau-ba, who was chief of the Ottowwaws, to which I belonged, and told him that I wished to take reprisals from the few Assinneboins still belonging to our party, but he would not consent, saying, very justly that the dissension growing out of such a measure, on my part, might lead to quarrels, which would entirely interrupt and frustrate the designs of the whole party.[8]

Tanner could easily be misunderstood. He had been asking Pe-shau-ba for help in seizing Assiniboin horses. He had not asked for Pe-shau-ba's permission. When Pe-shau-ba told him it was too dangerous and Tanner went ahead anyway, he was not defying authority. He tried to seize some Assiniboin horses but was unsuccessful, blaming his failure on the fact that he could persuade only one friend to join him.

At first glance Tanner's actions might not seem ideal for proving how greatly the urge for vengeance could dominate events on the western frontier. It might be thought that, as his horses had been taken from him and he needed horses for survival, he did what anyone with sufficient courage would have done under the circumstances. But his situation was not really desperate. He could have ridden the horses of friends, at least some of the time, or bought horses on credit. What was desperate was to disrupt the harmony of the war party. It was well inside the territory of the Sioux, a people deeply feared by the Chippewas if not by all the other nations in the war party. The warriors could not afford to become divided. Yet Tanner was ready to attack, perhaps even to fight a unit of the war party.

8. Tanner, *Narrative*, pp. 126-27.

And part of his motive, it should be noted, was vengeance. He had not planned to take just any horses, or the horses from the weakest in the party or from those who had the most to spare. He wanted Assiniboin horses because Assiniboins had taken his horses. Even assuming that he was in a desperate position and needed horses for survival, it has to be acknowledged that vengeance formed a large part of his motivation.

That Tanner planned to seize Assiniboin horses tells much of his story. The horses he wanted to take from Assiniboins were not the horses taken from him, or horses possessed by the Assiniboins who had taken his property. He was not particular. The horses of any Assiniboins would do. The reason was that he followed Indian principles of liability, not Christian principles of guilt. The Assiniboins who left the war party were the individuals who made off with his horses. Had he been asked, Tanner might have admitted that the Assiniboins who remained in the war party and whose horses he tried to take by force were innocent. But what did that matter? They were innocent as individuals, not as Assiniboins. That was what mattered: that they were Assiniboins, that Assiniboins had caused his injury, and, therefore, that they were liable. We might think that Tanner would have preferred to recover his own horses and pay back the individuals who had injured him, and he may well have preferred to do so, but it is unlikely that he thought it important—certainly not as important as we think it. The Assiniboins had done him in, and it was Assiniboins he would pay back.

It is doubtful whether in most cases of international homicide any attention was given to taking vengeance against the actual manslayer. The controlling doctrine was collectiveness. As we shall see, the nation of the manslayer was collectively liable and the nation of the victim could satisfy the blood debt by killing any member of the manslayer's nation. What is worth considering here is that Indians and fur men alike seem to have thought as Tanner did in terms of collective causation. Should a Crow be killed by the Sioux, for example, the victim's mother would ask the men of the Crow nation to slay any Sioux, apparently thinking of all Sioux as the cause of the homicide. "The Dakota have killed my . . . child," she would wail through the Crow camp, "who is going to kill one of them for me?"[9]

It is unclear how large the collectively liable group could be, although there is no problem with Indians. The Arikaras were not

9. Lowie, *Crow Indians*, p. 332. Similarly, *see* Mandelbaum, *Plains Cree*, p. 247.

out of the ordinary in taking vengeance against all Americans. It could as easily have been against all white people as against all Americans. The rule was different for fur traders and trappers, at least in most cases. It will be argued below that although few fur traders and trappers hesitated to adopt Indian notions and fix causation for homicide on individuals, families, bands, villages, camps, or nations, they did not extend liability to Indians in general. There were a very few exceptions to that practice, and it would be useful to consider one of them, as its facts help to delineate the reach of causation.

George Nidever was a trapper traveling with a fur brigade in the Sierras during 1833. A brother of his had been killed in Colorado three years earlier, and he knew that the manslayers had been Arapahos. We cannot be certain, but it is quite likely that he also knew that he would never run into Arapahos so far west. One day he and two other trappers were ahead of the main party scouting a campsite.

> [W]e became somewhat separated in our search, and upon entering the timber I discovered fresh signs of Indians. This alarmed me somewhat as I feared for the Capt.[10] and our companion,[11] who, like myself, had probably each taken a different course. I had just begun to look about for more signs when, glancing back in the direction I had come, I saw two Indians, with heads down and at a trot coming along my trail. I supposed that they were following my tracks, so I lost no time getting behind a tree and preparing for them. It took them some few minutes to reach me and in the meantime they would stop every few yards and look back, and listen as if pursued. I saw that they had not seen me or discovered my tracks, as they passed within a few feet of me, jabbering as they went along. I at first had a notion to let them go but the death of my brother, so treacherously murdered by these red devils was too fresh in my mind. The Indians were traveling in single file, and watching my chance, just before they would have to turn around a small point of rocks, I fired, shooting both of them dead at the first shot.[12]

10. The captain of the trapping brigade, Joseph Reddeford Walker, who had gone ahead with Nidever to locate a campsite.
11. Zenas Leonard, who also found this incident unusual enough to write an account. Leonard, *Narrative*, p. 75.
12. Nidever, *Life and Adventures*, p. 33.

From most perspectives, this double killing would not interest us. It was a clear case of payback vengeance and does not belong to any category of principled vengeance. Nidever's words, however, tell us something. He said his brother had been "murdered by these red devils." It is evident that he thought of all Indians as not just collectively liable for his brother's death but collectively the cause.

Ironically, perhaps the only North American people who would have understood and perhaps even accepted Nidever's concept of causation were Indians, or, at least, those Indians who would have held all white people liable to vengeance if a member of their own nation had been killed by a white. From the earliest days of the fur trade, both traders and trappers had realized that Indians were capable of extending causation almost beyond what to them were rational limits. They had long ago learned to tailor their behavior to avoid situations that could place them in what could be termed "causation jeopardy." A good example was the rule never to accept the protection of Indian war parties, and, certainly, never to join one as a member. There were, however, occasions when business needs might require that the rule be broken. In 1805 François-Antoine Larocque of the North West Company seized the chance to visit the Crows where no fur man had ever been, and perhaps open a trade with them. He was at the Missouri River villages of the Mandans and Hidatsa when a large party of Crows, led by Red Calf, arrived. The Crows refused to let Larocque travel with them until LaBorgne, a Hidatsa headman, pleaded on his behalf. Red Calf relented, on one condition. "Father, said he, if you are willing to go with us, we are willing to receive you—but should an enemy stand in our way, or attack us in our Journey—You and Your Young men must assist us in beating him off." Larocque promised "he would assist his friends on all occasions," surely aware that if he did so the enemy would hold him, his men, and most likely every other white trader liable for any killings.[13]

Seventy-one years earlier the great French explorer and fur trader Pierre Gaultier de Varennes La Vérendrye, seeking to cement a business relationship with the Crees, permitted them to adopt his eldest son and take him to war against the Sioux. His tactics worked in part, for he bound the Crees to the French trade. Unfortunately, the same steps made enemies of the Sioux. Two years after the son went on the warpath, he led a well-armed party of twenty-one men

13. "Charles McKenzie's Narratives," p. 248.

from La Vérendrye's fort. Within less than a day's journey they were all killed by the Sioux. The French knew why. The Sioux had taken vengeance.[14]

Merely to permit enemy Indians to travel with you could be cause enough. Warren Angus Ferris told of being a member of a brigade of trappers on the Lower Snake River in 1835 when they were confronted by a party of Snakes. The principal warrior demanded to know who the two Indians with the trappers were. They were Shawnees, members of a nation from east of the Mississippi, some of whom the summer before "had fought and killed a party of several Snakes." The trappers said they were Delawares, a nation from so far in the east it was likely the Snakes had had no experience with them. "[T]o have acknowledged them Shawnees would have exposed them and ourselves to instant death," Ferris explained. He said that the trappers and the Shawnees "were sworn to protect each other," but taking Shawnees into Snake territory could have been sufficient cause for the Snakes to have taken vengeance on the trappers.[15] In fact, trading with an enemy was enough. In 1818 Manuel Lisa, a St. Louis fur trader, reported "that the Arickaras have Killed one of his Men. It appears that they were provoked to it, from the circumstances of the Ottoes, with whom this Man Was trading, had killed in Action about thirty of them."[16] That was another reason why La Vérendrye's son had been killed by the Sioux: La Vérendrye had traded arms to the Cree.[17]

A person did not have to take specific action to incur liability. Passive causation triggered the same vengeance as active causation. John Tanner was hunting one day when he discovered tracks of the Sioux. Rushing home, he gathered his family and fled to a place where the Chippewas "had built and fortified a camp." He recounted: "On my arrival, the chiefs councilled, and sent two young men to look after the property left in my lodge, but as I knew the Sioux were lurking in that direction, and that should the young men be killed, or injured, their friends would consider me the cause of their misfortune, I went before them . . . determining that if any thing happened, I would be present, and have a part in it."[18]

14. Rich, *Fur Trade and Northwest*, pp. 88-89.
15. Ferris, *Life in Mountains*, p. 227.
16. Entry for 28 November 1818, Gale, *Missouri Journal*, p. 41.
17. Rich, *Fur Trade and Northwest*, p. 89.
18. Tanner, *Narrative*, p. 149.

Tanner was not apprehensive that vengeance would be taken against him. He only wanted to avoid being spoken of as the "cause" of their deaths. Someone unfamiliar with the doctrine of causation might think the Chippewa headmen more liable than Tanner. After all, they played an active role. They "sent" the two young men into potential danger. Tanner had done nothing but raise the alarm. But the Chippewa perspective was different. The young men did not have to go. The "chiefs" could not compel them. They went voluntarily. The more relevant cause was that Tanner and his family alone benefitted from the risk they took. It was his property they went to protect, and had they been killed the cause would have been protection of the property.

Just to invite Indians to trade could be dangerous. An officer of the Hudson's Bay Company described such an incident; one, he said, that caused him "alarm." To explain why, he quoted the Indians: "A party of seven or eight Indians having been drowned on their way to [Fort] Alexandria [a company post in New Caledonia], in autumn, their relatives imputed the misfortune to the whites. 'Had there been no whites at Alexandria,' said they, 'our friends would not have gone there to trade; and if they had not gone there, they would not have been drowned': *ergo*—the white men are the cause of their death, and the Indians must be avenged."[19]

That kind of reasoning could assign a cause for just about any death occurring to a person with whom you were associated. A British Columbia historian was probably correct in suggesting that when an Indian was killed while in the employ of Hudson's Bay Company "the traders could expect trouble," although it is doubtful that the Indians regarded them "as accessories after the fact."[20] The same causation flowed from the diseases that periodically swept through the nations, wiping out whole populations. The fur traders did not understand why the Indians threatened them with death. They assumed the Indians thought they had done something positive to spread the disease, by witchcraft or some such means.[21] In fact, the Indians knew who caused the plague, and causation determined liability.

In 1837 an American Fur Company steamboat stopping at Fort Clark carried the smallpox to the Arikara villages on the Missouri

19. McLean, *Notes of Service*, p. 148.
20. Fisher, *Contact and Conflict*, p. 38.
21. James Douglas to George Simpson, 18 March 1838, *Letters of McLoughlin First Series*, p. 282; White, *Middle Ground*, p. 77.

River. "A Ree that has lost his wife and child threatened us today," F. A. Chardon, the factor at Fort Clark, noted in his journal. "We are beset by enemies on all sides—expecting to be shot any Minute."[22] Chardon may have understood that, as a part of the fur trade and a member of the American Fur Company, he was, in medical fact, one of the contributing causes of the deaths of the Arikaras. What he did not realize was that he was also in danger because, in Indian law, he was a cause.

22. F.A. Chardon, journal entry, 16 August 1837, in Christopher and Hafen, "Wiliam F. May," p. 212.

SIX

Mechanics of Vengeance

AMERICAN AND BRITISH fur traders and trappers adapted to the culture of vengeance with remarkable ease. It became a defining ingredient of their philosophy of mountain life—certainly when dealing with Indians. "The Indians Killed one of my dogs," the factor at Fort Clark on the upper Missouri River noted, referring to a Mandan. "[R]etaliated by Killing two others in his place—sweet revenge."[1]

Vengeance was so natural to John Tanner that he could not break the habit once he reentered American society after spending his youth and early manhood as an Ottawa and a Chippewa.[2] While still a Chippewa, he had left home on a brief trip. In his absence Gi-ah-ge-wa-go-mo, another Chippewa, went to Tanner's lodge and seized one of his sons, a six-year-old. On his return, Tanner went in pursuit, overtook the party that had his son, scooped up the boy, and

> then turning, went back to meet Gi-ah-ge-wa-go-mo and Na-na-bush. They had now left the thicket, and were standing in the path, the former holding his favourite horse by the halter. When I rode up to them, I left my son on the horse, with the reins in his hands, got down, and stabbed Gi-ah-ge-wa-go-mo's horse twice with a large knife I had carried for the purpose. He clubbed his gun, and was about to strike me,

1. Entry for 14 March 1837, *Chardon's Journal*, p. 103.
2. "The circumstances into which he has been thrown, among a wild and lawless race, have taught him to consider himself in all situations, the avenger of his own quarrel," and he continued the practice up through the time he was writing his story. Edwin James, "Introductory Chapter," in Tanner, *Narrative*, p. xvii.

> but I caught it in descending, and wrested it out of his hands. He threatened he would shoot my horse whenever he could get a gun. I handed his own to him, and told him to shoot the horse now; but he dared not. . . . My friends could scarce believe I had killed his horse, but they did not blame me, neither did Gi-ah-ge-wa-go-mo. At least I never heard that he complained of it, and at the time he molested me no more.[3]

By killing the horse, Tanner paid back the injury Gi-ah-ge-wa-go-mo had done him. If he had an urge to kill Gi-ah-ge-wa-go-mo, Tanner suppressed it. Vengeance, he believed, should be proportionate to the injury. On another occasion, an enemy named Waw-bebe-nais-sa crept up behind Tanner and struck his head with a hatchet, almost killing him. While he was recovering, one of his friends, Oto-pun-ne-be, attacked Waw-bebe-nais-sa and would have killed him had not other Chippewas intervened. During the fight Oto-pun-ne-be broke two of Waw-bebe-nais-sa's ribs. "I was content with the punishment that had been thus bestowed upon Waw-bebe-nais-sa," Tanner explained, "as I thought two broken ribs about equal to the broken head he had given me."[4]

Tanner emphasized that Gi-ah-ge-wa-go-mo did not take vengeance after his horse had been killed, though he might have done so, and probably was expected to. Failing to exact vengeance could cost a man respect. Respect was a chief motivation for vengeance, as Tanner explained when describing how he paid back Wa-me-gon-a-biew, his best friend among the Chippewas. Wa-me-gon-a-biew had smashed a gun belonging to Tanner, uttering a disparaging remark that was overheard by a number of people. Later, when at Pembina to trade with the North West Company, the Chippewas held "a drunken frolick," as Tanner called it. "After I had drunk a little, I heard some one speak sneeringly about my gun," he explained. Angered, he went outside and killed Wa-me-gon-a-biew's horse, "using at the same time, in a loud voice, the same words I had been told he had spoken when he broke my gun." Tanner then remained at Pembina to face his friend should he want revenge, but "Wa-me-gon-a-biew made no complaints of my having killed his horse. Probably he was perfectly satisfied that I had done so, as an Indian always expects any outrage he commits shall be retaliated,

3. *Ibid.*, pp. 203-4.
4. *Ibid.*, pp. 233-34.

according to their customs, and a man who omits to take proper revenge is but lightly esteemed among them."[5]

The many reasons that the fur traders and trappers gave for adopting the practice of vengeance will be considered later, with the theory of vengeance. For the moment only one other reason for vengeance is relevant to the discussion. It is that among the Indians vengeance, especially for homicide, was quite often a legal duty. We need only one homicide to illustrate the rule. It is a homicide that was referred to in the introduction, but deserves to be considered in greater detail: the killing of Samuel Black by a young Shuswap.

Black was factor at the Kamloops post of the Hudson's Bay Company in New Caledonia when he was shot during 1841. Although there was little dispute about the facts of the case, there was much disagreement as to why he had been killed. John McLoughlin, Black's superintendent for the Oregon Country, reported to the governor of the Hudson's Bay Company in North America that Black had been killed without cause

> unless it could be traced to the sudden death of one of their [the Shuswaps'] rascally Chiefs, Tranquille. This Indian in the course of the summer applied to the deceased for a gun in the Fort, which he said the owner, a North River Indian had made over to him, a request that could not be complied with without a more convincing proof of the fact. In January he again applied, prior to his setting out for the Pavilion or Fraser's River with the same success, when I believe some angry words ensued. At the Pavilion he soon fell ill, and died five days after. Pending his illness, it was rumored among the Indians, and insidiously propagated by the doctors, that if he did not recover, his death must be ascribed to the bad medicine of the Whites, and revenged.[6]

McLoughlin's extensive experience among the Indians should have helped him understand the circumstances better. He was rationalizing by European explanations what he did not take the trouble to comprehend. An educated physician himself, he blamed the machinations of the Shuswap doctors, probably trying to shift blame for Le Tranquille's death away from their own incompetence. It

5. *Ibid.*, pp. 201-2.
6. John McLoughlin to George Simpson, 20 March 1841, *Letters of McLoughlin Second Series*, p. 247.

became an accepted story among the people of the Hudson's Bay Company. Another officer wrote: "To this melancholy affair no direct cause can be assigned, unless it could be traced to their superstition & the villainous practices of their man [*sic*] of medicine— One of their Chiefs died very suddenly, & the Conjurors made out that the medium of the whites was too powerful for them to avert, & hence took this frightful revenge."[7]

The man to whom McLoughlin wrote had a simpler explanation. "[T]his foul murder," Governor George Simpson told Hudson's Bay headquarters in London, "was committed without the least provocation on the part of the unfortunate gentleman, who has been the victim of savage superstition and revenge."[8] That was what most fur traders preferred to think. People they believed to be "savages" acted like savages, as should be expected, and to look for other motivations was a waste of time.[9] Everything was superstition and blind vengeance.[10]

Peter Skene Ogden had a different perspective. He had been Black's best friend in the Hudson's Bay Company as well as the company's chief factor for New Caledonia. Both the friendship and his position may have led him to investigate motivations. At least he went to the trouble of quoting the Shuswap words of vengeance. It is unfortunate we do not have more. Heed should be paid not only to what words Indians spoke, but what words were attributed to them by men in the fur trade. Ogden was told by an informant that after Le Tranquille died, his widow seized his gun and waved it in front of her eldest son. "With this must my husband's death be revenged," she scolded. "Go, my son, go, and revenge your father, whose death the foul machinations of others have occasioned."[11] These are Ogden's words, the words reported to him by some other person, whether Indian or Hudson's Bay Company official.

7. Cole, *Exile in Wilderness*, p. 196 (quoting McDonald).
8. George Simpson to the Governor and Committee, 20 June 1841, *Simpson's London Letters*, p. 30.
9. Or they made up motivations that seemed to them to fit Indian beliefs. The officer who was sent to avenge Black's death, for example, said that Le Tranquille's widow ordered her son to kill Black because "the father's spirit should not be left to go alone, but should be accompanied by the spirit of some chief of equal rank." Tod, "Scotch Boy," pp. 213-14.
10. Of course, some historians have adopted similar explanations. *See, e.g.*, Patterson, "Introduction of Journal," pp. xcii-xciii; Morice, *History*, p. 181 n. 1.
11. [Ogden,] *Traits of Indian Life*, p. 93.

Although there seems to be no direct Shuswap evidence, from what we know of North American Indian terminology, the expressions are authentic for western Indians in general, as well as for other Salishan nations in the transboundary area. Again it is important to distinguish between the international law of the North American nations and their domestic law, in this case Shuswap law. Under international law any Shuswap who believed Black had been the cause of Le Tranquille's death might have accepted the responsibility and have killed him or another member of the Hudson's Bay Company in revenge, at least if the company had not negotiated and paid compensation for the homicide to the Shuswap nation or to Le Tranquille's responsible kin. We can be less certain about domestic law as little is known about the specific rules governing retaliation for homicide among the Shuswaps. What can be said is that for those nations whose laws are known there was a legal principle conferring on certain members of the nation, often kin folk of a specific lineage or of a defined degree, a right—in some cases a duty, sometimes privileged—to retaliate in kind for the killing of a member of the nation or of the kin group. If the words Ogden attributed to Le Tranquille's widow were accurate to a reasonable degree, she appears to be asserting this domestic right in an international situation, telling her son that he has a right, perhaps even a duty, to avenge the death of her husband because it has been caused by "others" upon whom there was either an individual or collective liability.

To say that there was a duty to take vengeance, of course, raises other questions. A duty to avenge whom? Who had the duty to take vengeance? And against whom was there the duty to take vengeance?

Among Indians, the answer to the first question—which homicides created a duty to take vengeance—depended upon local law, and upon whether the homicide was committed by a member of the victim's nation or was an international homicide. Among fur traders and trappers, however, the general practice was to avenge all homicides committed by a full-blood Indian upon a white person or a fur trapper of mixed blood. Exceptions to that rule were very rare, perhaps more likely to be stated than to be carried out. An example was recorded by Robert Longmoor, the factor at Hudson's Bay Company's Hudson House in 1781. It had been a particularly hard winter, a time of great hunger among the Indians and a season when the company, because of the American war, was unable to keep posts supplied with trade goods. Indians arriving to sell furs were often angry when told there was little to exchange, and on at least one occasion became violent.

> [T]hey wanted to force the Gates and come in to take What they pleased, they had ten Guns loaded, Some with Ball, Some with Slugs and some Bristol Shot, they cut the Gates and likewise some of the Stockades the first Gun presented I broke, and then took all the rest from them,[12] and their Knives and Bayonets, and four I confined in the House, which was the Ringleaders, for some time, And then as I had all their Arms I let them out, Those is the same Villains that killed the Frenchmen and Robbed them, two years ago, but if in Case one Englishman should be killed I will not spare one Indian that I know has any hand in it.[13]

Longmoor was saying that he had in his power Indians whom he knew had killed John Cole at Eagle Hills two years earlier. But Cole had not been a Hudson's Bay Company employee, or what Longmoor called an "Englishman." He was a trader out of Montreal, a "Frenchman," and Longmoor felt neither a duty nor a need to avenge him.

Had Cole been "English," Longmoor would have taken vengeance. When any of their people were killed, Hudson's Bay Company officers assumed they had a right and, apparently, also a duty to avenge the homicide. They took vengeance while knowing it made them or other Hudson's Bay employees likely targets of countervengeance. Once James Douglas, the future governor of British Columbia, killed a Carrier in revenge for homicides that had been committed at Fort George, a Hudson's Bay trading post on a branch of the Fraser River in New Caledonia. Although Douglas understood the risk, he apparently expected the matter to be composed, for, when reporting the killing to James Connolly, the company's chief factor in New Caledonia, he did not seem concerned that he might become the object of counterretaliation. Describing the killing as "the accomplishment of a much desired event," he wrote of "the death of Zulth-nolly, whom we dispatched on the 1st of the Month in the Indian Village of this place, without confusion or any

12. He handled the Indians more easily than might be expected because they were drunk.
13. Entry for 4 March 1781, Longmoor, *Second Hudson Journal*, p. 182.

accident happening to any other individual."[14] Before too long, Douglas learned that he had been wrong. What he called an "accident" might happen to him. "Douglas's life is much exposed among the Carriers," Connolly wrote to John McLoughlin, the company's chief factor in the Oregon Country. "[H]e would readily face a hundred of them, but does not much like the idea of being assassinated, with your permission he might next year be removed to the Columbia."[15] Reassigning Douglas out of Carrier reach protected the Hudson's Bay Company's interests as well as Douglas. Had the Carriers killed him, the company would have surely retaliated again, making any accommodation much more difficult to negotiate.

Any member of the Carrier nation might have felt a duty to kill Douglas, and, in Carrier law, any member may have been competent to kill him, just as, from the perspective of the Hudson's Bay Company (although not, of course, from the perspective of the Shuswaps), any Hudson's Bay employee could have satisfied the debt owed for the killing of Samuel Black by executing his Shuswap avenger of blood. It was immaterial whether the person avenging blood was an officer of the company or of the same rank as the person being avenged. Nationality or kinship, not status, was what mattered. The Hudson's Bay Company's "official avenger" in New Caledonia, Jean-Baptiste Boucher, or Waccan, to use his native name, was an engagé, not an officer, and seems to have been of mixed blood.[16]

Although in international homicides it usually did not matter who served as the avenger of blood (any member of the avenging nation would do), the status of the avenger was of absolute importance in domestic homicide. In many nations certain close kin had the right to be the avenger of blood, and in some nations it may have been the duty to avenge a slaying if related by birth to the victim within a certain degree of kinship. It is sometimes said that in nations with either a matrilineal or patrilineal clan system, it was the clan that "avenged the death of any member."[17] That statement is a little misleading. In most cases it is more accurate to say that a close-clan kin, not the clan as a whole, was the avenger of blood.

Hudson's Bay Company officers and historians, when discussing

14. James Douglas to William Connolly, 3 August 1828, in "Notes," to *Simpson's 1828 Journey*, p. 27 n. 1.
15. Rich, "James Douglas," in *Letters of McLoughlin Third Series*, p. 312.
16. Morice, *History*, p. 253.
17. Bruner, "Mandan," p. 223.

the killing of Samuel Black, have variously described the Shuswap avenger of blood as either Le Tranquille's "nephew" or his "son." They did not think the distinction of much importance, but it could matter a great deal whether Le Tranquille's avenger was his son or his nephew. Whether he was one or the other depended on the rules of family relationship in the Shuswap nation. Under any kinship system, an avenger could be a brother. Under some, the avenger should not be a father, son, nephew, or uncle. As the Shuswaps were a Salishan people of the Plateau culture, their kinship system was almost certainly bilateral,[18] in which case the avenger of Le Tranquille's blood quite likely would have been Le Tranquille's son, if old enough, and the woman who urged him to kill Black could have been Le Tranquille's widow. For purposes of illustration, consider the alternatives. Under a patrilineal kinship system, the avenger of blood would also have been Le Tranquille's son, but the older woman was more likely to have been the young man's aunt, although she could have been his mother.[19] If, however, the Shuswap kinship was matrilineal, the avenger of blood should have been Le Tranquille's nephew, the son of Le Tranquille's sister.[20] The woman exhorting her male kin to exact the blood debt would have been the mother of the young man, the victim's sister, not his wife.

A more difficult matter was against whom vengeance could be taken. It was on this question that the moral and legal values of the white fur traders and trappers most sharply differed from those of the North American Indians. Where the whites tended to think in terms of individual guilt for homicide, the Indians thought of collective liability. Sir Nicholas Garry, a high-ranking Hudson's Bay Company officer, was surprised when told about the death "of an excellent Indian." "A friend of his had killed an Indian," Garry wrote. "The

18. Scholarship on the Shuswap is not extensive. It is known that Salishan kinship systems were uniformly bilateral. The cultures of the Salishan nations, which included that of the Shuswap, are said to have been so close that "a description of one is virtually a description of another." For example, "[t]heir marriage . . . customs are practically identical." Tout, "Ethnology," p. 131. Thus among the Shuswap there is one term for "uncle," referring to father's brother or mother's brother. The same is true of "aunt," "nephew," and "niece." Spier, "Kinship Systems," p. 74.

19. In the West, the Omaha had a patrilineal kinship system.

20. In the West, the Crow and the Mandan had a matrilineal kinship system. The relationship described in the text would also have been true of the Creeks, Chickasaws, and Cherokees.

Family to revenge this Death appointed one of their Tribe not to kill the Murderer, but his dearest Friend considering he would suffer more in the Death of the Person he loved than in dying himself."[21]

It can safely be assumed that the "Friend" was actually a near relative, perhaps a close-clan kin. Another significant fact, although Garry probably did not notice it, was that this was vengeance for a domestic, not an international killing. The slayer, the victim, the "Family," and the "Friend" all belonged to the same nation. Many facts about which Garry did not inquire, if known, would make the story quite different, such as whether the original manslayer had fled the nation, and the physical condition or age of the "Friend." Instead, Garry simply condemned the whole affair. "This is a Refinement of savage Cruelty and Revenge which only the Devil could put in their Heads. This is not a solitary Instance but it is their Custom," he concluded.[22]

From the perspective of law, the vengeance Garry criticized was not much different from the Chickasaw case in which an uncle killed himself as atonement for a homicide committed by his nephew. In both situations someone other than the manslayer paid the blood price. The main difference was that opposite parties selected the person to die. Garry did not understand what he was describing, and did not realize there were questions he could have asked. That was not his mistake, however. His mistake was to judge a case of North American Indian collective liability by the values of European individual responsibility.

Almost a half-century earlier, on the Saskatchewan River, William Tomison of the Hudson's Bay Company saw a pedlar named Captain Tute arrive to build a rival Canadian trading post and then flee the very next day. "Captain Tute went off this morning betimes, with men, Goods and every thing Else," Tomison recorded in the Hudson House journal. "What their reason is for so doing I do not know further than an Indian having died Suddently [*sic*] after drinking some at their Settlement at Sturgeon River this accident have put them in dread of the natives falling upon them again."[23] For some reason he did not explain, Tomison was not worried about the safety of himself or his men. The Indian had died while drinking at a Canadian post, not at a Hudson's Bay Company house. Tomison

21. Entry for 26 June 1821, Garry, "Diary," p. 113.
22. Entry for 26 June 1821, *ibid*.
23. Entry for 20 November 1779, Tomison, *Hudson Journal*, pp. 76-77.

apparently assumed the Indians would not "fall" on him even if Captain Tute escaped.

Tomison would have been well advised to follow Tute down the Saskatchewan. When a fur trader caused the death of a native, all fur traders could be collectively liable under international law. In 1823 trappers of the Missouri Fur Company killed two Arikaras. Describing the Arikaras' reaction, a historian wrote, "Making no distinction between white traders, the Indians were seeking revenge."[24] To say "making no distinction" may be another way of saying "collective liability." It is possible that Indians would make a distinction between traders of the Hudson's Bay Company and those of another firm, and take vengeance only against the traders associated with the person who committed a homicide. Sometimes they made that distinction when taking vengeance. Tomison, therefore, had a good chance of escaping liability but could never be sure he was safe, at least until he heard that vengeance had been taken against Captain Tute or some other Canadian.

Tomison could not be certain because these rules were not promulgated by a sovereign. Everything depended on the international nuances of the victim's nation. Under the customs of some tribes, Tomison would have made the right decision. Liability could be limited to the company of the manslayer. In still others, it was limited to the nationality of the manslayer, which would have meant that only Canadians were liable and that Tomison, as an "Englishman," was safe. But many nations—almost certainly the vast majority—made all whites liable, regardless of nationality.[25] When Alexander Ross was leading the Hudson's Bay Company's Snake country expedition for 1824 back to the Columbia River, he permitted some of his mixed-blood trappers to go off on a horse-stealing raid against a band of Snakes. At least one Snake was killed, perhaps more. These Snakes seem to have thought of the killers as "white men," for they looked to Americans as much as to British to pay the blood price. As events turned out, it was Americans who paid, because it was Americans whom the Snakes first encountered.[26]

24. Mattison, "Joshua Pilcher," p. 254.

25. For example, it was noted in 1794 that the Arikara, who were then only beginning to become acquainted with white people, "do not know any distinction between the French, Spanish, English, etc., calling them all indifferently White Men or Spirits." Truteau, "Journal," p. 296.

26. Hafen, "Etienne Provost," pp. 373-74, quoting Peter Skene Ogden, letter of 10 August 1825.

The next year Ross's successor as leader of the Snake country expedition, Peter Skene Ogden, exerted "considerable pe[r]suasion" to prevent another horse-stealing raid. "[T]he murder of 7 Americans & Patrick O'Con[n]or[27] was owing to that unfortunate thieving expedition," he explained. Ogden was saying that the Americans had been killed for revenge, and that Ross's men had been the cause of their deaths.[28]

Fur traders and trappers encountered the international situation so frequently that it is puzzling why they did not understand better the doctrine of collective liability that the Snakes had applied. To give just one other example, take an 1811 encounter with the Sioux by the overland Astorians—the members of John Jacob Astor's Pacific Fur Company who traveled to the mouth of the Columbia River by land rather than by sea.

> During smoking, Mr. [Wilson Price] Hunt asked them [the Sioux] why they killed white men, as he heard that they had killed three during the last summer? They replied, because the white men kill us: that man (pointing to Carson) killed one of our brothers last summer. This was true. Carson, who was at that time among the Ricaras [Arikaras], fired across the Missouri at a war party of Sioux, and it was by a very extraordinary chance he killed one of them, as the river is a full half mile in breadth, and in retaliation the Sioux killed three white men.[29]

Then, again, it may be that the Astorians did not understand what they were being told about collective liability. At least no one thought to ask the Sioux why, if Carson had been with the Arikaras and presumably fighting for them, liability fell on the whites rather than the Arikaras. The answer was not that the Sioux and the Arikaras were already at war. The answer was that Carson, the manslayer, was a white. The only relevant legal fact was that he caused the death of the Sioux. His intentions, to help the Arikaras, as well as the nature and quality of his actions, were immaterial.

27. Patrick O'Connor had been an employee of Hudson's Bay Company on the Columbia River. He had "deserted" to join the company of American trappers with whom he was slain.
28. Entry for 8 June 1825, Ogden, *First Snake Journals*, p. 58.
29. Entry for 2 June 1811, Bradbury, *Travels*, p. 111.

Among Indian nations it was not always easy to locate the unit to which collective liability attached. Certainly it was more difficult in the West than it had been in the Southeast—among the Creeks or Cherokees, for example. Under their domestic law, if a Creek killed a Creek, collective liability attached to the manslayer's clan, and the same was true if a Cherokee killed a Cherokee. By international law, if a Creek killed a Cherokee or a Cherokee killed a Creek, liability attached to the manslayer's nation, not to a clan, and the liable nation was readily identified. Rules in the fur-trapping regions of the transboundary West were less precise. One nation differed from another, with some fixing domestic liability on the "family," some on the "village" or camp, and some on the "band."

No matter how clear definitions may have been within groups, the terms "family," "village," and "band" could not match the preciseness of the matrilineal or the patrilineal clan. Recall the difficulty John Work had in formulating a plan to avenge his trapper killed by a family of Snakes. The "most fundamental social unit" among the Snakes was the nuclear bilateral family, which could have been hard to identify without help from some Snake who lived in the same neighborhood. Among many of the Indians of the Pacific coast, the most fundamental responsible unit was the village community.[30] To an outsider, a villager could include anyone in a village, even someone who was not a permanent resident but had just wandered in for a brief stay. Told that the individual against whom he had exacted vengeance was such a person, an avenger of blood might feel he had not obtained sufficient satisfaction and return, to kill someone else. Finally, among the Indians of the Plateau and some of the buffalo-hunting nations such as the Blackfoot and the Plains Cree, the basic group for maintaining order, control, and security was the band, generally traveling from place to place, often with flexible, open-ended membership.[31]

Two passages from the journal of Alexander Henry the Younger suggest how great the difference could be. During August 1808 Henry was reflecting upon the Chippewas. "They are so nearly connected together, that to injure one is to injure the whole tribe," he wrote, implying that collective liability should fasten on the entire Chippewa nation because, when one of its members was the victim of homicide, the whole nation would have an interest in the ven-

30. Sapir, "Social Organization of Coast," pp. 357-58.
31. Ray, *Cultural Relations in Plateau*, p. 7.

geance.[32] Two years later Henry was trading on the Saskatchewan River, far from the Chippewas. One day two Sussees hunting buffalo were fallen upon by a party of unidentified Indians. A Sussee was killed but the second, although scalped, survived.

> The wounded person says that one of them [i.e., the attackers] spoke the Cree Language. This affair was nearly the cause of an ugly affair between the Crees who are tented with them Ten Tents, and the Sussees but upon reflection the latter considered that if it was done by the Crees it must have been a party [of Crees] from below who of course are not considered as the same people as the Beaver Hills or Upper strong wood Crees. The affair has dropped for the present, but the Sussees declare they will have ample revenge, when it is found out who it was.[33]

There are few better descriptions of how difficult it could be to inflict vengeance on Plains Indians. Henry said that the Crees were so divided into autonomous, widely scattered, identifiable bands that the Sussees decided that all Crees would not be held collectively liable for the homicide of the Sussee hunter. In particular, they concluded that the Ten Tents Cree had had nothing to do with the attack and therefore were free from vengeance. They also exonerated the Beaver Hill Cree and the Strong Woods Cree, leaving open the question as to who was liable except that it was some band of Crees.

An aspect of the mechanics of vengeance that has previously been mentioned needs clarification. Whenever vengeance was taken for an international homicide, it was never a privileged act, and the nation against whose member vengeance was exercised was likely to retaliate. What was legal under the first nation's customs was illegal to the second nation, and was a common cause of Indian wars. For that reason, leaders of other Indian nations located in southern New Caledonia urged the Shuswaps to resolve the homicide of Samuel Black by satisfying the demands of the Hudson's Bay Company for retaliatory blood. They had an interest in the homicide because a Hudson's Bay Company war against the Shuswap would have disrupted trade in New Caledonia. "You, my friends of the Shuswap

32. Entry for 13 August 1808, Henry, *Journal Two*, p. 333.
33. Entry for 2 September 1810, *ibid.*, p. 467.

tribe, the murderer is one of you," Nicola, a headman of the Okanagans, told the Shuswaps. "Justice calls on him to die, and die he must."[34] Although the words used—"murderer," "justice," and that the Shuswap manslayer "must" die—indicate that this is a loose translation by some fur trader, we know the sense of what was said and Nicola's words should not be read in haste. He seems to be urging the Shuswaps to end the possibility of international conflict by killing Black's manslayer themselves. More probably, however, he thought that no Shuswap possessed the authority or the privilege to kill another Shuswap, and, therefore, had something else in mind. Perhaps he anticipated that an Okanagan or a member of some other local nation, to please the Hudson's Bay officers, might kill the manslayer, and he was asking the Shuswaps to overlook the slaying as a thing done in the dark. A stronger possibility is that he knew that the most likely avenger of blood would be an employee of the Hudson's Bay Company and wanted the Shuswaps to avoid war with the British by looking the other way.

It is remarkable how the British and the Americans working in the fur country of the transboundary North American West adapted to their own use the principles of collective liability even while refusing to credit their existence. Certainly they resisted admitting that they acted upon them. James Douglas, who killed more than one Indian manslayer in cold blood, took comfort in the fact that they were "guilty," boasting that when dealing with Indians he had "invariably acted on the principle that it is inexpedient and unjust to hold *tribes* responsible for the acts of *individuals*."[35] He was wrong, of course. It was surely expedient, and perhaps even just, to hold Indians to their own legal standards.

There are, unfortunately, too many cases of vengeance where we cannot be certain what the fur men had in mind. The reason is that their accounts are often too brief or written with too little attention to the mechanics of vengeance. When the Hudson's Bay Company decided to close the old North West Company's post of Fort St. John on the Peace River, local Indians became angry. They killed the clerk, Guy Hughes, and his only two remaining men. Hudson's Bay immediately gathered a force of mixed-blood employees and Crees, under the command of a clerk, to take vengeance. Before the party got far from its starting point it was told to return. A Hudson's

34. Patterson, "Introduction to Journal," p. xcvi.
35. Francis, Jones, and Smith, *Origins*, p. 369.

Bay Company officer explained: "These orders were no doubt dictated by feelings of humanity, as Mr. McIntosh had learned that some Indians, who were not concerned in the murder, were in the same camp, and he was apprehensive the innocent might be involved in the same punishment with the guilty."[36]

From this brief account we do not know why the officer, William McKintosh, canceled the vengeance. One interpretation is that he agreed with Douglas that whole tribes should not be held liable for acts of individuals, and decided that too many "innocent" people would be killed if the vengeance party got anywhere near the manslayers. Just as possible, however, is that the "innocent" Indians McKintosh was protecting were members of other nations who might be camped with the nation of the manslayers. If so, he was not rejecting Indian customs of vengeance for homicide. He was, rather, applying them by limiting vengeance to the nation of the manslayers and avoiding third-party or "innocent" Indians.

Peter Skene Ogden seems to have drawn somewhat the same line. He is of special interest for, as will be seen later, few other mountain men internalized Indians' values of vengeance more than he or gave less thought to the morality or legality of his actions when exacting vengeance. For the moment, recall that he once led the Snake country expedition far down the Colorado River into the Mohave nation. There he encountered Indians who, he suspected, had killed several of Jedediah Smith's men a year or two earlier when Smith crossed the desert into Mexican California.[37] "My men were eager to revenge the massacre upon them," Ogden later recalled, "but as I had no proof that these were the guilty persons, I withheld my consent to their entreaties." Although we cannot be certain, the implication from what Ogden said was that, had he been able "to confirm my suspicion of their identity,"[38] he would have permitted his Hudson's Bay brigade to retaliate for what had been done not to the Hudson's Bay Company or anyone belonging to it, or even to his fellow British, but to Americans. At first glance it might appear that Ogden was concerned that these Indians were not "guilty"; that they had not personally attacked Smith and hence were "innocent." That is quite unlikely. When Ogden said he had doubts as to whether they were "the guilty persons," he was not concerned with whether they

36. McLean, *Notes of Service*, p. 143.
37. Smith had had ten men killed. *Travels of Jedediah Smith*, pp. 29-31.
38. [Ogden,] *Traits of Indian Life*, p. 9.

were the individuals who had killed Smith's men. His doubts were whether they were members of the "guilty" nation. If they were of the same nation, it would have been immaterial whether they had played a role in the "massacre," opposed it when it occurred, or never known that the killings had taken place.

SEVEN

Compensation Vengeance

TO APPRECIATE more fully the rules of vengeance for homicide in either international law or domestic law, it is more useful to concentrate attention on the avenger of blood than on the person owing the blood debt. We might guess that the key to understanding vengeance would be found by studying the collective liability of the group against whom vengeance was being taken. In fact, the key lies with the collective solidarity or the collective sense of duty of the avenging group. If any decisions were made, if any variations were introduced to the procedures of vengeance, they were made and introduced by the avengers of blood. The story told by Sir Nicholas Garry illustrates the point. The Chippewas who chose to take vengeance on a "Friend" of the manslayer, rather than on the manslayer himself, were the avengers of blood.

Whom to take vengeance against was sometimes the second decision for the avengers of blood. On a few occasions they had to make another decision first: whether to take vengeance at all. That question might have to be decided, for example, in situations of international homicide if vengeance meant beginning a war with another nation or ending any chances of peace if negotiations were being conducted between the nation of the manslayer and the nation of the avenger of blood. In domestic law the question could also be important in those nations where killing the manslayer or a member of the liable kin could lead to vengeance ad infinitum.

John Tanner told two stories illustrating the issues faced by avengers of blood in nations in which vengeance could be ad infinitum. In the first, Tanner's Ottawa father, that is, the Ottawa who kidnapped him and adopted him as a son, was struck in the head by a younger Ottawa. After a few days the father realized he was dying. Taking his gun, he started off to kill the young man when he was stopped by his eldest son. "My father," the son said, "if I was well I could help you kill this man, and could protect my young brothers from the vengeance of his friends, after he is dead; but you see my situation, and that I am about to die. My brothers are young and weak, and we shall all be murdered if you kill this man." The father laid down his gun and in a short time died.[1]

Tanner's second story was about Wa-me-gon-a-biew, with whom Tanner was so close that he called him his "brother." Wa-me-gon-a-biew had his nose bitten off during a drunken brawl (a surprisingly frequent occurrence, at least among the Chippewas). One day, when returning to the camp where they lived, Tanner found a sign warning him that Wa-me-gon-a-biew had killed a man. "I was not deterred by this information," Tanner said, indicating that there was a risk he could somehow be involved, probably due to his closeness to Wa-me-gon-a-biew or some act of mutual adoption. When Tanner arrived at camp the victim was being buried.

> We-me-gon-a-biew went by himself, and dug a grave wide enough for two men; then the friends of Ke-zha-zhoons brought his body, and when it was let down into the grave, We-me-gon-a-biew took off all his clothes, except his breech cloth, and sitting down naked at the head of the grave, drew his knife, and offered the handle to the nearest male relative of the deceased. "My friend," said he, "I have killed your brother. You see I have made a grave wide enough for both of us, and I am now ready and willing to sleep with him." The first and second, and eventually all the friends of the murdered young man, refused the knife which Wa-me-gon-a-biew offered them in succession. The relations of Wa-me-gon-a-biew were powerful, and it was fear of them which now saved his life. The offence of the young man whom he killed, had been calling him "cut nose." Finding that none of the male relatives of the deceased were willing to undertake publicly the punishment of his murderer, Wa-me-gon-a-biew said to them, "trouble me no more, now or hereafter, about this business. I shall do again as I have now done, if any of you venture to give me similar provocations."[2]

1. Tanner, *Narrative*, pp. 19-21 (quote at 21).
2. *Ibid.*, pp. 154, 165-66.

In some Indian nations the law was different. Vengeance was privileged. Avengers of blood did not fear counterretaliation. If one clan, kin group, family, or household owed a life to another clan, kin group, family, or household, the avengers of blood were free to exact vengeance without interference or apprehension that violence would be turned back upon them. Among the Choctaws, manslayers not only helped to dig their victim's grave, as Wa-me-gon-a-biew did, they were told by the victim's clan how much time they had to arrange their affairs, and when and where to appear for their executions. No one thought of the manslayers' clans striking back.[3] The Cherokees referred to the avenging clan's privileged right as a duty imposed on the clan of the manslayer to be "indifferent," a duty "to remain neuter by the law of the Nation."[4]

To say that there was no privilege of vengeance in some nations would be to describe the matter too mildly. The rule was often so much the opposite of privileged vengeance that it seems to have been no rule at all. David Thompson, the great surveyor of the Canadian West, traded in the Mandan nation on the Missouri River in 1800. While there, he recorded what he learned of Mandan law: "They have no laws for the punishment of crime, everything is left to the injured party, the law of retaliation being in full force. It is this law which makes Murder so much dreaded by them, for vengeance is as likely to fall on the near relations of the murderer, as on himself, and the family of the Relation who may have thus suffered, have now their vengeance to take; Thus an endless feud arises."[5]

It might well be wondered if Thompson correctly understood what he was told, or got his rules right when explaining them. But there is too much evidence from other Indian nations to doubt that vengeance ad infinitum was law in some Indian nations of the North American West,[6] even among nations that seemed always at war,

3. *Law of Blood*, pp. 80-84.

4. *Ibid.*, p. 78.

5. Thompson, *Narrative*, p. 232.

6. The phenomenon of feuds "getting out of hand" is familiar to observers of societies regulated by blood vengeance. This is normally a social device containing its own automatic brake. Once the score between two feuding families is evened, by another death or some other compensation, a settlement is negotiated, guaranteed by third parties, by inter-marriage or in other well-understood ways, so that killing shall not proceed without end. Yet if for some reason (such as, most obviously, the intervention of the new-fangled state in some way incomprehensible to local custom, or by

surrounded and harassed by enemies. The Plains Cree are an example. Among them, if the avengers of blood put a manslayer to death, "his family in turn would seek revenge."[7]

In some nations the potential violence of domestic vengeance ad infinitum compounded the mores of civic conduct. Those were the nations not controlled by the ethic of the social systems of peoples such as the Zuni or the Cherokee. In those nations the good citizen overlooked an injury and did not pay back a hurt, except for homicide. The taught moral values, both social and legal, conditioned individuals to avoid face-to-face encounters when demands were made or threats were voiced. The standard of communal life was social harmony. The felt traditions of social harmony buoying up the Cherokee legal system have been summed up as "a consistent pattern of moral thought which disallowed face-to-face conflict." In national as well as village civil behavior, the imperative to avoid confrontation "came finally to pervade the group life and came to be the overriding measure of a good man."[8] The ideal Cherokee avoided social violence and maintained legal harmony by asserting rights or interests cautiously and respectfully, turning away from impending argumentation, and withdrawing from persons who did not behave as good Cherokees.[9] The ideal Zuni was a "person of dignity and affability," who "never tried to lead," and "never called forth comment from his neighbours." To engage in any conflict, "even though all right is on his side," was held against him.[10]

In some Indian nations somewhat the opposite behavior was the social norm, at least among males, and the admired role model, the individual likely to obtain positions of political leadership, was the aggressive, not the nonaggressive man. "[E]ven among themselves," Alexander Henry the Younger wrote of the Blackfoot, "[they were] perpetually embroiled on account of horses and women."[11] A case of domestic homicide among the Assiniboins that Henry described was

---

> lending support to the more politically influential of the contending families) the brake ceases to function, feuds develop into those protracted mutual massacres which end either with the extirpation of one family or, after years of warfare, the return to the negotiated settlement which ought to have been made at the outset. (Hobsbawm, *Bandits*, pp. 65-66.)

7. Mandelbaum, *Plains Cree*, p. 230.
8. Gearing, *Priests and Warriors*, pp. 34-36 (quote at 35-36).
9. *Law of Blood*, pp. 236-45.
10. Benedict, *Patterns of Culture*, p. 99.
11. O'Meara, *Savage Country*, p. 212 (quoting Henry).

not unusual, though it would have been sensational among the Zuni: "The Assineboines informed us of some serious disturbances that had taken place among their own nation below [that is, between two bands] the Little Girl Tribe and the Saskachewoine Assineboines wherein eight were killed and many wounded. This affair proceeded from the young men of the one tribe making too free with the women of the other. I was further supposed [to think] this affair was not yet terminated as the relations of the deceased were bent on revenge &c."[12] Apparently the young men of the Little Girl band of the Assiniboin nation became too familiar with some of the women of the Saskatchewan band. Eight homicides was an incredible number to be avenged among so small a population, and even more disastrous if retaliatory vengeance was permitted to go on and on. About the only solution was the self-exile of one of the bands. That seems to have been the way out of another series of killings among the Assiniboins. The story has been told by a historian of the fur trade. A point to be marked is that commercial rivalry was a factor.

> In 1831, Iron Flint's son, The Light, became the first Assiniboine to visit Washington, D. C. But that privilege and his loyalty to the American Fur Company . . . eventually led to his murder. A struggle for commercial supremacy and tribal leadership ensued in which two of The Light's brothers, Broken Cloud and Sweet, hunted down their brother's killers, who were supporters of Sublette and Campbell (the reorganized Rocky Mountain Fur Company). The two brothers would themselves be victims of intertribal strife, as one killing followed another. The death of chief Le Main, leader of the Sublette and Campbell faction, at the hands of First-who-Flies (another of The Light's brothers) ended the round of violence and also ended important Assiniboine trade with Sublette and Campbell. Those Assiniboines who opposed First-who-Flies were left to join the Crees for protection or to retreat to Canada where they could trade with the British.[13]

It is impossible to exaggerate. The differences are too absolute. These events could not have occurred among the Cherokees or certain other Indian nations. This is not because Cherokee government

12. Entry for 29 July 1810, Henry, *Journal Two*, p. 459.
13. Schilz, "Indian Middlemen," p. 8.

possessed coercive power to punish or stop homicidal behavior; the Cherokees seem to have had no experience with police, while the Assiniboins, like most Plains Indians, had groups of young men to regulate the buffalo hunt and keep order in camp. The reason, rather, was that the Cherokee controlled themselves by the standard of the ideal nonaggressive citizen, a conditioned civic mechanism making domestic aggression socially unacceptable.

Still, we must question whether differences could be so complete. We do not know as much as we ought to know, but it must be supposed that matters were not allowed to get entirely out of hand. Even societies tolerating the aggressive person had process for at least limiting retaliatory homicides, rules and procedures for restraining blood vengeance. Among the Plains Cree, for example, chiefs did not take vengeance for homicide, which may have meant only that tribal leaders should not risk being avengers of blood when relatives of lesser importance could do the job. The intercession of the worthy young men looks like a more significant process for preventing vengeance ad infinitum. "The Worthy Young men who were related to the participants in a feud forcibly escorted their relatives into a tipi. There the Sacred Pipestem was unwrapped. In the presence of this sacrosanct object, all quarrels had to be relinquished and resolved."[14]

It seems safe to guess that in most nations it was wise old men, not worthy young men, who mediated the end to a vengeance feud. David Thompson described the process among the Mandan, a people on the great bend of the Missouri River so exposed to enemies that they could ill afford the domestic strife of Mandans killing Mandans:

> [T]he old men attempt to compound for the crime [homicide] by presents to the injured party, which are always refused, except they know themselves to be too weak to obtain any other redress. If the presents are accepted the price of blood is paid, and the injured party has no longer any right to take the life of the criminal. This law of Retaliation, and compounding by presents for the life of the murderer, when accepted, appears to be the invariable laws with all the Natives of North America.[15]

14. Mandelbaum, *Plains Cree*, pp. 222, 230.
15. Thompson, *Narrative*, pp. 232-33.

Thompson would have been more accurate had he said that the practice of compounding liability for homicide by paying compensation was widespread in western North America. His guess, however, that it was universally known could not have been far off the mark. Although it may not have been part of every nation's domestic law, many Indian leaders would have had experience with it in international situations. In theory, compensation was a very practical doctrine. After all, it could accomplish much more than ending what might otherwise have been an interminable series of retaliatory killings. A price paid in lieu of vengeance in kind eased the harshness of a law otherwise absolute in application, a law that generally had no degrees of culpability allowing the avenger to consider any circumstances that might mitigate vengeance. By accepting compensation in lieu of blood, the relatives of the victim could weigh factors such as accident, self-defense, intention, malice, passion, national interest, or the feelings of friendship that the victim might have had for the manslayer.

When a Blackfoot, while putting away a gun, accidentally shot a child, "the matter [was] settled, by giving to the bereaved parents two or three horses."[16] In a band of Plains Cree

> three brothers attempted to hunt, against the orders of the Warriors. When the Warriors rode out to stop them, one of the brothers fatally wounded a Warrior. The three turned and fled, but during an exchange of volleys one brother was wounded and later bled to death. The two surviving brothers were caught and overpowered. To avoid further bloodshed, an exchange of blood presents was arranged. The brother who had killed a Warrior gave the dead man's relatives two horses and the Warrior who had shot one of the brothers gave his family a fast horse.[17]

Interestingly, although the practice of compensation may have been the element of the domestic law of homicide that most varied from nation to nation, its greatest usefulness was in international law. Payment of compensation was the surest—generally the only—way to avoid war following an international homicide when leaders in

16. MacLean, *Canadian Savage Folk*, p. 16.
17. Mandelbaum, *Plains Cree*, p. 231. This nation also had the capability of recognizing justifiable homicide. The brothers-in-law of a man who killed his wife forgave him because the wife, their sister, had provoked the incident (*ibid.*).

both the victim's nation and the manslayer's nation wanted peace. Although negotiations could be protracted and bitterness could arise over excessive demands, compensation had the advantage of being a practice everyone could understand, whether or not everyone accepted its legitimacy. It could end a conflict and even erase bad feelings. Recall the situation after James Douglas had executed an Indian manslayer, and his superiors in the Hudson's Bay Company removed him from New Caledonia to Oregon to save him from counterretaliation. Had the company wanted to keep Douglas in New Caledonia it would have sought out the brothers and sons, or brothers and nephews of the man whom Douglas killed, and offered to buy off the spear.

It took the first fur traders on the Columbia River, the Astorians of the Pacific Fur Company, only a short time to discover that compensation was widely practiced by the natives of the region. Robert Stuart, one of the officers, thought that he understood the process:

> Their system of criminal jurisprudence, in a particular manner, is very imperfect: the offences that are deemed deserving of capital punishments, are treachery, intentional homicide, and the robbing of any valuable article, nevertheless those found guilty of homicide can most generally screen themselves from punishment by a composition with the relatives of the murdered.—but should the assassin be inclined to make no reparation or concession, the injured family often assume the right of pursuing and punishing him, or some of his kindred, considering themselves under the most sacred obligations of supporting, even by force, the rights of their relations.[18]

Stuart was wrong, of course, to think the manslayer was being "screened from punishment." Punishment was not the correct word in the context of vengeance. Nor was he correct in thinking of the process in terms of permitting the manslayer to escape. The purpose of compensation was to restore social harmony or international peace. A third mistake was implying that the outcome was likely to hang on the manslayer's choice. It was the avenger of blood whose decision really counted. A manslayer who refused to compound had to have either a suicide wish, if the slaying had been domestic, or a

18. Stuart, "Narratives," pp. 10-11.

desire for war, if the slaying had been international. A difficulty among Columbia River nations may have been agreeing on a price satisfactory to the avengers. "We learn from the natives," Alexander Henry the Younger wrote in 1814, "that some of the Clatsop have killed a Chinook in a quarrel, and that preparations are making on the part of the latter to demand satisfaction which if not given in a remuneration of property a battle must be the consequence."[19] He meant that the Chinooks were waiting to hear from the Clatsops how much they would offer to buy off vengeance. It was up to the Chinooks, however, to decide whether to accept.

Compensation for homicide was the norm all along the Columbia River, and we should not be surprised. The Chinooks, Clatsops, and other nations were so small and so closely connected by travel, commerce, and marriage that compensation for homicide was almost a national necessity. Otherwise there might have been constant warfare. There is no evidence as to who made the decision for the Chinooks to accept or reject the compensation offered by the Clatsops, or who determined the amount. Possibly there was national machinery to effect a settlement. At the very least, public opinion must have played a role. These were very serious issues to have been left only to those who would have been the avengers of blood in situations of domestic homicide.

Whether the decision was national or familial, Columbia River Indians had a talent for making demands for compensation that fur men found surprising. At Celilo Falls in 1812 some Indians attempted to appropriate property belonging to the Pacific Fur Company, a struggle broke out, two natives were killed, and one of the fur men, John Reed, was badly wounded by blows to the head from an axe handle.

> [T]he War Chief with 3 others came to us in a Canoe; [*and after a long preamble*], said we had killed 2 of his nation, that their relatives, incensed had compelled him to take command of the Party against his will but that they were come purposely to fight, determined on having satisfaction in some shape or other; and proposed as the only means of appeasing their fury that we should deliver Mr. Reed (who he observed was already dead) to the friends of the savages who fell, to be by them cut in pieces—that would (he said)

19. Entry for 2 May 1814, Henry, *Journal Two*, p. 735.

> completely obliterate their present animosity and that the greatest harmony would prevail for the future.[20]

Although to British or American fur men it was a surprising demand, it was not unusual from the Indian perspective. As a substitute of vengeance in kind, they were asking for a compensation of symbolic vengeance, the pleasure of cutting the body to pieces while they danced and sang and stomped on certain parts. The Indian leader was wrong about one detail. Reed was not dead, but if he had been we may doubt if the officers of the Pacific Fur Company, to compose the conflict, would have given the Indians his body. They did, however, pay compensation: three blankets "and some Tobacco."[21]

Almost anything—property of value, a gesture of goodwill, a set-off of two homicides, one from each nation—could provide international compensation. John Tanner wrote of two examples. One occurred while he was with the war party of Crees, Ottawas, Chippewas, and Assiniboins out to revenge the Sioux attack on Chippewas trading at Pembina on the Red River. Some Assiniboins, it will be recalled, had run off with Tanner's horses and he had been unable to convert Assiniboin horses in retaliation. When the raid was over and the party had returned to Pembina, Tanner got partial revenge by taking a horse "from some Crees who were the friends of the Assineboins, by whom I had long been robbed of mine." For some reason that we may never understand, Tanner obtained satisfaction against the Assiniboins by helping himself to a horse of their Cree "friends." At Pembina, at the time, was a Chippewa named Ma-me-no-quaw-sink, who had killed a Cree and was "anxious to do something to gain friends among that people. It happened that Pe-shau-ba and myself were travelling together at a little distance from the main body, and I was leading the horse I had taken, when Ma-me-no-guaw-sink came up to us, accompanied by a few friends, and demanded the horse. Pe-shau-ba, cocking his gun, placed the muzzle of it to his heart, and so intimidated him by threats and reproaches, that he desisted."[22] Tanner's fellow Ottawas then surrounded him, "and fell in the rear of the main body, in order to avoid farther trouble on account of this horse, all of them being apparently unwilling that I should relinquish it."[23]

20. Stuart, "Narratives," pp. 58-59.
21. *Ibid.*
22. Tanner, *Narrative*, p. 130.
23. *Ibid.*

It would be easy to misinterpret what had happened. It might be thought that the Chippewas wanted the horse Tanner had taken to use as compensation to pay the blood debt he owed the Crees. That is quite unlikely. To spare Chippewa blood, the Crees would have wanted more than a single horse, but even if a single horse had been sufficient compensation, the Chippewa did not need that particular horse. The other Chippewas at Pembina could have furnished him with one. More likely, the Chippewa had in mind as compensation a goodwill gesture. By recovering that particular horse from Tanner, the very man who had converted it, while risking a Chippewa conflict with the Ottawas, the Chippewa could hope to show such respect for the Crees that they would accept the horse and treat the killing of the Cree as a thing done in the dark.[24]

Tanner's second case was more complicated. At a large peace council called by Governor Lewis Cass of Michigan, a young, drunken Ottawa stumbled across a young Potawatomi who was "sleeping, or lying in a state of insensibility from intoxication, and had stabbed him without any words having been exchanged, and apparently without knowing who he was." Next morning the Ottawa was told what he had done while Tanner and other friends

> made up a considerable present, one giving a blanket, one a piece of strouding, some one thing, and some another. With these he immediately returned, and placing them on the ground beside the wounded man, he said to the relatives, who were standing about, "My friends, I have, as you see, killed this, your brother; but I knew not what I did. I had no ill will against him, and when, a few days since, he came to our camp, I was glad to see him. But drunkenness made me a fool, and my life is justly forfeited to you. I am poor, and among strangers; but some of those who came from my own country with me, would gladly bring me back to my parents. They have, therefore, sent me with this small present. My life is in your hands, and my present is before you, take which ever you choose. My friends will have no cause to complain."[25]

24. The Chippewa may have been anticipating a gesture of goodwill from Tanner, perhaps hoping that Tanner would help him satisfy the Crees by allowing him to seize the horse. By resisting, both Pe-shau-ba and Tanner knew they were condemning the Chippewa, or, at least, indicating that they were indifferent to his fate.

25. Tanner, *Narrative*, pp. 238-39.

The Ottawa then sat down beside the dying Potawatomi. The man's mother, speaking for herself and her children, said she did not wish to take another life. She could not speak for her husband, who was absent. He might want vengeance in kind, but for herself she would take the presents, and she did. The woman had a purpose. After her son died and they had buried him, she said to the Ottawa, "Young man, he who was my son, was very dear to me, and I fear I shall cry much and often for him. I would be glad if you would consent to be my son in his stead, to love me and take care of me as he did, only I fear my husband." The Ottawa agreed.[26]

The presents had been earnest, not the real compensation. The woman wanted a new son and the manslayer was willing to pay that price. Whether he ever did most likely depended on the husband. If the husband did not want his son's killer in the family, the Ottawa probably went back to his own country.

Most Indians would have expected Governor Cass to pay a share of the compensation. He was the host of the conference at which the Potawatomi died. Like the governor of South Carolina in the case of the Acorn Whistler, his nation shared some of the liability. Host-and-guest was a relationship that could create claims to compensation in international law. When James Douglas killed the Frazer Lake Indian in retaliation for killing Hudson's Bay Company people at Fort George in New Caledonia, he did so in a village of another Indian nation, the Stuart Lake Indians whom both Douglas and the Frazer Lake manslayer were visiting. Douglas was not even avenging a killing perpetrated in that village, but one that had occurred in a distant part of New Caledonia. By killing the Frazer Lake in their village, Douglas made its people partially liable to the Frazer Lakes because he had killed his victim in the Stuart Lake jurisdiction, at a time when the Frazer Lake manslayer was a guest under their protection. "The Indians to whom he was on a visit," another Hudson's Bay Company officer wrote, "thought it incumbent upon them, in self defence, to claim for the relatives of the deceased, some property for them in indemnization for their loss, and accordingly they all assembled, and made a clandestine entry into the Fort [*i.e.*, Hudson's Bay Company's Fort St. James, where Douglas then was], and insisted upon getting a blanket."[27] It was a case of third-party compensation. The host Indians demanded the

26. *Ibid.*, p. 240.
27. Entry for 20 September 1828, McDonald, *Peace River*, p. 27.

blanket not to satisfy the blood debt owed by Douglas, but to pay their share of the liability if a demand were made by the Frazer Lakes.

It was more usual for nations that were friends or allies to pay and accept compensation than for nations that were traditionally at war. Compensation may have saved alliances. The Gros Ventres of the Plains, whom the British fur traders sometimes called the Fall Indians, were so closely associated with the Blackfoot, Piegans, and Bloods that they were often described as a fourth nation of the Blackfoot confederacy. In October 1801, some Blackfoot were trading at Chesterfield House, a Hudson's Bay Company post on the Saskatchewan. "Two Fall Indians came in," Peter Fidler recorded in the post journal, "and all the Blackfoot pitched away a little below the house; they are afraid of the Fall Indians."[28] The reason was that the son of The Feathers, a leading Blackfoot, had killed two Gros Ventres in February. To cover the two deaths The Feathers had just given the Gros Ventres "two good Horses." Even so, Fidler feared that the Gros Ventres "are neerly falling upon the blackfeet."[29] Before anything happened, some Tattooed Indians, people whom Fidler had never encountered before, came to Chesterfield House. "The Fall Indians in conjunction with the Tattood Indians are very near falling upon the Blackfeet on account of the latter killing one man, one woman and two children of the Tattood Indians, a few days before they arrived at the house. However, through our interference the affair was amicably settled between them, after the Blackfeet had given many valuable presents to the Tattood Indians."[30] Less than a week later, Fidler realized that there were still bad feelings, as a consequence of which his business might suffer. "I learn that a great many Blackfeet that are just left here will trade at the other river in the winter, as the Fall Indians are very near falling on them," he complained. "The above circumstances will be a great loss of trade at this house this year."[31]

The people Fidler called "Tattood Indians" were Arapahoes who lived far to the south. They were related to the Gros Ventres of the Plains and, occasionally, the two nations exchanged visits. Despite their alliance with the Gros Ventres, the Blackfoot apparently found

28. Entry for 30 October 1801, Fidler, *Second Chesterfield Journal*, p. 298.
29. Entry for 30 October 1801, *ibid.*, Alternative Journal, p. 299 n. 1.
30. Entry for 1 November 1801, Fidler, *Second Chesterfield Journal*, p. 299.
31. Entry for 8 November 1801, *ibid.*, pp. 299-300.

the temptation of foreign scalps impossible to resist, and the Gros Ventres had to retaliate. Yet, despite these and similar killings, the Gros Ventre alliance with the Blackfoot held up well. Over the next three decades they faced their enemies generally united and sometimes acting as one. No internal records tell us how they maintained harmony, but possibly the willingness to resolve homicides by accepting compensation in lieu of vengeance helped them to think good thoughts and to keep white the path to peace.

The payment of compensation did not serve the fur traders as well as it should have because they never understood its theory, usefulness, or legitimacy. They were predisposed by their cultural predilections to reject requests for payment in lieu of vengeance. Generally ready to insist that Indians accept compensation when a fur man killed an Indian, they were indignant if asked to allow an Indian who killed a trader or trapper to buy off vengeance with mere material goods.

James Ohio Pattie was trading and trapping on the Arkansas River in 1824 when his party was visited by a Comanche at war with the Spaniards. The Comanche told the trappers,

> "I suppose you are friends with the Spaniards, and are now going to trade with them." Our commander replied, that we were going to trade with them, but not to fight for them. That, said the chief, is what I wanted to know. I do not want war with your people, and should we accidently kill any of them, you must not declare war against us, as we will pay you for them in horses or beaver skins. We did not express our natural feeling, that the life of one man was worth more than all the horses or beaver skins, his nation could bring forth.[32]

Eleven years later, at Fort Clark near the great bend of the Missouri River, an employee of the American Fur Company named Dauphin had a quarrel with a Mandan. To get even, the Mandan approached Dauphin from behind and shot him so badly that he was thought to be dying. Next day the factor at Fort Clark "offered a reward to any one that will Kill the Mandan, either secretly or openly." Mandan headmen came to the post, carrying buffalo robes as compensation to Dauphin which were rejected. They also brought the factor "a *Pipe* to make me smoke—which I refused to do."[33]

32. *Personal Narrative of Pattie*, pp. 50-51.
33. Entry for 7 April 1835, *Chardon's Journal*, p. 28.

Pattie, dealing with the Comanche and the factor at Fort Clark, expressed the attitude of almost all the fur men. There is no principle of Indian law that fur traders and trappers so well understood, so effectively manipulated to their own advantage, yet treated with such crosscultural contempt as the practice of mitigating liability for homicide by paying compensation. They wanted Indians to accept compensation when one of their people killed an Indian, but would themselves accept compensation only for injuries less serious than homicide.[34] When a fur trader or trapper, whether British, American, or Métis, was killed by an Indian, his colleagues did not want to talk about compensation.[35]

During the first decade of the nineteenth century, a Chippewa killed an American employed by the North West Company. Most contemporaries—lawyers as well as fur traders—would have said the Chippewa acted with malice aforethought. It was true that he had not intended to kill the American, but he had planned to kill another North Wester, and was attempting to do so when the American, to save the life of the intended victim, intervened and got shot. L'Grande Noir, also a Chippewa and the manslayer's father-in-law, went to the company's Pembina River post, where Alexander Henry the Younger was bourgeois. "L. G. Noir, brought me a Pacton [pack] of Beaver Skins, which he laid down for me to do charity to his son in law," Henry recorded in his journal. "All the principal men in the Camp here came along with him, but the murderer was concealed and not to be found. I kicked his skins out of my house and would not listen to any of their speeches, telling them if I could see the murderer he would be a dead man, and that no number of skins could pay for the blood of one of our Servants who had been murdered designedly."[36]

Despite his decisive gesture of kicking the skins out of the door, Henry's intention is ambiguous. He may have meant that he would not accept compensation when the manslayer acted "designedly." More likely, he meant he would not accept compensation for any

34. For an example, *see* Begg, *British Columbia*, p. 145.

35. But they themselves might pay compensation if, during a conflict, more Indians than fur men had died. At one of the summer rendezvous of the American mountain men, Joe Meek shot a Crow for striking his wife. A general fight ensued, with two or three Crows killed. Although one trapper was also killed, the leader of the fur men, Jim Bridger, "had to make presents to cover the dead" of the Crows. Vestal, *Joe Meek*, p. 205.

36. Entry for 28 May 1806, Henry, *Journal One*, p. 184.

Indian homicide of a fur trader. That was what other fur traders would have said that he meant.

One case of fur-trader vengeance can be used to sum up the evidence in these last two chapters. It occurred in 1848. After what has been described as "considerable provocation,"[37] a New Caledonia native, an Indian identified as a resident of Quesnel village, killed a Métis, an employee of the Hudson's Bay Company. The company sent Donald McLean with a party of sufficient size to arrest the manslayer at his village. Finding him not there, and no one willing to tell where he had gone, McLean killed the manslayer's uncle in his stead. The men with him—apparently by accident—killed the manslayer's son-in-law and the baby of the manslayer's step-daughter.[38]

Caution should be used when evaluating such an event. As McLean was a Hudson's Bay officer he was applying the precepts of what he observed of Indian international conduct when he killed the manslayer's uncle. That he expected the death of a near relative could answer for the actions of the manslayer shows that he was thinking Indian legal thoughts, not European legal thoughts. Since McLean was not of the same nation as the Quesnel villagers, none of these killings would have been privileged under any law. One of them, however, or two, and possibly all three, could have been set off as compensation for the life owed to the Hudson's Bay Company as a result of the slaying McLean was avenging. Whether any of the killings was accepted as compensation might depend on local law, but more likely would be determined by the influence of headmen in the village and surrounding nations seeking to keep peace with the Hudson's Bay Company. By contrast, had McLean belonged to the same nation as the Quesnel villagers, domestic law and the Quesnel kinship system would have determined liability for the three killings. As they were probably Athapaskan, the villagers' kinship system may have been bilateral and liability fixed by rules we shall probably never know, since such matters have not been of interest to anthropologists.

That an uncle was killed, a fact largely irrelevant to international law, is of particular interest for illustrating the twists and turns of some of the domestic laws of blood vengeance. Under the domestic law of nations with a matrilineal kinship system in which vengeance was privileged if exacted by authorized kin members, the killing of

37. Mary Balf, "Donald McLean," *Dictionary of Canadian Biography* 9 (1976): 514.

38. Foster, "Kamloops Outlaws," p. 312.

the uncle would have been privileged and would not have led to retaliatory homicides had he been a brother of the mother of the Quesnel manslayer. If he were the manslayer's father's brother, the killing would not have been privileged and the uncle's kin could have exacted vengeance for his death. The reverse was true of a patrilineal system.

The other two killings, however, would not have been justified under either the domestic or the international law of most nations. Only one life was owed, and only one life should have been taken in satisfaction. McLean did not know any of this, and did not care. That he and other fur traders and trappers did not consider such questions does not excuse us from asking what was going on. Students of the fur trade should not be content with analysis that examines conflict and contention between societies of different legal cultures by the values of one culture only.

EIGHT

Company Vengeance

THE BRUTAL, uncompromising, and deadly efficient vengeance taken by Donald McLean upon the Quesnel villagers tells us much more than how liability might be accessed in a particular case. It bears on one of the best-known historical themes of the North American West. Once there were a very few givens of that history so certain and so accepted that, when stated, no authority needed to be cited in support. One of the best known of these givens drew a sharp comparison between the mild, humane policy of the British toward the native Indian population and the harsh, brutal policy of the Americans. Without citing authority, Frederick Merk summed up the thesis. Nineteenth-century British North America, he wrote, although "inhabited by a numerous and diverse Indian population, was an area of peace and order." In the territory of the United States, "violence and murder were the order of the day."

> This striking contrast between British and American Indian relations was no mere temporary phenomenon disappearing with the passing of the fur trade. It persisted as long as the red man and the white faced each other in the coveted land of the Far West. Trapper and trader gave way on both sides of the International boundary to miner and cattleman and they in turn to the pioneer farmer. The harbingers of the new day on the American side entered a region of already established strife and perpetuated there traditions two centuries old of Indian massacre and border retaliation. On the Canadian side civilization entered a region reduced by the Hudson's Bay Company to a tradition of law and order

and the history of this frontier was one of almost unbroken peace.[1]

The main thesis of British benevolence and American brutality has been so unchallenged that it has spawned a number of subtheses. The one that concerns us, mentioned by Merk when claiming that the Hudson's Bay Company had reduced the Canadian West to a tradition of law and order, has to do with the British fur companies. It contends that because the companies were "permanent organizations"[2] they could both appreciate and act on the fact that it was in "their pecuniary interest to be just and humane in their dealings with the natives."[3] The policy of the companies, then, was justice and humanity, and to implement it both the North West Company and the Hudson's Bay Company "set up certain standards of trade, and acted up to them fairly. They preserved order, and were ready to assist and protect those who lived up to the required standard, and [were] as ready and determined to punish offenders."[4]

The contrast with American policy could not have been greater, even on the isolated Pacific coast, where British fur companies experienced little direct control from either London or York Factory, Montreal or Fort William. Indeed, the leading historian of the Canadian West, without reservation and with hardly a hint of embarrassment, concluded that the Oregon Country, which was "managed by the English fur-traders for two generations with no more than a rare clash, was brought by the clumsy and inconsiderate methods of the Americans to savage warfare, and its soil stained with blood."[5]

Some Hudson's Bay Company officers not only believed that they behaved with less violence than American fur men toward Indians, they thought that they knew why. "[I]t must be borne in mind," one explained to a Hamilton, Ontario, newspaper in 1857, "that the American traders have always [had] a nation of enterprising, energetic men at their heels, ready and never failing to inflict a fearful retribution on the savages who may commit murders or outrages on any of their people; so that while the Indians on our side profess to

1. Merk, "Introduction," p. lx.
2. Howay, Sage, and Angus, *British Columbia*, p. 38-39.
3. Begg, *British Columia*, p. 120.
4. *Ibid.*, p. 119.
5. Morton, *Canadian West*, p. 763.

love their great Mother the Queen, those on the American side really fear their great Uncle, Kitche-Mokoman, the Big Knife."[6]

The subthesis of fur-company behavior has worked itself into history writing, shading the way some events have been interpreted. In 1755 the Captain of the Home Indians, his two sons, and his son-in-law surprised the Hudson's Bay Company post, Henley House, killed all the traders, and helped themselves to whatever property they fancied. "The Master of Albany [another Hudson's Bay post] seized the Captain of the Home Indians, and his sons, convened a court composed of all his men, condemned the Indians to death, and executed them." Consider how E. E. Rich, a leading British historian of the fur trade, analogized the trial and executions: "When the Master of Albany tried the Indians for murder he was at a loss as to procedure but convinced that he had powers to do what he intended, under the Charter of the Hudson's Bay Company. Little attention though this aspect of the Henley House massacre received, it meant that the sovereignty of the English Crown over the interior territories of Rupert's Land was vindicated in the rough-and-ready trial of those Indians."[7] Had this event occurred in the American West, it would most likely have been treated by historians as "murder," perhaps also as one more case of racism, with the "trial" dismissed as a sham. Even if the story were handled with sympathy and the killings excused as necessary executions, it is doubtful it would ever have been interpreted as it is in the paragraph just quoted: an application of the rule of law and the vindication of British sovereignty.

There was something about the British in the Canadian West that apparently gives the historical perspective a color of humanity and fairness. "In Oregon, [Hudson's Bay Company Chief Factor John] McLoughlin . . . meted out the same justice to an Indian as to a white man," an American historian wrote in a book published by a leading university press. "If a white man had exhibited an Indian scalp in Old Oregon he would have been tried formally and hanged."[8] This statement is utter nonsense. McLoughlin would not have hanged a fur trader or trapper for having killed an Indian with malice aforethought, let alone for having a scalp. He probably would have paid compensation had the victim's nation asked him "to wash away the blood," but that is as far as he would have gone.

6. Ermatinger, *Hudson's Bay Territories*, p. 12.
7. Rich, *Fur Trade*, p. 107.
8. Skinner, *Adventurers of Oregon*, p. 227.

Perhaps it is a mistake to say that the gentleness of British fur traders and trappers to Indians is a subthesis of Canadian native history. In truth, the subthesis has often absorbed the main historical thesis: the enlightened Canadian Indian policy has been explained in part by tracing it back to the era of the fur trade, particularly to the practices of the two great companies, North West and Hudson's Bay. "Their treatment of the natives was humane and protective," it has been contended. "They set up certain standards of trade, and acted up to them fairly."[9] When fine-tuned for popular consumption, the historical story has sometimes been that traders and trappers working for the fur companies not only paved the way for the kinder, gentler Indian relations that characterized Canada after the union, but that their program, attitudes, and actions perhaps gave rise to a more judicious policy than that which, in later years, the sagacious Canadian government wrought.[10] At least one writer in the 1930s was bold enough to make that assertion, even claiming that "[t]he Canadian Indian . . . would be better off today if the Hudson's Bay monopoly had continued in force."[11]

At first blush, the Hudson's Bay Company might seem irrelevant to the history of how the Dominion of Canada treated Indians. But if Canada inherited its early Indian relations from its colonial predecessors, the Hudson's Bay Company is pertinent because Hudson's Bay was one of Canada's colonial predecessors. For about two centuries, the Indian nations west of today's Ontario dealt only with the Hudson's Bay Company, not with British governmental or military officials or with representatives of either Quebec City or Toronto. For Indians west of the Ojibwas and north of the Flatheads, the Hudson's Bay Company was no mere business concern but a European colonial power, a virtual sovereign answering to no one. The British crown had granted to the "Company of Adventurers trading to Hudson's Bay" not only a commercial monopoly but territorial jurisdiction over all the lands drained by the waters flowing into the bay. In matters of criminal jurisdiction, the company's charter made it virtually a law unto itself when dealing with Indians.[12]

Although the North West Company also acted as if it were a law unto itself, it had no governmental authorization. It was a partner-

9. Begg, *British Columbia*, p. 119.
10. Washburn, "Symbol and Aesthetics," p. 202.
11. Pinkerton, *Hudson's Bay*, p. 217.
12. Dunn, *Oregon Territory*, p. 11.

ship, perfectly legal under the laws of Upper Canada, but try, as it might, North West never succeeded in obtaining a charter from London granting it rights in relation to the various Indian nations with which it came into commercial contact. Remarkably, that state of affairs remained in effect even after the Parliament of Great Britain extended the crown's criminal jurisdiction to the British lands in North America that lay west and north of the two Canadas. It is indicative of the place Indians held in the scheme of imperial criminal jurisdiction that Parliament was moved to act not out of any concern over how fur men treated natives, but over how they treated one another.

In the winter of 1801–2, there were three competing trading posts—belonging to the Hudson's Bay Company, the North West Company, and the XY Company—on an island in the North Saskatchewan River, and their fierce rivalry eventually led to a homicide. A trader of the XY Company shot a trader of the North West Company.[13] The slayer voluntarily went to Montreal for trial, only to have the judges rule that they had no jurisdiction over Rupert's Land, the Hudson's Bay Company territory that included the Saskatchewan region. The grand jury presentment remonstrated that lack of jurisdiction may "have been an incitement to the Commission of Crimes," and expressed the strange thought that it might "be the means of depriving an innocent person who may be unjustly accused, of ever having an opportunity of legally evincing to his Country and friends his innocence."[14]

The influential Sir Alexander Mackenzie, a founding officer of the fledgling XY Company, wrote the British Colonial Office, urging that some judicial system be created to "prevent the contending Fur Companies from abusing any power which superiority of numbers of strength may accidentaly confer."[15] The British Parliament responded by passing the Canada Jurisdiction Act of 1803. It provided that "all Offences committed within the Indian Territories, or Parts of America not within the Limits of either of the said Provinces of Lower or Upper Canada, or of any Civil Government of United States of America, shall be and be deemed to be Offences of the same Nature, and shall be tried in the same Manner and subject to the same Punishment, as if the same had been committed within the

13. The story is outlined in Morton, "Juridiction Act," pp. 125-26.
14. *Ibid.*, p. 126.
15. *Ibid.*, p. 127.

Provinces of Lower or Upper Canada." Persons accused of crime within that vast territory were to be conveyed to Lower Canada "to be dealt with according to Law."[16]

Despite the fact that there was little territory to which the act of 1803 could have applied except to Rupert's Land, the demesne governed by Hudson's Bay Company, "doubts" were "entertained" whether it extended there,[17] doubts probably strengthened by the technicality that the name, Rupert's Land, was not referred to in the legislation. As Arthur S. Morton noted, there was "no mention of any well-defined political region within which the Act shall run."[18]

Perhaps the most peculiar aspect of the Canada Jurisdiction Act was the grant of jurisdiction to Lower Canada over offenses committed in those sections of the United States where there were no courts. This provision could easily be misinterpreted. It might be thought to have anticipated the joint occupancy of Oregon, and to have been framed partly with acts committed by and against Indians in mind. In fact, it was concerned with the vast domain northwest of the Ohio River—the regions of Michilimackinac, Detroit, and the lower Red River—where there were probably more British subjects than American citizens.[19] In other words, Morton concluded,

> there is no definite statement as to the area over which the Canadian Courts are to have jurisdiction, but the plain affirmation that their jurisdiction was to apply to cases involving British subjects charged with murder in parts outside of the boundaries of the provinces, whether British or American, where there was no "civil jurisdiction." The Act would therefore apply to the Hudson's Bay Company's Territory as it was then without Law Courts organized, but it would cease to have force there as soon as the company should establish a "civil jurisdiction", as it had power to do in virtue of the Charter.[20]

That the Hudson's Bay Company might appoint its own judges in Rupert's Land must have made officers of the North West Company uneasy, especially when physical violence between employees

16. 43 George III, c. 138.
17. Preamble, 1&2 George IV, c. 66.
18. Morton, "Jurisdiction Act," p. 121.
19. *Ibid.*, p. 123.
20. *Ibid.*, p. 128.

of the two firms broke out in the 1810s. One North West officer, writing from Great Slave Lake during the height of the troubles, voiced some of the worries many felt: "The Act of Parliament extending the jurisdiction of the Canada Courts of Justice to the trial of offences committed in the wild parts ought also, I think, to have suggested something to protect individuals residing in the country from violence and oppression. A poor man might live and die a slave before he could find means to convey himself to Canada to have his wrong redressed. How, also, are we to have satisfaction afforded us if any of our people are murdered by the Natives?"[21] It is apparent that the writer was more concerned with civil redress than with criminal liability. But he did have one thing to say about crimes, and it was typical. He was upset that there was no tribunal to give fur men satisfaction against Indians, but he was not concerned that fur men might also be killing Indians.

Why he was worried about satisfaction is a puzzle. He had to know that if he were slain by a native, his colleagues in the North West Company would retaliate, possibly several times over. He also had to appreciate that, although his colleagues would exact blood for blood were he killed, if he killed an Indian the vengeance would most likely be compensation, not blood.

In 1821, following the merger of the North West Company with Hudson's Bay, another statute was enacted by Parliament declaring the act of 1803 "to be in full force in and through all the Territories heretofore granted to the Company of Adventurers of England Trading to Hudson's Bay; any thing in any Act or Acts of Parliament, or any Grant or Charter to the Company, to the contrary notwithstanding."[22] The crown was authorized to appoint justices of the peace within the "Indian Territories," empowering them to send accused criminals for trial in Upper Canada. Jurisdiction of both the Hudson's Bay Company and the crown was extended west of the Rocky Mountains, to lands that for a time would be known as the Oregon Country and New Caledonia, and later would be the states of Washington, Oregon, and Idaho, and the province of British Columbia.[23]

Even with the new legislation of 1821 there was no substantive

21. Willard-Ferdinard Wentzel to Roderick McKenzie, 23 May 1820, Wentzel, "Letters," p. 126.
22. 1&2 George IV, c. 66, sec. V.
23. 1&2 George IV, c. 66, sec. VIII, sec. X.

change from rule by the Hudson's Bay Company to governmental jurisdiction. In addition to being empowered to appoint justices of the peace, the crown had been authorized to commission justices "to sit and hold Courts of Record for Trial of Criminal Offences and Misdemeanors" in Hudson's Bay Company territory,[24] but the British cabinet decided not to issue commissions of any kind. The London headquarters of the company was advised that until "Courts and Justices" were constituted, its officers in the field should continue "to preserve the Peace and good Government of that part of North America under the Jurisdiction of the Hudsons Bay Company."[25]

The company's officers in London then instructed the governors and councils in North America that they should administer justice and enroll armed men, but suggested that in capital cases "it will be better to transmit the parties with the necessary witnesses for the defence as well as the prosecution to Upper Canada for trial." [26] For noncapital cases they were to summon a jury, "but where from the thinness of the population it is not practicable to get 12 impartial men, a smaller number may compose the jury, and when their verdict of guilty is given moderate and reasonable punishment should be awarded by the Court, composed of the Governor and his Council." [27] The governing council for the Hudson's Bay Company in North America created at least one court. Resolved, it voted "That any one of the Governors together with any two of the Council shall be competent to form a Council for the Administration of Justice, and the exercise of the Powers vested in them by the Charter."[28]

Any lawyer reading this legislation would have advised Hudson's Bay Company officers dealing with Indians not to be concerned. Parliament had given no thought to acts of violence committed by, and against, the native peoples of North America. It was reasonable for the officers, therefore, to conclude that Parliament had authorized them to deal with the Indians just as the fur men had always dealt with them. True, at least one Hudson's Bay Company officer believed the acts of 1803 and 1821 had made illegal the "killing [of] Indian murderers summarily," and refused to be a party to execu-

24. 1&2 George IV, c. 66, sec. XI.
25. Earl of Bathurst to Governor Joseph Berens, 31 May 1822, *Minutes of Northern Department*, p. 31.
26. Governor and Committee to William Williams, 1 June 1822, *ibid.*, pp. 333-34.
27. *Ibid.*, p. 334.
28. Council of 20 August 1822, *ibid.*, p. 29.

tions. The general attitude, however, as that officer himself admitted, was that the acts "were ill-considered and practically useless in relation to crimes committed in the wild western territory."[29] No matter what Parliament intended, the legislation of 1821 was never applied to Indians. What can be labeled "company law" rather than common law became the prevalent rule in both Rupert's Land and in the territories west of the Rocky Mountains.[30] On one hand, W. Kaye Lamb has explained, "the Indians were left alone, and the Company sought to modify only the most barbarous of their customs. On the other hand the company regarded its posts and servants as things apart, and aimed to make it clear that if either were molested, certain retaliation would follow."[31] That was the legal process in Rupert's Land, the Oregon Country, and New Caledonia—retaliation in kind, blood for blood, life for life.

Parliament's decision to leave questions of how to react to Indian homicides under the act of 1821, to Hudson's Bay Company officers, in most cases meant leaving vengeance to the masters of the various trading posts or to the leaders of the fur-trapping expeditions acting in the field. It also meant leaving overall policy to George Simpson, who was the company's governor in North America, that is, the officer in charge of all the company's field operations. Even more than the governor and management committee at the London headquarters, Simpson decided how the company dealt with Indians. As much as any man could control so vast an enterprise, he was in control. Policy was formulated from his ideas, prejudices, and philosophy, and he had ideas, prejudices, and certainly a philosophy about how to govern Indians.

For one thing, Simpson thought Indians could be easily managed. "An Indian trader who cannot obtain personal influence and secure himself the respect and esteem of the Indians he has been dealing with for three years successively is unworthy the title he bears and unfit for the situation he holds," he insisted.[32] "I have made it my duty to examine the nature and character of the Indians," he explained, "and however repugnant it may be to our feelings, I am convinced they must be ruled with a rod of iron."[33] That comment

29. Tod, "Scotch Boy," p. 196.
30. It was also labeled "Club Law" in New Caledonia. Morice, *History*, pp. 260-90.
31. Lamb, "Introduction to McLoughlin," p. lxii.
32. MacKay, *Honourable Company*, pp. 190-91.
33. Pinkerton, *Hudson's Bay*, p. 222.

comes as close as any other to summing up in a single sentence the humanitarianism of Hudson's Bay Company Indian policy. According to Alexander Simpson, another Hudson's Bay officer, mild Indian relations meant not interfering in internal disputes or tribal wars. He expressed pride in the company's record of Indian relations, which he compared with the wretched failure of American policy. Alexander Simpson insisted that the Hudson's Bay Company left the Indians of Rupert's Land alone except when they committed offenses against the company's property or personnel. It was the "invariable rule" for Hudson's Bay, he noted, to avenge "the murder by Indians of any of its servants, blood for blood, without trial of any kind."[34]

The same word that had described company vengeance in the eighteenth century continued to describe it after Parliament had passed the act of 1821: summary. In fact, summary execution was so much the norm that Hudson's Bay people did not even limit it to homicide. Alexander Henry the Younger told of an incident of suspected horse taking that occurred during the period of intense competition between the North West and Hudson's Bay companies, when their posts were situated close together, partly for protection, but mainly so that commercial rivals could keep an eye on one another. Two young Crees arrived at the nearby Hudson's Bay Company fort, one of whom was identified as a "notorious character," a "horse thief." The man was interrogated, apparently by officers of both companies. "[H]is defense was lame, and his excuses vague and without foundation," Henry wrote. "Every thing appeared to confirm the character we had heard of him and to allow him to escape unpunished, after hearing such great proof, of his bad manner of life would be the height of imprudence and would be the means of encouraging others to commit similar crimes." Everyone in the two companies agreed on the principles; it was the penalty that divided them. Henry, who was in charge of the North West Company post, wanted corporal punishment. Hudson's Bay people, however, "insisted on killing him," and the Cree was shot by a large firing squad.[35] It is not necessary to note, as part of the historical record, that there was no trial, because the Hudson's Bay Company hardly ever gave Indians trials. The striking aspect of the case is that Henry's account gives no indication that the Cree appropriated

34. Simpson, *Simpson*, p. 418.
35. Entries for 9, 10, 11 October 1809, Henry, *Journal Two*, pp. 404-6.

horses belonging to either post. He appears to have been executed for a bad reputation as much as for anything. This would have served Hudson's Bay legal strategy: putting Indians on notice that taking company horses could cost someone his life. If horses were run off, the person executed did not have to be the culprit who took the horses.

A similar incident occurred two and a half decades later, also in Rupert's Land. There are at least two versions of what happened. According to one, a party was dispatched from a Hudson's Bay Company fort, led by two clerks,

> to look for some horses that were grazing at a considerable distance from the post. As they approached the spot they perceived a band of Assineboine Indians, eight in number . . . on an adjacent hill, who immediately joined them, and, delivering up their arms, encamped with them for the night. Next morning a *court martial* was held by the two clerks and some of the men, to determine the punishment due to the Indians for having been found near the company's horses, with the *supposed* intention of carrying them off. . . . [T]he whole band, after having given up their arms, . . . were condemned to death, and the sentence [was] carried into execution on the spot.[36]

In the second version, the party had been sent from the trading post to kill meat. When encamped one night, the hunters discovered Assiniboins "(who are noted horse-thieves) prowling round the camp, and there can be no doubt as to their intentions." The Indians were captured, and the next morning they were killed. "The only justification attempted by the murderers was that they had no other means of preserving their horses."[37] When the incident was reported to company headquarters, an officer later recalled, "the punishment awarded to the murderers was—a reprimand!"[38]

If there is anything unusual about these two situations, the execution of the Cree and the killing of the Assiniboins, it is that a

36. McLean, *Notes of Service*, p. 324.
37. Account of A. C. Anderson, a Hudson's Bay Company officer, McLean, *Notes of Service*, p. 325 n. 2. Another officer, in a book defending the company's reputation, claimed that "[t]here is not [a] particle of truth to the story." Ermatinger, *Hudson's Bay Territories*, p. 23.
38. McLean, *Notes of Service*, p. 325.

debate occurred in each case. Usually Hudson's Bay Company officers acted with summary dispatch, even against horse thefts. "While I was at Okanagan in Jan[uar]y a fellow, who killed a man here, some years ago, stole a horse," the officer in charge of a company post in New Caledonia wrote a brother who had retired from the service. "Immediately upon my return, altho' we mustered only five strong, I had him shot." If there was any blame to be given, he thought, it ought to fall on his predecessor, who had failed to kill the Indian when he had committed homicide. "I am prepared it will be said by those who have preceded me, that it was a rash act, merely to screen themselves from blame, for . . . when he committed the first fault . . . [they] certainly ought to have made an example of him; but I am satisfied we shall feel the good effects of what we have done."[39]

What may have been the most summary execution occurred on the other side of Hudson's Bay Company's vast jurisdiction, involving Indians whom one officer called the "Hannah Bay" manslayers. "They were conveyed to Moose Factory, bound hand and foot, and there shot down by orders of the Chief Factor."[40]

Perhaps the most famous case of a summary execution is one that has previously been considered, involving Sir James Douglas, the future governor of British Columbia. As Hubert Howe Bancroft remarked, "This story has been harped in variations by almost as many authors as has given us the gunpowder plots."[41] In 1823, two Fraser Lake Indians killed two Hudson's Bay employees at Fort George in New Caledonia. One of the two manslayers was killed not long afterward, apparently by a Cree.[42] The second fled the area, remaining undetected until about five years later, when he thought it safe to emerge and pay a visit to a village of the Stuart Lake Indians, near the company post at which Douglas was factor. The Stuart Lake Indians were away when Douglas learned that the manslayer was in the neighborhood. Finding the suspect hiding under a pile of skins, Douglas dragged the man out and, with a blunderbuss, tried to shoot him. "[O]wing to the efforts of the [Fraser Lake] youth to free himself from his grasp the ball went wide of the mark, whereupon with

39. Francis Ermatinger to Edward Ermatinger, 14 March 1829, McDonald, *Letters of Ermatinger*, p. 119-20.

40. McLean, *Notes of Service*, p. 323.

41. Bancroft, *History*, 28:475 n. 26.

42. Coats and Gosnell, *James Douglas*, p. 105; McLean, *Notes of Service*, pp. 162, 166.

hoes and the remnants of a camp-fire near by, his [Douglas's] assistants stunned the Indian and reduced his lifeless body to the condition of a shapeless jelly."[43]

The killing at Stuart Lake, Douglas wrote the Hudson's Bay Company's chief factor in New Caledonia, was "the accomplishment of a much desired event." He had, he boasted, "dispatched" a manslayer "[w]ho had hitherto Contrived to escape the punishment his crime so deservedly merited."[44] Douglas used the word "murderer" as well as the word "crime." Although he had acted under the authority of no statute, and had only the implied consent of the Hudson's Bay Company, we may be certain that he would have resented anyone using those words to describe his own actions. He would not have thought of using them himself, nor would his superiors in the company, or even Canadian lawyers of a later day. Forty-five years after Douglas had executed the Fraser Lake Indian, an Ontario barrister would write: "Mr. Douglas was just the man to do so righteous a deed, and with those similarly situated throughout the country, it was the regular practice of the day, to meet all exigencies of a case, at all personal risk."[45] It would seem that bravery, like necessity, created legality in the old Canadian West.

Had Douglas been forced to defend himself before British authorities, we may suspect that he would have placed the legality for killing the Fraser Lake in the customary acquiescence or, at least, the disinterest of the Hudson's Bay Company. Applying that standard, there was an even greater tinge of legality when, instead of a lone executioner's providing his own authority as Douglas had done, acting on his own initiative without consulting other local officers of the Hudson's Bay Company, or communicating with one of its higher-ranking officers, a chief trader or even a postmaster ordered the execution of an Indian manslayer and dispatched an official company brigade to be avenger of blood. Although statistics must be guessed at, it is likely that company-ordered vengeance took place more often than did individual retaliation. An instance occurred in 1832 when John McLoughlin, chief factor on the Columbia, sent Michel Laframboise with a small band of Hudson's Bay Company trappers from Fort Vancouver to the Killimook country to "punish" Indians for the "atro-

43. Morice, *History*, p. 142.
44. James Douglas to James Connolly, 3 August 1828, Rich, "James Douglas," in *Letters of McLoughlin Third Series*, p. 311.
45. Malcolm M. McLeod, in McDonald, *Peace River*, p. 27.

cious murder of Pierre Kaharaguiron and Thomas Canasawarette who were savagely murdered by the above Tribe Twenty days Since." Laframboise executed the commission threefold. Although only two Hudson's Bay employees had died, he killed six Indians.[46]

McLoughlin's instructions to Laframboise were typical of the control that the Hudson's Bay Company exercised over its men when sending them out to exact vengeance upon Indians. Apart from inconsistently directing officers both to demand blood and to take blood while telling them to exercise restraint, most orders to leaders of vengeance brigades were hardly instructions at all. "As it is impossible for me at a distance," McLoughlin wrote,

> to point out the manner in which this can be effected with the least effusion of blood, I shall not shackle you with copious instructions, particularly as your experience in that part of the country, and your Knowledge of the Indian character, will point out to you the best mode of obtaining the object of your mission, permit me, however, to recommend that as 'tis likely some innocent beings may in such cases unavoidably become victims as well as the guilty the severity necessary, for our own safety & security may always be tempered with humanity and mercy.[47]

When Laframboise reported he had killed six Indians, McLoughlin did not ask why he had killed so many, or who they were. There does not even appear to have been an investigation. The important fact McLoughlin stressed in his letters to other company officers on the Columbia River was that "none of our people were hurt."[48] That fact, he told Laframboise, made him "happy." He wrote: "I pray to God that we may not be exposed again to have recourse to violent measures at the same time I think it but right that you send word to these sauvages—that what we have done is merely to let them see what we can do, and that as we do not wish to hurt the innocent we expect that themselves will Kill the remainder of the Murderers of our people.—if they do not we will return and will not spare one of the tribe."[49]

46. Nunis, "Michel Laframboise," p. 150.
47. Instructions, John McLoughlin to Michel Laframboise [April 1832], *Letters of John McLoughlin*, p. 268.
48. John McLoughlin to Samuel Black, 8 May 1832, *ibid.*, p. 270.
49. John McLoughlin to Michel Laframboise, 9 May 1832, *ibid.*, p. 272.

We might suppose that McLoughlin was using words loosely. It defies credibility that an officer with such authority in the benevolent Hudson's Bay Company would contemplate killing an entire nation, not sparing "one of the tribe." Yet he seems to have meant it. At least, he repeated the thought to a clerk of the company when explaining what he had wanted Laframboise to do:

> I desired him to Kill a few men only of the first party of that tribe that he fell in with and tell those he allowed to escape that we did this to let them see what we could do and that as we only wished to Kill those who had killed our people we allowed them to escape to tell their Countrymen this and that they themselves must Kill those who had been concerned in the Murder of our people—if they would not we would come back and Kill every one of the tribe that came in our way and would not stop till we had Killed every one of them.[50]

It may be that McLoughlin was not sure what he wanted. In this last letter, he seems to contradict what he had told Laframboise in his instructions. There, he had asked Laframboise to spill blood sparingly and to give some attention to the fact not all members of the nation were "guilty." Here, he said that Laframboise was to have killed indiscriminately an unspecified number of whomever he met first.

McLoughlin was almost describing payback vengeance, except for one thing. He expected the killings to deter these Indians from committing homicides in the future, and, somehow, he thought they could be persuaded to kill the manslayers themselves. That may have been the purpose of killing the first men encountered. If they understood that vengeance was both certain and indiscriminate, next time the Indians might head off random slaughter by executing the manslayers themselves. It was a totally unrealistic expectation, but indicative of how Hudson's Bay Company officers frequently thought.

50. John McLoughlin to James Birnie, 15 May 1832, *ibid.*, p. 273.

NINE

Efficiency of Vengeance

IT IS DIFFICULT to generalize about company vengeance. Most incidents occurred on the northern side of what then was still a changing, shifting boundary, and most of our accounts are filtered through the peculiar rose-colored lenses that once shaded a good deal of the history of Indian relations in the Canadian West. Of course, observers admit that "there were incidents of individual cruelty towards Indians," but they were nothing compared with what was happening south of the border: "On a couple of occasions Indians who made off with traders' women had their ears cut off, and once, on a similar pretext, an Indian was castrated at Fort Vancouver." There were excuses as to why such things happened: "The monotonous and uncouth life led by many traders undoubtedly had a brutalizing effect on them." But, even though harsh, company vengeance was more evenly applied than we might think: "[T]he company's punishment of its own servants who were found guilty of misdemeanors was often just as brutal."[1] It may be unfair to protest and to ask for evidence that Hudson's Bay Company treated "its own servants" with the same pains and penalties it inflicted upon Indians. The historically significant aspect about company vengeance was not its brutality or its cruelty. It was, rather, its certainty of application and efficiency of execution.

To measure the certainty of company vengeance, and to obtain an idea of its efficiency, we need not search for incidents throughout Rupert's Land during the two centuries of fur-trader rule. For our purposes, the evidence can be limited to the Oregon Country and to

1. Fisher, *Contact and Conflict*, p. 37.

New Caledonia during the era when the Hudson's Bay Company was at the peak of its prosperity and when centralized management, both from London and the North American headquarters, was most efficient.

Company vengeance first crossed the Rocky Mountains with the Pacific Fur Company of New York and the North West Company of Montreal. North West was also the company that brought eastern Indians, especially Iroquois, to the Far West to trap beaver. The Iroquois were constantly in trouble with the local natives, generally for overtrapping the countryside and for making too free with the women. During their first decade west of the mountains, a party of Iroquois was sent out from North West headquarters at Fort George on the Columbia to trap the Cowlitz River. While the men were attempting to kidnap a Cowlitz woman, one of the Iroquois was killed. The party returned to Fort George and reported the death to the officer in charge. He sent Peter Skene Ogden back with the Iroquois, perhaps to investigate, more likely to take vengeance. Ogden apparently hoped to seize the manslayer, and even obtained the cooperation of a Cowlitz headman, Chief How How, but he could not control the Iroquois. As soon as they reached the Cowlitz camp they rushed to the attack, indiscriminately killing twelve men, women, and children.[2]

Two aspects to the Cowlitz vengeance party characterize all the company vengeance expeditions mounted over the next three or four decades in the Oregon Country and New Caledonia. One was that they could be sizable affairs, by local standards often the equivalent of large war parties. The second was that they could get out of hand. John McLoughlin, who authorized most of the expeditions of company vengeance that will be discussed, understood the difficulties better than anyone else. He also knew that expeditions of company vengeance were more likely to be freewheeling than to be disciplined. "[I]t is but justice to all in charge of such Expeditions," he once explained,

> to state they are the most disagreeable Duty to which a person can be appointed to take Charge of and extremely difficult to manage Composed as they are of Canadians Iroquois a few Europeans Owhyees [Hawaiians] and native Indians whose language we do not speak nor they ours and even

2. Cline, *Ogden*, p. 28; Carey, *General History*, 1:242.

> hardly understand us [and?] of hired servants who consider themselves bound to defend our persons and property when attacked but conceive it no part of their duty to go to war and merely go to oblige and of freemen[3] who may be led but will not be commanded. In such a Group when obedience cannot be enforced great management is required.[4]

Maybe so, but McLoughlin never hesitated to mount expeditions whenever there were Hudson's Bay Company people to avenge. Sometimes he even allowed "native Indians" to join them. And despite what he says, the problem with controlling these Indians was not language. It was that they were after blood. Local natives would almost surely be national enemies of the Indians against whom vengeance was being taken. They were not interested in avenging fur trappers or in deterring future homicides. They wanted to get scalps and, probably, plunder, which for them could be easy pickings when they were part of a Hudson's Bay Company expedition.

One other generality should be noted. McLoughlin, when reporting to London, could always say that an expedition had been successful. He may not have appreciated why, however. Although Hudson's Bay Company officers would not have admitted the fact, for an expedition to succeed it was not the manslayer who had to die, be captured, or even be identified. The death or deaths of any member of the manslayer's nation satisfied McLoughlin, and London headquarters apparently did not notice and, therefore, never asked questions about the theory of culpability applied in the field. It is no exaggeration to say that in practice, if not in explicit policy, the Hudson's Bay Company was unconsciously adopting the principles of Indian international law. It judged success not by Christian or common-law standards of punishment, but by the precepts of Indian liability.

In December 1827, Alexander McKenzie, a company clerk, accompanied by four employees and the Indian wife of one of the employees, carried dispatches from Fort Vancouver to Fort Langley, a newly established post on the Fraser River. On their return trip to the Columbia in January, the party was sleeping by Hood Canal, near Puget Sound, when members of the Clallum nation killed the men

3. Trappers who were not in the company's employ. Generally they were mixed-blood sons of former traders or Iroquois who had not returned east.
4. John McLoughlin to George Simpson [March 1830], *Letters of John McLoughlin*, p. 83.

for their clothing and arms and made the woman a slave.[5] By June McLoughlin had learned of the homicides, identified the liable nation, and organized a retaliatory brigade. It was the "decided impression of all," one member of the party noted in his journal, "that an expedition to that quarter would be most necessary, if not as a punishment to the tribe in question, at least as an example . . . to deter others from similar attempts in the future." Putting together a force of four company officers and fifty-nine "labourers,"[6] under the command of Alexander Roderick McLeod, McLoughlin urged them "to make a salutary example" of "the murderous tribe," adding that "*the honour of the whites was at stake*, and that if we did *not succeed in the undertaking* it would be dangerous to be seen by the natives any distance from the Fort hereafter."[7]

On the way to Puget Sound there was a significant occurrence. McLeod met Indians who wanted to go along as auxiliaries. Avoiding one of the problems of discipline mentioned by McLoughlin, McLeod turned them away. They "were told, I believe," a member of the expedition wrote, "that we fought our own battles."[8] If that was not only what McLeod said but what he meant, he may have thought that to impress Indians of other nations who were not party to the two sides of the blood debt, company vengeance was best exacted by the Hudson's Bay Company's acting by itself. Mercenaries or allies could do the job, and were often used, but Hudson's Bay officers must have assumed that the lesson would not be quite as effective as when the company employed its own men to do the killing.

Before reaching the Clallum villages, the retaliatory brigade is said to have fallen "in with a Party of the tribe of the murderers of whom they killed eight."[9] Actually, what seems to have happened is that a small party of Clallums was discovered camped at a portage. Ordering the lodge surrounded, McLeod apparently neglected to tell his men that they were not to kill the Clallums and that he wanted them alive, to serve as hostages. At dawn, when they rushed out of their shelter, all were shot down. "Two families were killed," a participant recorded, "three men, two or three women, a girl and

5. Fleming, "Alexander McKenzie," in *Minutes of Northern Department*, p. 447.
6. Nunis, "Introduction to McLeod," p. 7.
7. Entry for 13 June 1828, Journal of Frank Ermatinger, in McDonald, *Letters of Ermatinger*, p. 97.
8. Entry for 29 June 1828, Journal of Frank Ermatinger, in *ibid.*, p. 106.
9. Nunis, "Alexander Roderick McLeod," p. 285.

a boy." McLeod became angry, but at least one of the other officers said the killings were his fault.[10]

The most telling fact may be that McLeod then pushed on to take vengeance at the main Clallum settlements. Eight deaths for five could have been enough satisfaction for a group of American fur trappers, but not for the Hudson's Bay Company. Unlike most American trapping expeditions, the Hudson's Bay Company had the financial resources and the manpower to keep avengers of blood in the field until the Indians were taught the lesson the officer in charge wanted to teach, and usually it kept them out.

That the Hudson's Bay Company, rather than a party of American freemen, sought vengeance made a decided difference in the quality and certainty of the vengeance obtained; just its ability to muster large numbers of men could be enough to dampen the fighting spirit of Indian nations against whom it was proceeding. Size did not necessarily mean greater bloodshed, though it often did, because retaliatory brigades could be little more than wilderness mobs let loose in the western mountains. If they were disciplined, however, the expedition's leader could use size to intimidate the subjects of vengeance, keeping bloodshed at a minimum, perhaps even avoiding it altogether.

The men of a North West Company retaliatory brigade had that objective in mind when flaunting their numbers in 1814. They were attempting to force Indians at the Cascades of the Columbia River to return guns, ammunition, kettles, and other things confiscated after a North West party had fled the scene of an attack and left the property behind. Since the "intention was merely to frighten the Indians, without spilling blood," one of the North West Company officers wrote, "[w]e made a great show of our numbers and fired our field piece occasionally, to demonstrate that we could reach them even across the river."[11] Another officer, who was a partner in the North West Company, described some of their tactics in his journal:

> We fired the swivel to show them we had such a thing . . . We then drew up all our people and paraded them on the field facing the village, fired a round of musketry, and marched them around and through the camp . . . We then called out to the Indians that we were ready for Peace or War, as they

10. Morton, *Canadian West*, p. 721.
11. Franchère, *Journal of Voyage*, p. 141.

> thought fit. Horsemen were instantly dispatched at full speed above and below to the several villages, and a large canoe was also set off down river with six persons.[12]

After nightfall, when the Indian village was encased in darkness, "[w]e fired our brass swivel and sent up two most beautiful sky-rockets, which must have alarmed the natives very much, never having seen nor heard of any thing of the kind before."[13] As we shall see, this strategy of intimidation by numbers was reasonably successful. The Indians remained defiant, refusing to return all the property, but most items were recovered, including the all-important guns; partial satisfaction was obtained by the North Westers without shedding blood.

The conclusion must be proven largely by inference, but there can be no doubt that large numbers and substantial resources made vengeance by companies more certain than vengeance by individual mountain men or ad hoc partnerships. Had he been an American fur-brigade leader, McLeod, after killing the eight Clallums found camped at a portage on the way to the Clallum nation, would most likely have said he had obtained satisfaction and gone back to trapping beaver. But McLeod was a Hudson's Bay Company officer and felt no pressure from the men who were with him and who, had it not been a company vengeance expedition, might have been unhappy at not earning a living. While he kept them out against the Clallums they were making money, for they were on the Hudson's Bay payroll.

McLeod kept the expedition in the field even after killing eight Clallums, in part because he had been ordered by McLoughlin to free the woman whom the Clallums had made a slave. Some members of the expedition complained that there was an easier way to get her back. They "admitted it to be a most laudable wish to set the poor woman at liberty," but "we thought [it] could always be done at the price of a few Blankets and without so many men coming so far. . . . [T]o make it the primitive object of our expedition, we never understood."[14] They were right. The woman's freedom could have been purchased at a ridiculously low price by European standards.

For some reason McLeod chose not to resolve the matter with a few blankets or a kettle. Perhaps he feared that paying ransom would

12. Entry for 17 January 1814, Henry, *Journal Two*, p. 652.

13. *Ibid.*

14. Entry for 26 June 1828, Journal of Frank Ermatinger, in McDonald, *Letters of Ermatinger*, p. 105.

teach the Clallums the wrong lesson. They might conclude that although they had to pay a heavy blood price for killing Hudson's Bay Company employees, kidnapping their wives could be a profitable business. He wanted, instead, to teach them that making slaves of women married to company men could cost them dearly. For whatever reason, he decided to remain in the field, and was able to do so because he worked for the Hudson's Bay Company. It is a simple but not unimportant point. McLeod could afford to stay the course until the woman was released, and he did. This was another of the elements making Hudson's Bay Company vengeance more certain than American vengeance. Company employees obeyed orders long after Indians and most free trappers would have gone home.

Arriving at one Clallum village, McLeod held a conference with two headmen who came out to meet him. We do not know what was said. Perhaps McLeod asked that the manslayers be surrendered or that the woman be released, and the headmen replied that they were powerless. For some reason McLeod became angry. As the two headmen made their way back to the village, McLeod had them shot. One was killed and the other wounded. The Iroquois wanted to scalp the wounded man, but McLeod stopped that.[15] The Clallums fled into the woods, and the men of the Hudson's Bay Company expedition "helped themselves to what they chose," then burnt the property they did not want, as well as every building.[16] Some items belonging to Alexander McKenzie, the officer whose death was being revenged, were recovered, as was the kidnapped woman, exchanged for the wounded headman.[17] Not content, McLeod burnt a second village.

In all, the Clallums paid a stiff price for five Hudson's Bay Company deaths and one kidnapping—twenty-two of their people were slain, and "two villages put to the torch."[18] Still, some of the officers on the expedition were unhappy, displeased that retaliation had not touched at least one of the Clallum manslayers. As we would expect, they wanted to punish individual guilt. But that did not mean—and this is our lesson—that they also disapproved of collective liability:

15. Morton, *Canadian West*, p. 721.
16. Entry for 4 July 1828, Journal of Frank Ermatinger, in McDonald, *Letters of Ermatinger*, p. 112.
17. Morton, *Canadian West*, p. 721.
18. Nunis, "Alexander Roderick McLeod," pp. 285-86.

they would have taken both individual retribution and collective satisfaction. "Upon the whole the damage done to their property is great and will, I trust, be seriously felt for some time to come, but I would wish we had been allowed to do more to the rascals themselves," one officer observed.[19] "[W]e took an abrupt departure, without having come to any settlement with the natives, either for war or peace, or ever having, to my knowledge, once mentioning to them the object of our coming through the [Puget] Sound; at least the murder of Mr. McKenzie and his men was never enquired into, nor their names once mentioned."[20]

Pursuing a notion common to many company men, that Indians had no "feeling" for human life, McLoughlin disagreed. Thinking of the Clallums collectively as "the murderers," he insisted that the vengeance obtained would have gained little in substance if the actual manslayers had been identified and killed: "[T]hough the loss the murderers have suffered may appear great & ought to deter them & their countrymen from committing any acts of violence towards us, still I doubt if it is sufficient for that object, as though the report that twenty one of their people were killed by us, & two of the murderers by the relatives of those killed,[21] yet they are so devoid of feeling that this does not effect them so much as the burning of their Village & property & destruction of their Canoes."[22]

Despite Clallum callousness, McLoughlin, as usual, reported that the retaliation had been a success. "[I]n my opinion," he decided, "the whole Expedition was most judiciously conducted, the woman was recovered, the murderers were punished & not a man of ours received the least injury."[23] Governor George Simpson agreed. He, too, was satisfied with what had been accomplished. There had been one unfortunate side effect, which he was confident would be remedied by time. McLeod's vengeance had so terrorized the Indians around the mouth of the Fraser River that many were "deterred" from going to Fort Langley for trade. "[B]ut this panic will now wear

19. Entry for 4 July 1828, Journal of Frank Ermatinger, in McDonald, *Letters of Ermatinger*, p. 113.
20. Entry for 8 July 1828, in *ibid.*, p. 114.
21. If this fact is true, the manslayers would have been killed for *causing* the deaths of the people killed by McLeod, a rather surprising application of the doctrine of causation.
22. John McLoughlin to the Governor and Committee, 7 August 1828, in Nunis, "Introduction to McLeod," pp. 8-9.
23. *Ibid.*, p. 8.

off, while the Salutary measures that gave rise to it, are likely to leave a lasting impression, and render our intercourse with them, less dangerous than it has heretofore been."[24]

London headquarters, however, found fault either with something the expedition did or with McLeod's leadership. There was a suggestion that McLeod had mismanaged the affair, and his promotion from chief trader to chief factor, an office to which he had already been nominated, was rejected.[25] This reprimand may well have been unprecedented in the annals of the Hudson's Bay Company. Aside from policy matters such as selling liquor or the propagation of religion, it is one of the rare occasions when headquarters in London expressed any interest in how the company's officers in North America treated Indians.

Simpson feared that his superiors in Great Britain did not understand that McLeod had to kill Clallums. He sent them an explanation of what had occurred, an explanation that might better be termed a defense. It was a defense less of the expedition's conduct than of the theory of vengeance for homicide on which it had acted. Deterrence was the objective of retaliation in kind, Simpson wrote, and necessity was its justification. Although regrettable, it was not really material that the Clallum "murderers" had not been killed. "[T]here is a price . . . set upon their heads," he explained, "which makes their situation very hazardous." It should not be overlooked, moreover, that others had been killed in their place and many wounded, a fact that he indicated, at least by implication, had his approval. There was, of course, an uncertain element, a calculated risk involved in the execution of vengeance in kind, for no one knew how the kin of the executed persons would react. That uncertainty, however, apparently did not trouble Governor Simpson. He thought retaliatory killings positive steps, at least for the Hudson's Bay Company. "[W]hat has been done," he assured London, "will be productive of much good, and render our intercourse with the Natives on this side of the Mountains, . . . a less dangerous Service."[26]

In the same document Simpson reported that Duncan Livingston, a Hudson's Bay Company interpreter, had been killed in

24. *Simpson's 1828 Journey*, pp. 42-43.

25. Nunis, "Introduction to McLeod," p. 9; Fleming, "Alexander Roderick McLeod," in *Minutes of Northern Department*, p. 449.

26. *Simpson's 1828 Journey*, p. 77. Simpson was writing from Fort Langley, on the western side of the Rockies.

New Caledonia by two Indians. One of the manslayers, he wrote, "was put to death soon afterwards by his own Countrymen, and the other destroyed about the same time by one of the people belonging to the Establishment."[27] He meant that the second manslayer had been "destroyed" by a Hudson's Bay employee. What he did not mention, and what London probably did not suspect, was that the employee was "the Company's gendarme and chief executioner in New Caledonia." At least, that is how the avenger of blood was described by A. C. Morice, a historian of early British Columbia. "[H]e was the official avenger of the killed," Morice wrote, "the policeman who was dispatched to the villages in order to stir up the natives and send them hunting, or put a stop to the endless gambling parties."[28]

It may have been an exaggeration to call the man, Jean-Baptiste Boucher (or Waccan, his Indian name), "the official avenger," but he was used in that capacity, and he was effective. To retaliate for the death of Livingston, he went boldly into the camp of the manslayer and killed him before armed men who were friends of the manslayer.[29] With Waccan in Hudson's Bay service, company vengeance in New Caledonia was nearly inescapable, a fact Simpson stressed in a talk that he gave to the Indians around Fort St. James on Lake Stuart. Another company officer who was present reported the governor's talk: "He represented to them how helpless their condition would be at the moment were he and all his people to enter upon hostilities against them. That a partial example had been already made of the guilty parties, but that the next time the Whites should be compelled to imbrue their hands in the blood of Indians, it would be a general sweep; that the innocent would go with the guilty, and that their fate would become deplorable indeed."[30]

We may doubt that either vengeance in kind or talks such as this one by Simpson had any effect on the Indians. Hudson's Bay Company officers had no doubts. "[E]verything is quiet," the chief factor of New Caledonia wrote less than two years later. "The examples which were made of some of the rascals who assisted in murdering

27. *Ibid.*, p. 27.
28. Morice, *History*, p. 253.
29. *Ibid.*, pp. 254-55. Morice said that Livingston was Waccan's half-brother. Another authority said he was his adopted brother. McLean, *Notes of Service*, pp. 164-65.
30. Entry for 20 September 1828, McDonald, *Peace River*, p. 27.

our people, have had a wonderful effect, & I hope will keep the natives quiet for years to come."[31]

Good fur-country theory was mixed with wishful thinking. International homicides continued, and, if anything, the company retaliated with greater determination. When the postmaster at Fort Babine was killed by an Indian, the new chief factor in New Caledonia, Peter Skene Ogden, ordered a party of eleven men, including Waccan, to exact vengeance. "I deem it expedient," he instructed the leader, "that you . . . proceed to investigate this affair and take such decisive measures as circumstances may warrant to punish the murderer and restore peace and order."[32] He apparently also directed the retaliatory party to kill the manslayer himself, if possible, and not settle for the object lesson of a few random killings.

When they reached the Babines, the Hudson's Bay people found that the manslayer had fortified himself in a place that would cost them dearly to assault. Moreover, he was supported by the men of the village. The avenging party decided upon a stratagem. "They sent him word that if he would come and surrender the gun with which he had killed Morwick, and deliver to them his daughter, the matter could be compromised, and there would be no effusion of blood." The manslayer agreed, and with his daughter, who carried the gun, came out and walked toward the avengers of blood. The Hudson's Bay men lost no time in obtaining satisfaction and teaching the Babines that there was a predictable price to be paid for a committing a company homicide. The manslayer was immediately shot.[33]

When Samuel Black, the factor at Fort Kamloops, was killed by a young Shuswap Indian, Hudson's Bay Company men converged on the Kamloops from at least three posts in New Caledonia and the Columbia. "The party from headquarters at Fort Vancouver," John Tod later recalled, "began to terrorize the Indians within reach of Kamloops as a means of enforcing delivery of the murderer. Horses were seized, property destroyed, and, practically, short of killing men, war against the people was undertaken." The harassment was too brutal and too indiscriminate. The men were recalled, "a tem-

31. Connolly to James Hargrave, 19 February 1830, *Hargrave Correspondence*, p. 43.

32. Morice, *History*, pp. 214-15. Morice described the expedition as "the avenging party—for it was none other," p. 215.

33. *Ibid.*, pp. 216-17.

porizing policy was approved," and Tod was transferred from Fort Alexander to succeed Black at Fort Kamloops, "with instructions to try to continue trading and [to continue] the business of the District as usual, and with an intimation that towards the end of the year a well armed force would be sent to aid me in 'prosecuting hostilities.'"[34] The armed force would not be needed. The Indians along the North Thompson River had felt the wrath of the Hudson's Bay Company. Black's manslayer was killed before the year had ended.

An important point must be made about this survey of Hudson's Bay Company's policy of retaliation-in-kind in the transboundary country of the North American West. It is not complete. No consideration has as yet been given to instances of vengeance taken by Hudson's Bay people in the field, whether in the Snake country, along the Sacramento River, or among the Blackfoot. It was on those occasions, when conditions were more harsh and life filled with peril, that vengeance became more brutal and fur trappers were most contemptuous of life.

The evidence that we have examined has been limited to Hudson's Bay Company conduct as directed by commissioned officers stationed in permanent posts with sufficient time to reflect on the execution of policy. It is those officials who are said to have been the precursors of the Canadian practice of enlightened benevolence toward Indians so much praised today. It was they who laid the foundation of the superiority of Canadian Indian policy over American Indian policy, and who, as one of them wrote of the Oregon Country in 1844, produced "a state of astonishing quiet, peace, and good government."[35]

The word "astonishing" might have had a touch of irony for Robert Campbell, had he read it. About five years earlier, Campbell would probably have thought it astonishing to use the words "quiet," "peace," and "good government" to describe the lands governed by the Hudson's Bay Company west of the Rocky Mountains He had then been in charge of the Hudson's Bay post on Dease Lake when supplies grew so low that, to survive the winter, he had to scatter his men about the lake to search for food. Isolated in small groups, the British were soon harassed by local Indians. Outside the walls of the stockade they were in continual danger, or thought they were. On one occasion, some Indians encountered a few of Campbell's men

34. Tod, "Scotch Boy," pp. 214-15.
35. Dunn, *Oregon Territory*, p. 81.

and "relieved them of 2 guns & other articles, & also of some dried meat they were bringing for us & themselves." Finally, on 8 May, Campbell decided the weather had turned warm enough to abandon the post and strike out overland for Fort Simpson. For the first time since winter had set in, the men were together and in sufficient force to command respect from Indians.

> Some miles down the river we came on a camp of our late pillagers who were much alarmed at seeing us in such force, & were now as abject & submissive as they had formerly been bold & arbitrary. It was now our turn to bully & intimidate but we retailiated [*sic*] only to the extent of resuming possession of our own. Some of our people wanted to take revenge on them for their savage treatment of us throughout the winter by killing a few of them, but this I would not permit.[36]

There is a unique aspect to this case. Campbell's men wanted to retaliate against Indians whom they could positively identify as individuals who had continually done them a series of injuries. He stopped them. We may suppose that Campbell was still uneasy about their situation and would not risk starting something that he might not be able to control or finish. What should be borne in mind, however, is that when he failed to retaliate he was disregarding Hudson's Bay Company policy. He knew he should obtain satisfaction for Indian wrongs whenever possible.

There is a problem with the evidence. Campbell's account is not as clear as we would wish. It is possible that he let his men physically thrash those Indians, taking vengeance through corporal punishment. All that he would not permit is what he said—to take revenge "by killing a few of them." If so, he would have been following Hudson's Bay Company policy. When Indians against whom retaliation was taken had not killed Hudson's Bay people or other whites or Métis, the company preferred not to kill them. The official practice, as McLoughlin had asked William Connolly to explain to William Kittson, was to kill only manslayers. That rule was not always adhered to, however, because, despite the efficiency of Hudson's Bay Company's leadership, retaliation often took directions that could not be foreseen or controlled.

In 1829 the Hudson's Bay Company ship *William and Ann* sank in the waters near the mouth of the Columbia River. The crew was

36. Campbell, *Journals*, p. 55.

lost and the cargo disappeared. At first, Chief Factor McLoughlin believed that men of the Clatsop nation had killed the sailors, but on investigation he concluded that, although the Clatsops had the property, the crew had drowned in the storm. The retaliatory force he sent to the Clatsops was to demand only the return of the property. It was not to take blood.[37]

The large Hudson's Bay Company expedition to the Clatsops—five officers and sixty men[38]—went by ship. On arrival, the leader "sent a message to the Clatsops demanding restitution of the property to which they replied they would restore all they yet had and pay by giving us slaves for what they had appropriated to themselves and requested us not to land."[39] The weather was stormy, however, and the company officer in charge of the expedition was worried that the landing boats, banging against the hull, were damaging the ship. Besides, his men were "Crowded on Board." He "sent the Clatsops word he must land with his people but that since they promised to give up the property they need be under no apprehension from us."[40]

The Clatsop headmen had been right. The expedition should not have landed. When the British force came ashore it was fired upon. The Hudson's Bay party returned the fire, and kept firing until one Indian was killed and the others fled. Then, "Our people burnt their village and all their property." On the return to base, some Hudson's Bay Company men saw two Indians in the woods, chased them, and killed both.[41] The expedition had started out to recover property and avoid bloodshed. It ended by killing four Indians, burning an entire village, and scattering the Clatsops to such an extent there was no one with whom the British could deal.[42]

37. John McLoughlin to the Governor and Committee, 5 August 1829, *Letters of John McLoughlin*, pp. 19-20 [draft], 29-30. *See also* "Editorial Comment," pp. 38-39.

38. John McLoughlin to John Warren Dease, 4 July 1829, *Letters of John McLoughlin*, p. 18.

39. Letter from John McLoughlin, 5 August 1829, McDonald, *Letters of Ermatinger*, p. 125.

40. John McLoughlin to the Governor and Committee, 5 August 1829, *Letters of John McLoughlin*, pp. 20 [draft], 30. The word "with" is not in the draft letter.

41. Letter from John McLoughlin, 5 August 1829, McDonald, *Letters of Ermatinger*, p. 125.

42. McLoughlin is the authority for saying that four Clatsops were killed. He added, "I have the satisfaction to say not one of our people got the slightest wound." John McLoughlin to John Warren Dease, 4 July 1829, *Letters of John McLoughlin*, p. 19.

We must not draw too simple a conclusion. The lesson is not only that Hudson's Bay Company retaliatory expeditions could get out of hand. It is, also, that they could be too large. With his men crowded aboard ship, the leader felt he had to land. The size of the force apparently alarmed at least some Clatsops, and the short battle was soon under way. Size was supposed to frighten Indians and it usually did, making them more submissive. That was the Hudson's Bay Company's advantage. It was organized, it was relatively disciplined, and it could, when necessary, muster a large number of fighting men. For that reason it seldom failed to take vengeance, and, more importantly, for that reason its vengeance seldom failed.[43]

There is another general point. To make the claim that Hudson's Bay Company vengeance was more effective than the vengeance of any American party of mountain men was likely to be does not mean that an American company could not have exerted the same degree of discipline that the Hudson's Bay Company enforced. It means, rather, that American fur trapping was not controlled by a large, centralized monopoly. Just about the only American firm that could exercise comparable influence and command comparable obedience was the American Fur Company, with its subsidiary, the Upper Missouri Outfit. When its employees committed offenses against Indians, the company was strong enough to negotiate with the offended nation. In 1833, for example, an employee named Durocher killed a Blackfoot near Fort McKenzie. The Upper Missouri Outfit's chief agent, Kenneth McKenzie, offered to pay "for the body of the slain man." He also instructed the master in charge of the American Fur Company post where Durocher was employed to promise the Blackfoot that "if the man can be found, I will deliver him up to the nation to be dealt with as they think fit." It was a promise he probably would not have kept had he been able, but he

43. One historian has concluded that the company's vengeance did not fail against the Clatsops:

> [T]he lesson proved salutary, as was evidenced by the fact that when, a year later, the British ship, Isabella, was similarly wrecked in the same locality, her crew was not injured or assaulted, and no other demonstration of force was ever required to insure the supremacy of the authority of Fort Vancouver.

Carey, *General History*, 1:365. The facts may be true, but the crew of the *William and Ann* had not been injured or assaulted, nor had the "authority" of Fort Vancouver been challenged. At most, the Clatsops had exercised rights of salvage, and for that four died and an entire village was destroyed.

was not put to the test. Durocher stole a company canoe, persuaded another employee to desert with him, and escaped down the Missouri River.[44]

Although American fur companies maintained some trading posts such as Fort Union and Fort Clark, most American trapping parties were ad hoc affairs, made up not of employees but of individual contractees, who joined a brigade because of its leader or because it was going in a direction where they wanted to trap. As a result, most American vengeance against Indians for homicide was random, swiftly organized, and, if the manslayers or some other Indians of the manslayers' nation were not quickly found, quite likely to be abandoned. Most important of all, Indians may well have understood that American vengeance was not as certain or effective as Hudson's Bay Company vengeance. Indian headmen whose people killed Hudson's Bay employees knew there was no escaping paying a blood price, perhaps several times over. If they fortified themselves, the company had the resources to wear them down or to plan some stratagem that would entice the manslayer into the open. And if the company did not wish to mount expeditions, it could assign one of the many Indians or mixed-bloods in its employ to act as avenger of blood. We may be certain that most Indian headmen knew there would be a heavy cost to their nation should they resist or even show resentment. The Hudson's Bay Company could always have the upper hand. If everything failed, the company could have paid a neighboring nation to make war on Indians who resisted demands for satisfaction.

We may be more certain about the vengeance policy of the Hudson's Bay Company than we are about the lessons that it teaches. There is no need to agree or disagree with the arguments quoted in the first paragraph of the previous chapter: that American settlers populated a West "of Indian massacre and border retaliation," while Canadians settled a West "reduced by the Hudson's Bay Company to a tradition of law and order and [where] the history of this frontier was one of unbroken peace."[45] The evidence discussed in this chapter, however—of the swiftness, the certainty, and the brutality of Hudson's Bay Company vengeance—does not tell us why the Canadian and American experience differed. Too many other variables separate the history of Canadian and American relations with Indi-

44. Swagerty, "View from Bottom," p. 30.
45. Merk, "Introductions," pp. lix-lx.

ans. Canada had a smaller population and a harsher environment, which meant, consequently, a less intense drive for land, and Canada, both before and after the union, was ruled by a more authoritative central government less responsive to the politics of a democratic electorate.

Variables in the fur-trade experience itself also contributed to the differences. British fur-company employees were more likely than American mountain men to marry or live with Indian women, creating at least a temporary personal relationship with the local people;[46] they were more likely to be skilled in the ways of Indian diplomacy than were American government or military officials;[47] their tenure was more permanent, especially their residence within or near particular nations, and, as a result, they felt a greater incentive than did more transitory trappers to cooperate with the Indians, learn and respect their social system, and not destroy their means of livelihood.[48] Still, the evidence of Hudson's Bay Company's policy of swift, certain, and brutal vengeance must be placed somewhere on the historical scales. At the least, it should make us question earlier beliefs, such as the assertion that "[u]nder the management of the two great fur companies . . . treatment of the natives was humane and protective,"[49] or even wonder about more recent claims such as, "In those parts of the Hudson's Bay Company's territories where the Indians were dependent, they were to be kept in a 'proper state of subordination,' but in areas like the Pacific Northwest where Indians retained a large degree of independence 'mild and cautious measures' would have to be used."[50]

A further historical question that must be researched, although it may never be answered to everyone's satisfaction, is: What contribution did the certain, brutal, and unilateral vengeance that British fur companies inflicted upon Indians make to Canada's alleged history of "almost unbroken peace"?[51] Did company vengeance beat into Canadian Indians a fear or respect for Canadian law and order?

46. Van Kirk, *Many Tender Ties*; Brown, *Strangers in Blood*. But contrary, *see* Swagerty, "Marriage and Settlement Patterns," p. 158. Marriage could produce social conflict as well as commercial advantage.
47. *See* Washburn, "Symbol and Aesthetics," pp. 201-2.
48. Fisher, *Contact and Conflict*, p. xv.
49. Begg, *British Columbia*, p. 119.
50. Fisher, *Contact and Conflict*, p. 36.
51. Merk, "Introductions," p. lx.

TEN

Restraining Vengeance

ALTHOUGH THE DYNAMICS of blood vengeance in the North American West during the first half of the nineteenth century meant that company retaliation was more certain to occur, and often more brutal, than retaliation exacted by less well organized groups of mountain men, there was another side to the picture. Company vengeance could be less bloody than noncompany vengeance. The very command structure that made company vengeance more certain could, on occasions, keep vengeance within bounds of restraint. Fur-company expeditions sent out by either the North West or Hudson's Bay companies were made up largely of employees brought into the mountains by the firms. Anyone who did not obey could be expelled from the fur country. Even should the men on an expedition want to take vengeance upon Indians, a company brigade leader had greater authority than did a leader of free trappers to restrain them if he thought the situation too dangerous for retaliation,[1] or if he was not certain that the Indians whom the men wished to kill had committed the offense they wanted to avenge.[2]

Another difference made the vengeance of American bands of mountain men appear ad hoc when compared with retaliation by British companies. Because most company vengeance was directed by commissioned officers stationed at permanent posts, long-range goals could be enunciated and policy could be implemented. All offi-

1. For example, what seems to have been the case of Robert Campbell, *see* ch. 9 *supra*.
2. As in the case of Peter Skene Ogden when restraining his men from attacking the Mohaves, *see* text at ch. 6 nn. 37, 38 *supra*.

cers knew, Peter Skene Ogden observed, that "we have nothing to gain; on the contrary, everything to lose" from violence.[3] Sometimes —especially when preferring to kill the manslayer rather than taking vengeance against anyone connected with him—they could sit back and wait for the manslayer to come to them. "I sent a bit of Tob[acco] For the Crapaud," Alexander Norman McLeod noted in the journal of Fort Alexandria, a North West Company post. The purpose was "to invite him to come to the House he has not been oppenly at any of our Forts since he killed B[aptise] La France four years ago at Fort des Prairies, he may perhaps be led by a fatall security to come see me, which I very earnestly wish."[4]

At Fort George in New Caledonia in 1824, two employees of the Hudson's Bay Company were killed by two local Indians who fled the area. Instead of ordering immediate retaliation against the relatives of the manslayers, the officer in charge of the post acted much as he would have had he been an official of Upper Canada or an eastern American state. Investigation determined that the killings had been a personal, not a tribal, affair. "The practice of the company in such cases," a Hudson's Bay officer explained, with questionable accuracy, "was to outlaw the murderer and kill him when caught—it might be years afterwards."[5] The point probably does not have to be iterated, but perhaps it should be, just to be sure that it is not misunderstood. To a degree the officer was operating as if he were in the East—but only to a degree. Once individual liability was determined and the manslayer was identified, mountain law took over from eastern law. When the manslayers—or suspected manslayers—surfaced, there would be no trial and anyone could be the executioner.

There is one other way in which the officers of the large British and Canadian companies had an advantage over the leaders of American fur brigades. Following an injury by the Indians, they were in a better position to weigh the facts of the situation and consider whether circumstances mitigated against the imposition of summary retaliation. A case in point involved a North West Company expedition out of Fort Nez Percés on the Walla Walla River and led by William Kittson. The trappers had not progressed far on their jour-

3. Letter of 22 October 1845, in Fisher, *Contact and Conflict*, p. 38. *See also* remarks of James Douglas, p. 36.

4. Entry for 30 March 1801, McLeod, "Alexandria Diary," p. 168.

5. Tod, "Scotch Boy," p. 164.

ney into the Snake country before they had horses taken—twice. Some of the horses were recovered, however, and the brigade was not handicapped. "[W]hile they were encamped one night on a small river where everything around indicated security, two more horse thieves were detected in the night by the unhobbling of their horses. In this instance, the people on watch were more fortunate; they got hold of them, and kept the rascals in safe custody until daylight." The two Indians would have been dead men had they been captured by almost any other group of mountain men, especially as each "had a quiver, containing from fifty to sixty arrows . . . and long lines for securing horses." They were in luck, however. "[T]he whites had suffered no loss, and therefore Mr. Kittson had the clemency to let them go unhurt."[6] For a mountain man not to kill Indians who obviously had planned to run off with his horses because they had not yet done so was unusual rationalization.

Some decisions were determined by commercial considerations, such as company profits. When a few homicides occurred at the Hudson's Bay Company's Fort McLeod in 1823, George McDougall, the officer in charge, decided not to kill the first Indians on whom he could get his hands, partly because they were the best beaver hunters, "who if once destroyed would leave only the most worthless probably to trouble us again."[7] In fact, the company was so big that it could do the opposite of what McDougall thought important. To avoid trouble or to put pressure on nations to which manslayers belonged, it would write off its immediate income by shutting posts and moving elsewhere. In 1824 Beaver Indians killed five Hudson's Bay employees at Fort St. John. The council for the northern department of the company decided to close the posts where the Beavers traded. It voted to abandon Fort Dunvegan and Rocky Mountain post "in consequence of the late much lamented murders and daring atrocities committed by the natives in Upper Peace River and with a view to accelerate the deserved punishment of the principals and abbettors thereof, prevent a recurrence and at the same time impress the Indians in general with a due sense of their relative situation and dependence."[8] The last fact was the significant one: dependence. Hudson's Bay's commercial monopoly meant that the Indians depended on the company and on the company alone to

6. Ross, *Fur Hunters*, p. 142.
7. Fisher, *Contact and Conflict*, p. 37.
8. Holmgren, "Fort Dunvegan," p. 177.

obtain guns, ammunition, and manufactured goods. The threat of removing their one source of trade, company officials believed, might keep Indians obedient and, hopefully, deter other homicides in the future. "[T]he absence of a Post," Governor George Simpson observed when moving Jasper House to a new location, "will in the course of a year or two humble the Natives and ensure its safety when re-established."[9]

In 1814 an incident occurred that graphically illustrates how a fur company, exercising discipline over its officers and employees and implementing decisions calculated to promote the company's continual commercial prosperity in the area, could limit retaliatory violence. It took place at Fort George, the North West Company's westernmost outpost, on the southern side of the Columbia River not far from the Pacific Ocean. Early in January, a party led by David Stuart was sent up the Columbia carrying dispatches, guns, ammunition, and other trade goods to posts being established in the interior.[10] At the Cascades,[11] local Indians of a nation that historians have not identified, and who, for our purposes, can be referred to as the Cascades Indians or the Cascades, attempted to make off with some of the property being carried across the portage. They were detected, there was resistance, shots and arrows were exchanged, and, before both sides retreated, two Indians were dead and Stuart was badly wounded.[12]

It is not surprising that trouble occurred in the Cascades area of the Columbia River. Lewis and Clark had experienced one of their few difficulties with Indians at the Cascades, even ordering their sentries to shoot anyone attempting to convert the expedition's property.[13] When David Thompson of the North West Company and Alexander Ross of the Pacific Fur Company passed that way in July 1811, Thompson was convinced that the natives "were determined to pick a quarrel for the sake of plunder."[14] "At first we formed a favourable opinion of them," Ross explained, "but their conduct soon changed, for we had no sooner commenced transporting our goods then they tried to annoy us in every kind of way—to break our

9. Entry for 11 October 1824, Simpson, *Journal*, pp. 30-31.
10. Ross, *Adventures*, p. 256.
11. Today's Cascade Locks.
12. Franchère, *Journal of Voyage*, pp. 137-38.
13. Ronda, *Lewis and Clark*, p. 217.
14. Thompson, *Travels*, p. 303.

canoes, pilfer our property, and even to threaten ourselves, by throwing stones and pointing their arrows at us."[15]

Over the next two years both the Pacific Fur Company at Astoria and the North West Company, also at Astoria but renamed Fort George, continued to experience trouble with the Cascades.[16] A historian has recently labeled these Indians "native highwaymen,"[17] but the fur traders found their conduct too puzzling to be reduced to a single trait. "On talking over the events of the day," Thompson wrote after passing the Cascades portage,

> we hardly knew what to make of these people; they appeared a mixture of kindness and treachery; willingly rendering every service required, and performing well what they undertook, but demanding exorbitant prices for their services, and dagger in hand ready to enforce their demands. . . . They steal all they can lay their hands on, and nothing can be got [back] from them which they have stolen; . . . still there were some few kind men among them, and more than one man came close to us with his dagger, and in a mild voice warned us of our danger, and to be courageous.[18]

The fur men would never realize the fact, but they had encountered a set of Indian nation villages with a foreign policy seeking economic profit from geographic position. Location was the advantage exploited and toll the measure of friendship. The Upper Chinookans at the Cascades and The Dalles controlled key stretches of the Columbia River and much of the trade passing over it. They claimed and exercised rights of way, seeking tribute at the portages, opposing trade that brought arms to their enemies, and resenting all threats to their domination of the river. Violence and what the fur men called "theft" seem to have been among the ways that the Cascades collected toll.[19]

When they first encountered the Cascades, fur traders were caught unawares. Indians with whom they had in the past dealt had not claimed ownership rights over sections of the Saskatchewan,

15. Ross, *First Settlers*, p. 124.
16. *Ibid.*, pp. 187-88, 254-55; entry for 7 July 1812, Stuart, "Narratives," p. 34; Franchère, *Journal of Voyage*, pp. 113, 138.
17. Ronda, *Lewis and Clark*, p. 217.
18. Thompson, *Travels*, pp. 305-6.
19. Teit, "Middle Columbia Salish," p. 121; Ruby and Brown, *Chinook*, p. 153; Ronda, *Lewis and Clark*, pp. 171, 216, 280.

Missouri, or Red rivers.[20] Traders and trappers had usually paddled right by other tribes, giving no thought to proprietorship, toll, or right of way. When they did the same on the Columbia, they were not prepared for the clashes that resulted.[21] They should have paid more heed to the villagers' sense of importance.[22] That, at least, is what a scholar has concluded about one of the peoples of the area. "[T]he Wasco-Wishram had defined themselves as *the* important people. In a number of traditional ways visitors and travelers had paid attention to them. They could be generous or parsimonious, belligerent or gentle, as they saw fit. The Whites were ignoring them when they could, and, in general, acting without reference to them. The harassing behavior of the Indians can be interpreted, then, as attempts to maintain or re-establish their position of importance."[23]

Such possibilities were unknown to the officers of the North West Company when David Stuart returned to Fort George to report the attack at the Cascades. The first important fact, at least from the perspective of assessing liability and determining what actions to take, was that no officer or employee of the North West Company had been killed, although Stuart had been badly wounded.[24] The second was that two Indians said to have been "chiefs," one each from the two villages that had attacked Stuart, had been slain.[25] Another fact, which the North West people thought the most important of all, was that when Stuart fled he had abandoned the supplies being carried over the portage. "The goods that fell into the Indians hands," one North Wester wrote, "were of importance to the Company for they could not be replaced. Furthermore these barbarians

20. On these rivers, except for such nations as the Arikaras or the Mandans, the Indians did not live in permanent villages as did the Columbia River nations, and could not assert a claim to permanent right to toll. When the claim was made it was more likely to be ad hoc, because a band was passing by or it was the tribe's summer fishing rendezvous. *See, e. g.*, Meyer and Thistle, "Saskatchewan Rendezvous," p. 430.
21. It should be noted, however, that other nations, such as the Nez Percé and the Cayuse, "resented the throttlehold of the villages from the Dalles to the Cascades upon the passage of European goods coming up from the coast." Stern, *Chiefs & Traders*, p. 32.
22. Morton, *Canadian West*, p. 618.
23. French, "Wasco-Wishram," p. 353.
24. Alexander Ross would later recall that the North West Company's retaliatory party demanded that the Indians deliver up "the murderers," surely a mistake by Ross. Ross, *Adventures*, p. 259.
25. Entry for 13 January 1814, *Journal of Henry*, p. 799.

were in possession of 50 guns and a quantity of ammunition that they might use against us."[26]

The guns alone would have led the North West Company to organize an avenging expedition. Even if no property had been taken, however, the dynamics of western Indian customary law required retaliation. To use the language of the day, "Revenge for the insult, and a heavy retribution on the heads of the whole Cath-le-yach-é-yach nation"[27] was absolutely necessary because the company could not "allow it [the insult] to pass with impunity."[28] If the company overlooked the attack, it would be inviting more of the same and worse, not only by that nation but by every nation along the Columbia. That argument was no mere supposition, but was fact proven by the very attack that had just been made on Stuart.

Shortly before the Stuart affair, a large North West Company party had been attacked while camped between the first and second portages of the Columbia. "The boldness of these barbarians in attacking a brigade of 40 men," Gabriel Franchère wrote, "led us to presume that they would be even more likely to attack the small brigade that had left a few days before under Messrs. Stewart [Stuart] and Keith, which was composed of no more than 17 men."[29] Fort George ordered Franchère up the river with reinforcements to convoy Stuart beyond The Dalles and other portages of danger, but he was too late. The next expedition to leave Fort George would be sent up the Columbia to avenge the attack on Stuart.

The legal context of the situation determined the instructions given to the retaliatory brigade: "Pacific measures were to be taken, and no blood spilt, unless the natives should be the aggressors."[30] A Canadian historian has recently suggested that, because "establishing a good relationship with the upriver Indians was fundamental to Nor'Wester trade and security, . . . the expedition was under orders to pursue a peaceful course to its limits."[31] This explanation is typical of assumptions historians are likely to make when failing to consider the legal dynamics of a situation. The fact is that had Stuart or one of his men been killed, the instructions would have been quite

26. Franchère, *Journal of Voyage*, p. 140.
27. Ross, *Adventures*, p. 257.
28. Cox, *Columbia River*, p. 149.
29. Franchère, *Journal of Voyage*, p. 137.
30. Entry for 9 January 1814, *Journal of Henry*, p. 792.
31. Gough, "Introduction to Henry," p. lviii.

different. The retaliatory party would have been sent to obtain the blood of the manslayer or of someone of the manslayer's nation. Bloodshed was to be avoided because no North Wester had been killed.

Before arriving at the place of the attack, the leaders of the retaliatory brigade sought the advice—perhaps even the legal advice—of various Indian nations along the Columbia. The headman of the tribe nearest Fort George was of little help. He "said it was right to go up and kill them all." He was, of course, speaking from a Columbia River Indian point of view, but the North Westers, thinking from different values, misunderstood him. "[W]e told them that was not our object, as we did not come here to kill the natives, but to show them charity. It was our property that we wanted; if it should be refused us, we should take forcible measures to secure it."[32]

Coalpo, headman of the Clatsop nation, said much the same. He was "an inveterate enemy" of the people who had attacked Stuart, and "was, of course, for war, and would certainly join us." His wife, "a woman of high birth and of some consequence," was more helpful, especially on matters of law: "She gave us much useful information regarding their customs in adjusting any misunderstanding between hostile nations, such as giving a slave, or making some other payment for anyone killed. They seemed to have some principles of honor in settling their differences. They do not appear to be bloodthirsty; they steal as much as they can, but do not wish to kill if booty can be got without murder."[33]

The most significant legal point mentioned by Coalpo's wife was that the Cascades Indians accepted compensation in satisfaction of international homicide. As mentioned earlier, this was a distinct feature of Indian law along the Columbia River, but we know next to nothing about how the system worked, and the North Westers knew even less. Robert Stuart of the Pacific Fur Company had heard of a homicide that had been composed by payment of "3 Blankets to cover the dead, and some Tobacco to fill the Calumet of Peace,"[34] but it is doubtful that he asked who negotiated the compensation and who was paid. It has been claimed that among one of the nations at the Cascades, the Wishram, the amount of blood money in each case of domestic homicide was fixed by the chiefs after a hearing,

32. Entry for 9 January 1814, *Journal of Henry*, p. 793.
33. *Ibid.*
34. Stuart, "Narratives," pp. 58-59.

not by the kin of the victim bargaining with the kin of the manslayer. The decision supposedly turned on the rank of the victim, the rank of the manslayer, and such matters as the orphans left by the victim.[35] If this is true, it was a surprisingly unusual process for North American Indians, but if enforceable in domestic law it would almost certainly have been applicable in international law.

The North West Company officers also sought advice and help from a headman of the Willamette nation named Casino. Agreeing to join the expedition, he gave them some information that may also have been intended as a warning. He had, he said, "relatives" living in the village along the portage where the attack had occurred. "This circumstance alone," Alexander Henry the Younger noted, "shows us the necessity of conciliatory measures, in our proceedings above, to avoid incurring the ill will of the Willamette natives,"[36] suggesting that he thought it a reasonable guess that other Willamettes besides Casino had kin among the Cascades.

Depending on the types and degrees of relationships, the situation could become very dangerous for the fur men. If any people living in the Cascades villages were Casino's close kin to the degree that he had a duty to avenge their blood should they be killed, then the killing of one of them by the North West party would have put Casino in the position either of having to retaliate in kind against the North Westers or of negotiating for compensation in lieu of blood. If he did avenge the death of the kin by killing a North Wester, he surely would have been killed in return by some member of the North West Company, and Fort George would have been at war with the Willamette nation.

To understand the risks facing the retaliatory expedition, the North West Company had to do more than consider Cascades law, the law of the nation against which retaliation was sought. It should also have given attention to the laws of other nations up and down the Columbia River. Because of those laws, especially the laws of kinship and the customs of retaliation for homicide, those nations could be drawn into, and become parties to, the conflict.

Casino, the Willamette, was remarkably well informed about politics in the Cascades nation and, if he could be believed, even knew why Stuart's party had been attacked.

35. Spier and Sapir, "Wishram Ethnography," pp. 214-15.

36. Entry for 11 January 1814, *Journal of Henry*, p. 797.

> He informed us that the principal instigator of that affair was a chief called Canook, of the Cathlathlaly village. . . . This fellow it seems, on seeing our party of two canoes only passing up river, formed a plan to pillage them. He assembled the warriors of the two villages below and made a long speech, telling them that we never traded anything of consequence with them, but took our property further up, to their enemies, the Nez Percés, and that here was a favorable opportunity to better themselves. They agreed, and all went armed up to the Cathlayackty village, where the harangue was repeated. That village also joined the party and . . . they all came down to meet our people at the portage on the S., with Canook as their war chief.[37]

The leaders of the retaliatory brigade learned at least two useful facts from Casino's story. First, they now knew that the attack on Stuart was not a raid merely for plunder, but had, rather, some serious international overtones. Fur traders had been in the country west of the Rocky Mountains for only a few years in 1814, yet every Indian nation had experienced at least one important result: the balance of power among the tribes had been radically altered and was in a constant state of flux. Nations to which the traders came were furnished with European weapons. Nations which the trade passed by had only bows, arrows, clubs, hatchets, shields, and spears. Those without trade, such as the Cascades, who lived where there was little beaver, seeing their enemies growing stronger with the purchase of every gun, either had to become parties to the trade or stop the traffic. Some nations virtually made war on the traders.[38] Survival was at stake. That was the theme with which Canook stirred up the Cascades warriors, telling them that Stuart's guns were on the way upriver to the Nez Percés.

The second piece of valuable information learned from Casino's account was Canook's role as instigator. Should the North West Company men decide they should take a hostage, they now knew whom to seize. Any recognized leader of the villages would have served the purpose of forcing the Cascades to negotiate. That was

37. Entry for 13 January 1814, *ibid.*, p. 799.

38. For example, the Blackfoot, especially opposing traders furnishing guns to the Flatheads and the Crows. Leonard, *Narrative*, pp. 34, 52, 62; Thompson, *Narrative*, pp. 212, 546 (*see also* "Introduction," p. li); Elliott, "Fur Trade to 1811," pp. 5-6, 7-8.

especially true if the Cascades were the Wishram or another one of the nations in the area that not only had hereditary chiefs, but chiefs who wielded actual governmental power. In addition, there is some authority for thinking that they were generally men of considerable wealth.[39] It would have given the North Westers the upper hand to capture Canook, the man responsible for the attack. At the least, the Cascades would think that threats to harm any hostages would, in his case, be executed.

The North West Company expedition that set out from Fort George consisted of "62 persons in all, well armed and fortified with a small field-piece." They left in too much haste, however. Soon it was discovered that "our little army lacked the most vital thing—food."[40] When the party arrived at the first Cascades village, they found the women, children, and old men scattered in the woods, a sure sign that the warriors were ready to fight. To prepare their side for battle, therefore, the first thing the fur men did was to secure their own needs by buying a few old horses and over twenty dogs. "[H]aving thus made sure of our food supply for several days, we announced our intention of punishing them with death and burning their villages if they did not return within two days the goods stolen."[41] It was an ultimatum, but by no means as drastic as it might have been. "For the present we demanded only guns and kettles, without mentioning other goods—the guns being our principal object."[42]

Pushing on to the next village, the brigade learned that the enemy was not intimidated. In fact, the headmen of that place had a counterdemand. "The whites have killed two of our people," they said, "let them deliver up the murderers to us, and we will deliver to them all the property in our possession." According to Alexander Ross, the Cascades said that this demand was made as a matter of law. "When the whites had paid according to Indian law for the two men they had killed," Ross quoted the Indians as saying, "they would smoke the pipe of peace, but not till then. Their wives and children were safe, and as for themselves they were prepared for the worst."[43]

The demand for blood to cover the two chiefs killed by Stuart's

39. Ray, *Cultural Relations in Plateau*, pp. 19, 22. But *see* French, "Wasco-Wishram," p. 361.

40. Franchère, *Journal of Voyage*, p. 140.

41. *Ibid.*

42. Entry for 14 January 1814, *Journal of Henry*, p. 800.

43. Ross, *Adventures*, p. 258.

party did not mean that the Cascades Indians refused to negotiate, that they either wanted war or thought war inevitable. For the headmen to call for payment of blood was one way of opening negotiations for compensation in lieu of vengeance in kind. They accompanied their demands for satisfaction with token gestures of returning the North West Company's property. On the second day a few Indians, probably slaves for the most part, came into the company's camp "and delivered up a small parcel of cloth and cotton, torn up into pieces, and scarcely worth picking up." More important than the gesture was the message that came with it. "We have sent you some of the property," it was purported to have said, "deliver us up the murderers, and we will send you the rest."[44]

The Cascades might not have got away with such taunts had the North Westers' leadership been more decisive. There were serious disagreements on how to proceed. Whenever Indians brought in a few items, putting themselves within the control of the fur men, there were arguments over whether to force the issue by taking hostages or to continue negotiating. "Some were for hanging the Indians up at once; others for detaining them; at last, however, it was resolved to let them go."[45] Interestingly, the Clatsops who had accompanied the North Westers on the expedition did not want the Cascades killed. It might be thought that, having come so far, they would have been urging some violence so that they might gather up some booty, but again international customs of retaliation may have made them cautious. Had any Cascades been hanged, even if the Clatsops had publicly and strenuously opposed killing them, as allies of the North West Company, the Clatsops would have shared liability for the deaths and could have been dragged into a North West Company–Cascades war.

Instead of hanging Cascades, the Clatsops wanted to invite them to parley, and then seize some as hostages, to be exchanged for the property.[46] This was the plan finally adopted. The man everyone hoped to capture was Canook, but he kept out of the way. "Our intention was to seize Canook," Henry explained, "but he kept in the crowd and could not be prevailed upon to approach, though he and all the others were invited in to smoke."[47] Not only Canook but all

44. *Ibid.*, p. 259.
45. *Ibid.*, pp. 258, 259.
46. Cox, *Columbia River*, p. 149.
47. Entry for 16 January 1814, *Journal of Henry*, p. 808.

the Cascades must have known what was being planned, for nobody came in, not even for a smoke, where, by the customs of Indian diplomacy, they could have expected to have been safe.

There was a single exception. When Casino, the Willamette, persuaded a Cascades, identified as a "chief," to visit the North West Company camp, the frustrated North West officers decided he was the best they could get, and they grabbed him. "He appeared surprised, but not terrified, and said not a word. Casino, who was sitting near him, started up instantly, but we desired him to explain to the prisoner our intention of keeping him until our property was returned; that not only the guns and kettles were wanted, but every article they had taken from us; that we had heretofore been trifling, but were now in earnest, must have our goods, and were ready to fight if necessary."[48]

The hostage stratagem worked—or, more accurately, the North Westers claimed that it worked. At least John McDonald of Garth, who had remained at Fort George, later wrote in his autobiographical notes that the North West Company "recovered part of the goods by taking a chief prisoner and keeping him till all that could be got was collected."[49] Women, led by the wives of the prisoner, began to come in with guns and kettles. The hostage "desired them to collect the property quickly, and we told them we would remain two nights to give them time, when, if the goods were not returned, we would take him to sea with us."[50] But the expedition did not have so much time. The dynamics of a perilous situation were catching up with it. Once they had arrived at the enemy villages, the leaders had been startled to learn that Coalpo's wife "was related to one of the Indians that our people [Stuart's party] had shot at the portage." This meant that at least one of the Clatsop allies, like the Willamette, Casino, had kin ties with people among the enemy. The Indian nations up and down the Columbia River apparently were more interrelated than the North Westers could have imagined. "Such a menace was more than we expected," one of them bemoaned. "[W]e feared that, on our pushing over to the village, they would shoot at us in desperation, and thus oblige us to fire upon them—a thing we ardently wished to avoid."[51]

48. Entry for 17 January 1814, *ibid.*, p. 806.
49. McDonald, "Autobiographical Notes," p. 51.
50. Entry for 17 January 1814, *Journal of Henry*, p. 801.
51. Entry for 14 January 1814, *ibid.*, p. 801.

What he meant was that the North Westers realized, after what Coalpo's wife had told them, that any attack on the Cascades could raise blood debts in nations with which Fort George was at peace and on which it depended for trade. The options of the company's leaders were much more limited than they had realized when they left Fort George to start the expedition. They decided "merely to frighten the Indians without spilling blood," by shooting off their "field pieces."[52] Important as the display was to impress the Indians, the most important aspect of this strategy was not to hit anyone.

As the hours passed, the expedition found that it was becoming too dependent on its Indian allies. Even if Casino and Coalpo's wife had had no kin at the Cascades, they did have interests different from those of the North West Company. Warfare for them was wrapped up in interminable talk and pipe smoking, and they were constantly in and out of the Cascades villages. None of the fur men knew what was being discussed, although they had suspicions, for the North Westers had no control over them and knew that there was no possibility of establishing control. To have tried to keep them away from the Cascades could have manufactured unneeded trouble. "[W]e began to suspect Casino's fidelity," Alexander Henry the Younger acknowledged, "but it would have been imprudent to show any suspicions of him."[53]

A final problem was food. After about three days the Cascades Indians stopped selling horses and dogs. On the fourth day the leaders "put all hands on an allowance of one meal a day, as our stock of horseflesh was getting short, and we had no hopes of a further supply from the natives."[54] By that time they had received most of the guns, many of the kettles, and about half of all the other property. The Cascades then "declared they could not recover any more," and suggested a settlement based on the law of compensation for homicide. They "asked our gentlemen, 'would they not allow them any thing to place over the dead bodies of their two relatives, who had been killed by Mr. Stewart?'"[55] As the North West Company might eventually have to pay something for the two deaths that occurred during the attack on Stuart, that solution was accepted. "[W]e made

52. Franchère, *Journal of Voyage*, p. 141.
53. Entry for 15 January 1814, *Journal of Henry*, p. 803.
54. Entry for 18 January 1814, *ibid.*, p. 807.
55. Cox, *Columbia River*, p. 149.

a present of the rest of the goods to compensate for the death of the two Indians killed on the 7th of January, though they had been the aggressors."[56]

The reasoning of the North West Company officers is a remarkable instance of cross-cultural legal thought. They realized that, no matter what else happened, if they wanted to establish peaceful relations with the Cascades they would have to pay some compensation. Whether or not they understood it, this was an acknowledgment by them of the force of Indian law. They may have rationalized it less as legitimate law or as binding custom than as a form of extortion, but they were saying that, for whatever reason, compensation would have to be paid.

After the expedition had ended and the North Westers were back at Fort George, both the fur men and the Indians on the Columbia River took stock. A company officer wrote that the retaliatory expedition had been successful; it had "succeeded in recovering all the guns and a third of the other effects."[57] The Indians, however, were not certain what had been accomplished. Had the North West Company vindicated its rights to passage at the Cascades and the other portages, or had it failed to avenge the attack on Stuart and the conversion of the property that he had been transporting? Coalpo's wife told Indians near the mouth of the Columbia that the "pacific measures [at the rapids] were due more to timidity in us than to any view of humanity," and repeated her belief that the fur men "ought to have killed them all." When he heard what she had said, Alexander Henry the Younger, one of the leaders of the expedition, was annoyed. "This reasoning may do very well for her," he wrote, "but would not answer our business in future, and would only have been making bad worse."[58] The officer who had done most of the negotiating—with the Clatsops and the Willamettes as well as with the Cascades Indians—agreed. "We had gone with a strong enough force to punish the Indians in an exemplary manner," Gabriel Franchère contended. "But after all what satisfaction would there have been in massacring a number of natives? If we did not do so, it was not through fear—for our young men were spoiling for a fight—but rather from the humane motive of wishing to prevent bloodshed, and the partners preferred losing

56. Franchère, *Journal of Voyage*, pp. 141-42.
57. *Ibid.*, p. 141.
58. Entry for 27 January 1814, Henry, *Journal Two*, pp. 666-67.

goods worth 500 or 600 *louis* to making enemies of all the Indian tribes living near the portages."[59]

There should be no doubt that most North West Company officers saw the affair as Henry and Franchère did—from the perspective of Anglo-American social values and Anglo-American legal principles. One of them—a man who judged the outcome entirely by European, non-Indian assumptions—was Ross Cox, a clerk from Ireland. "The most important object of the expedition having been thus attained without bloodshed," he wrote, "and as the aggressors had been pretty severely punished in the first instance, the party deemed it both human and prudent to rest satisfied with what they recovered." The one concession Cox made to Indian customs was to weigh the consequences that might have resulted had the expedition killed more Cascades. "They," he wrote, referring to the company's senior officers on the Columbia River, "also felt that an unnecessary waste of humane blood might prove ultimately prejudicial to their own interests, by raising up a combined force of natives, against whom their limited numbers would find it impossible to contend."[60]

Cox was thinking too much as a European. Given the animosity felt toward the Cascades Indians by several of the other Columbia River nations, there was little likelihood that a combined force would have risen up—unless the North Westers had been less disciplined than they had planned to be and had killed at the Cascades people of many different nations and those nations, as a consequence, had been dragged into the conflict to avenge their people who had been killed.

At least one fur trader at Fort George evaluated the events at the Cascades with Indian thoughts, much as if he had internalized Indian social values and Indian legal principles. He was Alexander Ross, a clerk with the North West Company, and he agreed with Coalpo's wife that some blood—it did not really matter whose or how much—should have been spilled. Ross would have conducted Indian diplomacy by Indian precepts, hanging, for example, some of the Cascades Indians who had come into the North West camp to return the property. When the war council of the expedition would not take even a few of these down to Fort George in irons, he was disgusted. "[T]o the disgrace of the expedition," he complained, "they were set at liberty."[61]

59. Franchère, *Journal of Voyage*, p. 142.
60. Cox, *Columbia River*, pp. 149-50.
61. Ross, *Adventures*, p. 259.

The word "disgrace" should not be misunderstood. Ross did not mean it was disgraceful to be lenient and to spare Indian lives. He meant that the North Westers had lost face in the eyes of the Columbia River Indians; their standing had been diminished with people who did not share their values. Among Indians, or generally any people with Indian expectations, they appeared weak and indecisive. It was a disgrace that could easily have been avoided by a few random hangings.

The expedition sent out from Fort George to wreak at least some vengeance on the Indians of the Cascades had been large and well enough armed to have struck the fear of certain retaliation into all the nations of the Columbia River, should any of them think of attacking North West Company brigades. Instead it was, for Ross, an "inglorious expedition, which promised so much and did so little." More than three decades later, he was still angry at how his fellow North West Company officers, by thinking more like Europeans than like Indians, let the Cascades turn the affair "into ridicule." "They, therefore," he complained in the 1840s, "without recovering the property, firing a gun, or securing a single prisoner, sounded the retreat, and returned home on the ninth day—making the matter ten times worse than it was before."[62] He did not mean it was "ten times worse" because none of the Cascades had been killed. He meant that it would have been better had the attack on Stuart gone unrevenged than for the expedition to get less satisfaction than every Indian on the Columbia River expected it to exact from the Cascades.

Ross, however, was wrong. The expedition had been more effective than he realized. He weighed only the vengeance element of Indian international law, and did not ask whether the Cascades had a legitimate claim to compensation to cover the two "chiefs" killed by

62. *Ibid.*, p. 260. We may understand what Ross meant and, given his situation, accept his values. But what do we make of historians who, like Ross, criticized the expedition for not acting like an Indian retaliatory party?

> The fiasco is inexplicable; one would think that with such an outfit as started in the warpath from Fort George the river would have been swept clear of its native freebooters and most of the looted property recovered, had the party been properly officered and handled. . . . They even got a tongue-lashing from Mrs. Coalpo; and to be reviled by a squaw for cowardice is *scandalum magnatum*. The fiasco is inexplicable, I repeat; the North [West] men were no cowards, and none knew better than they did how to deal with Indians in peace and war.

Elliott Coues, n. 36, in *Journal of Henry*, p. 809.

Stuart's men. Perhaps he did not take the claim seriously because, by attacking Stuart's party and seizing his property, the Indians had been the "aggressors." If so—if he considered that a claimant had to have what common lawyers call "clean hands"—he was in that respect thinking as a European.

The Cascades Indians would have answered that they were not the aggressors. Stuart, by carrying guns up the river to trade with their enemies, the Nez Percés, was the person who instigated or who caused the affair. He was the aggressive party. By the premises of Indian international law, the Cascades could make a persuasive case that the North West Company was the cause of the homicides. Certainly there were questions as to just what the Cascades had intended and why they had attacked Stuart. If they regarded the portage as their national territory, and if they usually obtained toll for its use, they could have argued that the North West Company brigade, by pushing its way across without permission or so much as a by-your-leave, was the aggressor, the cause. Besides, who had been the aggressor was not relevant to the main question of whether compensation was due. It was owed because Stuart's men had killed the two chiefs, not because someone else started the fight. For other Indians of the Columbia River, the matter of aggression was perhaps a factor to be argued when negotiating the amount of compensation. Most likely it was not a consideration in determining liability to pay for the deaths, and, therefore, the North West Company people were collectively liable.

For that reason Ross was mistaken in saying that most Columbia River Indians would think the compensation paid to the Cascades proof that the North West Company was debilitated; that it was extortion demonstrating how easily fur men were intimidated. Perhaps some Indians had this idea, but there is no reason to think that many did. Of course, those who were enemies of the Cascades, such as Coalpo's wife, wanted them wiped out, and thought the North Westers had missed a wonderful opportunity to spill Cascades blood. But a majority of other Columbia River Indians were culturally conditioned to view the surrender of the property by the North West Company as payment of compensation, legally owed, not intimidation.

ELEVEN

Controlling Vengeance

FUR MEN such as Alexander Ross, who had internalized Indian values, did not say that retaliatory expeditions had to be bloody. If asked, they probably would have preferred less killing than more, although as a matter of policy they were indifferent to the cost of life. What they wanted was not blood but decisiveness: that a retaliatory brigade should have a specific goal, that the avengers should be of sufficient strength to do all that had to be done to achieve that goal, and that they should understand they must persevere until it was accomplished. Those three objectives became the rule of the Hudson's Bay Company, the standard that officers in the field applied when deciding if and how to organize retaliatory expeditions. "When it is necessary to punish Indians for murders or other crimes," the governor and the committee of Hudson's Bay Company in London instructed the field officers in North America, "it should be done as mercifully as possible. Clemency and forbearance should be exercised wherever possible. But when punishment is undertaken there must be no chance of defeat, as that would endanger all establishments."[1]

These instructions were written after the governor and the committee had been told of a most unusual Hudson's Bay Company punitive expedition sent out to retaliate against Kalawatset Indians for an injury inflicted against an American trapping brigade led by Jedediah Smith. It is a case of company vengeance that deserves detailed examination, as it may shed light on a question raised (but not answered) by the decision of the North West Company to

1. Instructions from the Governor and Committee, 28 October 1829, Simpson, *Journal*, p. 318.

"cover" the two chiefs killed by David Stuart by paying compensation to the Cascades Indians. That question asks whether the North Westers were applying Indian international law. Did the fur traders and trappers of the transboundary North American West adopt, adapt, and follow some of the norms of customary Indian behavior in cases of homicide?

To answer with an uneqivocal no would be risky. After all, the implication is not just that the officers of the North West Company adapted the Indian international law of compensation to free themselves from an increasingly dangerous situation. Surely the norms of Indian customary behavior—the felt social imperative to avenge an injury—had much to do with why they had taken that strong force up the Columbia River in the first place, or, as Alexander Ross put it, "[r]evenge for the insult, and a heavy retribution on the heads of the whole Cath-la-yach-é-yach nation."[2] That was one of their two main aims in confronting the Cascades. Their other aim had been achieved: they had gotten back the guns and much of the ammunition that had been converted by the Cascades. If we were to conclude that they failed in their first purpose because by paying compensation they were backing away from vengeance and not adhering to Indian law, it should be recalled that one reason why they paid was that they knew they would have to "cover the dead" anyway. They might not have been saying they knew the Cascades insisted upon compensation as a "right" to atone for the two slain chiefs. But at the least they were predicting that they could not reestablish peace with the Cascades without making even a token payment. They were acknowledging the force of Indian custom.

As a measure of the possibility that the fur traders and trappers could have absorbed Indian legal rules, consider how easily they adopted Indian legal language. In his "Narrative" describing the first overland journey made from the Oregon Country to St. Louis via the Platte River, Robert Stuart told of the skirmish that occurred at Celilo Falls in 1812, when two natives were killed and their relatives asked as compensation for the body of John Reed to cut to pieces. Stuart refused, but he did pay compensation. "The business was soon after compromised," he wrote, "for 3 Blankets to cover the dead, and some Tobacco to fill the Calumet of Peace."[3]

2. Ross, *Adventures*, p. 257 (quoted ch. 10, text at n. 27 *supra*).

3. Stuart, "Narratives," p. 59 (for a discussion of this incident, *see* text at ch. 7, n. 20 *supra*).

It is Stuart's words, his way of describing compensation, that merit our attention. They were not words that nineteenth-century American white people ordinarily used. "To cover the dead" and "fill the Calumet" were Indian expressions. That they were employed in an account written for non-Indians by a fur trader shows how easily a mountain man could fall into Indian ways of speaking. We may never know why fur men spoke in Indian idioms, but a possibility is that they had internalized Indian ways of thinking about vengeance and Indian ways of reacting to homicide.

Between four hundred and five hundred Indians, probably Sioux, surprised Fort Manuel on the upper Missouri in 1813. There were twenty-six men inside the compound and only one outside. The Indians killed him. "[T]hey took the Scalp and cut him nearly to pieces," John Luttig recorded, "leaving us to lament the Death of [a] fellow Citizen unrevenged."[4] That was an Indian lament. In sections of the United States other than Indian country, the more likely American thought would have been that the killing was unpunished, not that it was "unrevenged." British and Canadian trappers also reacted to Indian homicides by expressing values more Indian than European. Consider words that Peter Skene Ogden wrote on the day that Blackfoot killed a member of a Hudson's Bay Company expedition he was leading. "It is certainly most galling to the feelings of all, who are doomed to seek their bread in this country," he reflected, "that these villains commit so many murders without its being in our power to retaliate in kind."[5]

These examples could go on and on. They are not direct proof that the fur traders and trappers of the transboundary North American West knowingly adopted, adapted, and followed the norms, rules, and process of the native American Indian law of homicide, only that they had absorbed ways of expressing that law. If we want proof that they applied Indian law when practicing vengeance we shall find it, if it exists, only in actual cases such as the incident at the Cascades of the Columbia River when compensation was paid to cover the dead. Possibly no other case is so revealing in this regard as when the Hudson's Bay Company sent out an expedition to retaliate for injuries inflicted upon American fur trappers by the Kalawatset Indians in 1828. It is important to keep in mind that the company was not reacting to an attack on one of its own brigades, or for in-

4. Entry for 22 February 1813, Luttig, *Journal*, p. 125.
5. Entry for 24 May 1828, Ogden, *Third Snake Journal*, p. 85.

juries committed by Indians against other British fur men. The expedition, rather, was organized to avenge the deaths of Americans belonging to a party led by Jedediah Smith. Today, we think of Smith as America's greatest mountain man. In 1828 the Hudson's Bay Company thought of him as a rather annoying commercial rival.[6] That the company's officers felt they had to obtain satisfaction for what relatively unknown Indians had done to him is impressive evidence of the weight these men gave to resenting every Indian homicide, if not every injury committed by the Indians against fur trappers.

Smith's trapping and exploring party of nineteen men had been attacked on the Umpqua River by members of the Kalawatset nation.[7] At least fifteen of his people had been killed, and Smith and three others barely escaped with their lives.

Smith and his men had entered California illegally and had been ordered by Mexican authorities to leave. He had headed north from San Francisco Bay, apparently for Fort Vancouver, the Hudson's Bay Company's Columbia River headquarters, intending, as Governor George Simpson later understood, to "proceed either by the Columbia or across Country from thence to Salt Lake, being desirous of avoiding the circuitous route by the Rio Colorado, and unwilling to attempt cutting across the Sandy desert," because of an attack on his party by the Mohaves on his way into California.[8] The Americans had found the previously unexplored coastal route "more rugged & mountainous than they expected"[9] and the Indians, especially after they had arrived in the region of the Rogue River, unusually hostile and even planning to attack, or so Smith said.[10]

When Smith told the Hudson's Bay Company that the Indians were planning to attack, he may have been recalling things from the hindsight of his terrible ordeal. Whether it was true did not much interest Hudson's Bay officers. They wanted an answer to the opposite question: whether the Americans brought trouble with the Kala-

6. Smith first annoyed the Hudson's Bay Company by intruding himself into the company's Snake country expedition of 1824 and returning with it to the Columbia Basin, where he was suspected of being an American commercial spy. "Beaver's Law in Elephant's Country," pp. 197-98.

7. In today's Douglas County, Oregon. Pollard, "Smith Massacre," pp. 133-37.

8. *Simpson's 1828 Journey*, p. 59. For Smith's legal problems in California, *see* Weber, *Californios v. Smith*.

9. *Simpson's 1828 Journey*, p. 59.

10. Maurice Sullivan, Editorial Comment, in *Travels of Jedediah Smith*, p. 107.

watsets on themselves by their own reckless actions. On 12 July, just after Smith had crossed the Umpqua, a Kalawatset helped himself to the company's only axe. This event was more serious than we might suppose, for the Americans had few tools and needed the axe for survival. About a month earlier, when the axe and a drawing knife had been taken by other Indians, Smith had tied up one of the natives, intending to keep him prisoner until the axe was recovered.[11] Now the same tactic was followed. A Kalawatset suspected of taking the axe was seized and tied with a rope while the Americans stood guard with loaded rifles. The frightened man told them where the axe was buried. Once released, he urged his fellow tribe members to avenge his humiliation. However, it seems that he was opposed by a Kalawatset reportedly of high rank and greater prestige, and it is possible that nothing would have come of the incident. Unfortunately for the Americans, the second Kalawatset climbed on one of the expedition's horses, not to take the animal, the British were later told, but to learn what it was like to sit on a horse, or, perhaps, to ride one that was saddled. He was immediately ordered off by one of Smith's men. Now the second Kalawatset became angry and agreed to attack the Americans.[12]

We shall never be able to explain all the nuances of the situation. One problem is that we know nothing of Kalawatset culture. Even if we did, it might not matter. All our evidence from the Kalawatset side is secondhand hearsay filtered through reports written by Hudson's Bay Company officers of what translators told them Indians said, or, more often, what translators told them Indians said they had learned in talking to other Indians, especially non-Kalawatsets talking with Kalawatsets. It is not necessary to be certain about the facts. All we have to know is what Hudson's Bay Company officers believed had happened. Their decisions were based on what they understood had occurred, after all, not on events that did happen but that they were never told about.

The horse-riding incident occurred two days after the affair with the axe. Smith had already left the camp to find a path the brigade could follow to the north, and had warned his second-in-command to keep all Indians out of camp. It is not known why his

11. Entry for 11 June 1828, "The Second Journal of Harrison G. Rogers," in Dale, *Ashley-Smith Explorations*, p. 255; entry for 11 June 1828, Smith, "Journal," in *Travels of Jedediah Smith*, p. 99.

12. Maurice Sullivan, Editorial Comment, in *Travels of Jedediah Smith*, p. 108.

orders were disobeyed, but the camp was filled with about a hundred Indians when the second Kalawatset climbed on the horse. Chief Factor McLoughlin later claimed that he knew why Smith had been disobeyed. "[T]o gratify their passion for women," he charged, "the men neglected to follow the order."[13] Recently, a historian of the event has cast doubt on the accusation, pointing out that McLoughlin did not mention it in any of the several official communications to his superiors discussing the affair on the Umpqua. He wrote it during a "later year" in his autobiography. It is true that McLoughlin's superior, Governor George Simpson, was told that Smith's second-in-command, Harrison Rogers, tried to force a Kalawatset woman into his tent. The same historian also doubts the accuracy of that charge. "Rogers's journal shows him to have been a sober, religious, and intelligent leader," he notes, "for whom an attempted rape on the eve of departing the Umpqua River seems out of character."[14]

Smith's best biographer gave a quite different explanation as to why so many Indians were allowed to loiter in the American camp. He thought Rogers "trusted to the influence of the Hudson's Bay Company on these Indians."[15] The Americans had been surprised to discover that the Indians on the Umpqua possessed British goods, and even more surprised that they knew the names of the British leaders at Fort Vancouver, about 150 miles to the north. This discovery, it has been suggested by another of Smith's biographers, may have given the Americans a sense of security.[16] It is pure conjecture, but if it is true, the men were relying on some rather faulty guesswork. As the Hudson's Bay Company had made contact with some of these Indians only two years before,[17] it is unlikely that as yet it had much influence over them.

The Kalawatsets, however, did know who the British were, and later claimed that they thought the Americans were enemies of the British whom the British would want to have driven away. Either they made up this story to excuse what they did to Smith's brigade, or they went to great lengths for a people whom they knew little and

13. McLoughlin, "Document," p. 47.
14. Douthit, "Hudson's Bay," pp. 44, 60 n. 78.
15. Morgan, *Jedediah Smith*, p. 268.
16. Maurice Sullivan, Editorial Comment, in *Travels of Jedediah Smith*, p. 107.
17. Letter from John McLoughlin, 5 November 1826, in "Appendix D," in McLeod, *Umpqua Journal*, p. 222.

who apparently did not know them at all. When hearing of the killings, McLoughlin would refer to them as "Umpqua Indians," and say that Alexander Roderick McLeod, on a trapping expedition, "had visited these Indians two months previous to this outrage and had promised to pay them another visit on his return to his hunting grounds."[18] McLeod, however, when he got back to the Umpqua River, referred to a different group of Indians as the Umpquas, suggesting that the Kalawatsets, who had attacked Smith, were not the Indians he had visited.

Whatever their motivation, one fact was indisputable. The Kalawatsets attacked the Americans, killed fifteen of them within minutes, and divided their property, including 120 horses and mules, 180 beaver pelts, two hundredweight of beads, and a hundredweight of other goods such as tobacco.[19] Only one of the trappers who had been in the camp escaped, making his way to friendly Indians who took him to the Hudson's Bay Company's headquarters on the Columbia River. By coincidence, he was the man who had ordered the Kalawatset from the horse. Some days after that trapper had arrived at Fort Vancouver, Smith also appeared with the two other men who had survived the attack.

After listening to the stories of the four men, McLoughlin decided that the Hudson's Bay Company had to seek vengeance because, even though only Americans had died, Indians had to be taught they would pay a fearful price for killing trappers. "I conceive in our intercourse with such barbarians," he explained to Smith, "we ought always to keep in view the future consequences likely to result from our conduct as unless those Murderers of your people & Robbers of your property are made to return their plunder, as we unfortunately too well know they have no horror or compunction of Conscience at depriving their fellow Man of Life—If strangers came in their way they would not hesitate to murder them for the sake of possessing themselves of their property."[20]

Doubting neither his right nor his duty to take vengeance against the Kalawatsets, McLoughlin immediately organized a retaliatory

18. Letter to George Simpson, 24 March 1829, *Letters of John McLoughlin*, p. 77.

19. George Simpson to Governor and Committee, 1 March 1829, *Travels of Jedediah Smith*, p. 147; John McLoughlin to Governor and Committee, 10 August 1828, in Cleland, *Reckless Breed*, p. 110.

20. John McLoughlin to Jedediah Smith, 12 September 1828, *Travels of Jedediah Smith*, pp. 109-110; Morgan, *Smith*, p. 275.

expedition under the command of McLeod.[21] As McLoughlin told Smith, however, there were limits to vengeance. Like the governor and the committee at the London headquarters of the Hudson's Bay Company, McLoughlin believed "it would be worse than useless to attempt more than our forces would enable us to accomplish." Therefore, many decisions had to be left to McLeod's discretion. Because "McLeod knows those Indians & knows best whether we can effect any good, he will decide on what is to be done."[22]

As McLoughlin explained to McLeod, Hudson's Bay had to choose between two extremes: "either we must make War on the Murder[er]s of his [Smith's] people to make them restore his property or drop the business entirely." He wrote, "You know those Indians you know our means, and as a failure in undertaking too much, would make this unfortunate affair worse—& as you are on the spot—you therefore will decide on what is best to be done and depend that whatever that decision may be at least as far as I am concerned every allowance will be made for the situation you are placed in."[23]

The main point raised in McLoughlin's instructions, that much was being left to McLeod's discretion, was explicitly endorsed by his superior, the governor of the Hudson's Bay Company in North America. McLeod, George Simpson wrote London, had "the double object of recovering Smiths property . . . and of enquiring into the cause of, and punishing those who were concerned in the horrible outrage if found practicable and considered expedient."[24]

After the expedition was concluded, and McLoughlin realized that McLeod had acted so cautiously that little had been accomplished, he regretted putting so much emphasis on discretion, practicalities, and expediency. He had wanted McLeod to be more decisive and to show greater boldness when asserting the demands of the Hudson's Bay Company. "I neaver [*sic*] meant or expected you were to run along the Coast from place to place for a few articles my Idea was that you Should go to the main band of the murderers

21. Letter of 1 September 1828, *Letters of McLoughlin First Series*, p. 30.
22. John McLoughlin to Jedediah Smith, 12 September 1828, *Travels of Jedediah Smith*, pp. 109-10.
23. John McLoughlin to Alexander Roderick McLeod, 12 September 1828, *Travels of Jedediah Smith*, p. 111; Morgan, *Smith*, pp. 275-76.
24. George Simpson to Governor and Committee, 1 March 1829, *Travels of Jedediah Smith*, pp. 147-48; *Simpson's 1828 Journey*, p. 60. *See also* George Simpson to Jedediah Smith, 26 December 1828, *Travels of Jedediah Smith*, p. 136.

and make them return what they had and which I conceived you Could have done without any great loss of time in fact by incurring little more delay than if you went simply to trade"[25]

McLoughlin's mistake was not these instructions; they were standard. Much was left to the judgment of every leader of Hudson's Bay Company retaliatory expeditions. They could kill or not kill, as they saw fit. If McLoughlin's instructions to McLeod were different, it was only in the emphasis that everything was left to McLeod's discretion and the promise that McLoughlin would support him with headquarters. If McLoughlin can be charged with a mistake, it was in putting the expedition under the command of Alexander Roderick McLeod.

After arriving on the Umpqua River, McLeod had several options. At one extreme, he could have demanded the deaths of fifteen Kalawatsets to "satisfy" the deaths of the fifteen American trappers. He could have insisted on fifteen bodies—any bodies—and have refused, for example, to take fourteen. At the opposite extreme, he could have done nothing at all. What interests us is not how close he came to the second extreme, but how he reached or justified decisions on the basis of a combination of European and Indian legal principles, drawn from the circumstances of the case and from the testimony of third-party Indians who had not been present at the killings, but had spoken to the Kalawatsets, and were believed by McLeod to tell the Kalawatset side of the story.

To be sure, McLeod also drew his facts from American testimony. Before sending the expedition off, McLoughlin had interviewed Smith, asking if he had experienced any trouble with the Indians. Smith told him about the hidden axe, and that, previous to reaching the Kalawatsets, "they had two skirmishes with the natives in which they killed two of them."[26] He meant that on their way up the coast from California, the trappers had killed two members of other nations.

The first thing McLeod did after arriving on the Umpqua was to bury the dead. Next, he questioned members of neighboring nations about what they knew of the affair or what the Kalawatsets had told them. These people, some of whom wanted to join forces

25. Letter to Alex[ander] Roderick McLeod, 3 March 1830, *Letters of John McLoughlin*, p. 79.

26. John McLoughlin to Governor and Committee, 10 August 1828, Cleland, *Reckless Breed*, p. 111.

with the British and make war on the Kalawatsets, became his main informants. They said that even before Smith's expedition had arrived at the river, "they had notice of the approach of his party, from some of the Tribes he had passed, with intimations that they were Enemies destroying all the Natives that came within their reach."[27] McLeod was right to credit this tale as indicating the apprehension of Indians on the Umpqua. It would have been reasonable for the Kalawatsets and their neighboring nations to have considered the American trapping party, appearing without warning and without precedent, to be dangerous, a threat to their security. McLeod was also right to discredit the tale itself. Among the property of Smith's brigade recovered by the British at the Kalawatset village was the journal of Rogers, Smith's second-in-command, and it showed that no massacres had occurred.[28]

The Kalawatsets were reported to have taken the rumors seriously, and to have had them "confirmed by their [the trappers] severely beating and binding the hands and feet of one of their own Tribe who had pilfered an axe (a very slight offense in their estimation)."[29] When questioned by McLeod, Smith admitted to tying the Kalawatset "but denies having used blows or any manner of violence except Seizing him."[30] In the various reports by McLeod to McLoughlin and by McLoughlin and Simpson to the company's London headquarters, no one mentioned that in January the year before McLeod had taken the same action. When an axe had been lifted from his trapping party in the area of the Rogue River, he had done exactly what Smith would do. He seized a local Indian as a hostage and held him until the axe was returned.[31]

Although the conversion of the axe was but "a slight offense" to the Kalawatsets or to the Indians of the Umpqua River who told this tale to McLeod, it had been a serious matter to the Americans. As

27. George Simpson to Governor and Committee, 1 March 1829, *Travels of Jedediah Smith*, p. 148.

28. The journal, together with Smith's journal written after the event, "indicate[s] that in northern California Smith and his men probably killed three or four Indians, and they used limited force to protect animals, human life, and property against Indian attack." Douthit, "Hudson's Bay," p. 44.

29. George Simpson to Governor and Committee, 1 March 1829, *Travels of Jedediah Smith*, 148; *Simpson's 1828 Journey*, p. 61.

30. Entry for 12 October 1828, "Alex. R. McLeod's Journal of Southern Expedition," in *Travels of Jedediah Smith*, p. 125.

31. Douthit, "Hudson's Bay," p. 34.

one of the men who escaped with Smith told McLoughlin, it was the only axe that they had left and "they absolutely required it." It was only "after doing all they could in vain, to get it from the Indians, they had recourse as a last alternative to tying the Chief."[32]

Here is an instance of how easy it was for a misunderstanding to arise in a crosscultural legal situation. McLeod's Indian informants said that "stealing" an axe was "a very slight offense," in their estimation, in the estimation of the Kalawatsets, or both. The American whom McLoughlin questioned replied that the axe was "absolutely required," indicating that he understood the Indians to mean that the "stealing" had been "a very slight offense" because they did not think the axe of much value. As the American was answering a question put to him by McLoughlin, and as it was McLoughlin who recorded this answer as material evidence, it can be assumed that McLoughlin also understood that the Indians meant that the taking had been "a very slight offense" because the axe was not worth much. This assumption was quite natural for the two men to have made. After all, a Briton or an American of that era who said that appropriating someone else's axe "was a very slight offense" would probably have been referring to the value of the axe.

But it was not a Briton or an American who said that the axe taking had been "a very slight offense." It had been a Kalawatset quoted by an Indian of one of the Umpqua River nations, or an Indian of one of the Umpqua River nations, or both. Whoever said it, we should remember, spoke in a crosscultural context. That is the context in which McLeod and the American heard the words, and that is why both misunderstood what was said. When the Indians of the Umpqua River said that either they or the Kalawatsets thought the taking of the axe "a very slight offense," they were referring to the act of conversion, not to the value or the size of the item. We may be certain that an axe was valuable to them. Quite possibly the Kalawatsets did not possess a single axe, a marvelous instrument compared with any tool that they could manufacture. They would not have considered it inconsequential to their well-being had they possessed one and it had been taken from them. "A very slight offense" to them was the appropriation of things they needed or coveted from people of other nations, even from people who were their guests. Here again, we can see the difficulty caused by crosscultural

32. John McLoughlin to Governor and Committee, 15 November 1843, *Letters of McLoughlin Second Series*, p. 115.

language. Taking the axe was "theft" to the fur traders and trappers, just as it would be to twentieth-century historians. If their words could have been idiomatically translated, the Indians would not be quoted as saying "theft." They might, though, be quoted as saying "slight offense." No harm was done in this case, however, for McLeod had only to understand that the offense was slight to the Kalawatsets. The reason it was "slight" was not material to his inquiry.

McLeod may have better understood what the Umpqua River Indians told him about the Kalawatset who had wanted to ride one of the American horses. Their story was somewhat rougher than the American version. It was they who informed the British that their man had "overruled" the first suggestion that the Kalawatsets attack the Americans. He was "higher in Rank and possessing greater influence" than the man who had been tied up and forced to tell where the axe was buried. He had wanted "to ride a horse for amusement about the Camp" and had mounted one when "one of Mr. Smiths men, having a Gun in his hand and an irritated aspect desired the Indian angrily to dismount, the Indian instantly obeyed, hurt at the Idea and suspecting the Man disposed to take his life." It was then that "he gave his concurrence to the Plan in agitation" to attack the Americans.[33] Questioned by McLeod, the trapper admitted he had "seen a Chief mount a Horse without leave and [had] ordered him to desist but not in an angry tone neither did he present his Gun, but had it in his hand."[34]

Again McLeod and the American trapper probably misunderstood the nuances of the crosscultural situation. Whether the American spoke with an angry tone may have depended on the property concepts and sharing values of the Indians who heard his words and saw his gestures. The Kalawatset who climbed on the horse had clearly been caught in a crosscultural conflict if sharing property was a dominant norm of his society, especially if sharing customarily extended to property brought into the host nation by an alien. The cultural conflict would have been even more evident if sharing property among the Kalawatsets was so entrenched that people who would be called borrowers in European society would not be thought of as borrowers by the Kalawatsets, because they possessed

33. Entry for 11 October 1828, "Alex. R. McLeod's Journal of Southern Expedition," in *Travels of Jedediah Smith*, p. 123.

34. Entry for 12 October 1828, McLeod, *Journal*, p. 125.

claim rights on or property interests in things that they wished to share. It is possible that when he got on the Americans' horse for what today we would describe as a joy ride, the Kalawatset could not conceive that he was committing a wrong because he and his fellow tribal members thought he had a "right" to a ride. When the American ordered him off the horse, the demand may have been so rude by Kalawatset behavioral expectations that the American's tone seemed angry to Kalawatsets, though it would not have seemed angry to a European such as McLeod, had he been present.

The evidence that made the strongest impression on the British was the Kalawatset argument with the least crosscultural implications, the one closest to their own political and legal way of thinking. McLeod heard it from an elderly headman belonging to one of the Umpqua River nations. The Kalawatsets, McLeod reported him as saying, "were much influenced by the Assertions of the other Party [the Americans], telling them that they were a different people from us [the British], and would soon monopolize the trade, and turn us out of the Country."[35] Reporting this evidence to London, Simpson embellished it a bit, saying that the Americans "declared themselves to be people of a different Nation from us, and our Enemies, and therefore intended to drive us from the Columbia where we were intruders on their Territory."[36]

This story of Americans saying they were a different people from the British bridged the cultural gap. On the Indian side, it persuaded the Umpqua River headman to question the wisdom, even to doubt the right, of the British to make war against the Kalawatsets on Smith's behalf. The headman's argument so impressed McLeod that he reported it in detail:

> [T]he Old Fellow, entered more minutely into the subject, and expressed his surprise at our interference in aiding and assisting People that evinced evil intentions towards us, as he had been informed by the people [the Kalawatsets] who defeated the party, they [the American trappers] having communicated something about territorial Claim, and that they would soon possess themselves of the Country, makes the Natives about us very inquisitive not having ever heard

35. Entry for 11 October 1828, *ibid.*, p. 123.

36. *Simpson's 1828 Journey*, p. 61; George Simpson to Governor and Committee, 1 March 1829, *Travels of Jedediah Smith*, p. 148.

such a thing before, and we avoid giving them any information,[37] and treat the subject with derision.[38]

Asked whether the story were true, Jedediah Smith told McLeod "that he did not doubt of it"—that is, that the Kalawatsets had been told something similar to what the headman reported. What they had been told, however, "was without his knowledge and must have been intimated to the Indians through the Medium of a Slave boy attached to his Party, a Native of the Willamette—he could converse freely with those Indians."[39]

One other fact was given weight by the British when deciding what retaliation to take against the Kalawatsets, though McLeod did not record it in his journal. We know about it because Simpson mentioned it in his report to company headquarters in London, so McLeod must either have told it to Simpson or Chief Factor McLoughlin, or included it in a written communication supplementing his journal. It concerned the alleged attempt by Harrison Rogers to force a woman into his tent. Simpson attributed the attack to this incident. The anti-British talk had caused the Kalawatsets to "look upon the party with suspicion," he concluded, "but they had not formed any plan of destruction" until Rogers grabbed the woman and knocked down her brother.[40]

Officially, McLeod gave an entirely different explanation as to why he had concluded not to seek vengeance in kind, and to limit satisfaction from the Kalawatsets to the recovery of Smith's property. Talk of turning the British out of the Oregon Country, he decided, combined with the "harsh treatment"—tying up the axe taker and forcing the second man off the horse—"caused" the Americans' "untimely fate."[41]

For us, McLeod becomes an enigma with that statement. Did he realize what he was saying? Did he, in fact, base his decision not to take vengeance in kind on an Indian legal principle? That is what he said. With Simpson and McLoughlin both agreeing with him, Mc-

37. Information about the treaty of 1818, claiming for Great Britain and the United States joint occupancy of the Oregon Country, something that would have upset the Umpqua River nations had they understood its implications.

38. Entry for 12 October 1828, McLeod, *Journal*, pp. 124-25.

39. *Ibid.*, p. 125.

40. *Simpson's 1828 Journey*, p. 61; George Simpson to Governor and Committee, 1 March 1829, *Travels of Jedediah Smith*, p. 148.

41. Entry for 11 October 1828, McLeod, *Journal*, p. 123.

Leod resolved the matter on a finding of causation. He concluded that certain unfriendly, aggressive acts committed by the American trappers were the *cause* of the Kalawatsets' killing them. That was why he demanded only the return of Smith's property and told the Kalawatsets that the Hudson's Bay Company would not take vengeance in kind against them if it were returned. He had the full support of the company's governor for North America. It was true, Simpson wrote headquarters in Great Britain, that some parts of the evidence McLeod had collected "Smith denies; but the whole story is well told, and carries the probability of truth along with it."[42] We may wonder whether he realized how odd his reasoning would have seemed in London had anyone bothered to analyze it.

Of course, there were practical considerations that went into McLeod's decision. Like the North West Company officers at the Cascades of the Columbia River, he had to weigh the consequences of spilling Indian blood. "Mr. McLeod might have taken the lives of several of the Murderers," Simpson explained to London, "but had he done so, it would have involved us in eternal Warfare with a very Numerous and powerful Nation, with whom we have been on Friendly terms for several years, whose Trade is important to us and in whose power our Trapping and Trading parties would frequently be; he therefore considered it prudent as regarded our own safety, and politic as regarded the interests of the Service, to abstain from violence."[43]

Why Simpson so misrepresented the situation is not clear. The best guess is that he was trying to defend McLeod with his superiors in London. Headquarters was then displeased with McLeod, believing that he had mismanaged the retaliatory expedition against the Clallums that he had led earlier in the year. The governing committee of the Hudson's Bay Company was about to reject his promotion to the rank of chief factor. Criticism of McLeod's conduct against the Clallums, when he had been careless with Indian life, may have had something to do with his caution in dealing with the Kalawatsets. Even before starting on the expedition, he had written to McLoughlin, "I am unable even to form an Idea what measure to adopt at this early period however I am not disposed to hostile

42. *Simpson's 1828 Journey*, p. 61; George Simpson to Governor and Committee, 1 March 1829, *Travels of Jedediah Smith*, p. 148.

43. *Simpson's 1828 Journey*, pp. 61-62; George Simpson to Governor and Committee, 1 March 1829, *Travels of Jedediah Smith*, pp. 148-49.

measures. I must learn more than I Know before proceeding to extremities."[44]

Trying to persuade London that McLeod's decisions were sound, Simpson exaggerated both the size of the Kalawatset nation and the significance of their trade with Hudson's Bay Company. But he was right about international law. Had McLeod avenged the deaths of Smith's men, the Kalawatset nation most likely would have considered itself at war with the British—any British—or with white people in general. Despite what Simpson told London, a Kalawatset war did not pose a serious threat to the company, because the Kalawatsets appear to have been too small a nation to cause it any damage. What could have been troublesome was the likelihood that Kalawatsets would be seeking Hudson's Bay blood for years to come. The number of Smith's men killed could have been a greater consideration than the size of the Kalawatset nation. As fifteen had been killed, McLeod, to take vengeance, should have killed at least fifteen Kalawatsets. To have killed so many could have meant that, even if the nation did not go to war against the British, there would have been a substantial number of kin of those people slain with a perceived duty to avenge their deaths. Any British trappers, traders, or seamen passing the Umpqua River area would have been in danger—a danger that could have lasted as much as a generation unless that part of the Kalawatset nation were wiped out.

The better view, in light of the established practice of the Hudson's Bay Company and the psychological premises of Indian behavior on which the officers acted, is that McLeod decided not to kill Kalawatsets after weighing the mitigating facts of the situation. Among these were rules of Indian international law. He did so although not thinking of them as "legal," just as the North West Company officers had unknowingly applied the international law of the Columbia River Indians when agreeing that the Cascades could keep some of the property taken from the Stuart party as compensation for the two men killed.

He may not have thought of them as legal, but McLeod was aware of some of his premises. One was his decision to credit the doubt expressed by both the Kalawatsets and the headman of the Umpqua River nation that the British had any business avenging American deaths. The trappers' jingoism, he concluded, led the

44. Letter to George Simpson, 24 March 1829, *Letters of John McLoughlin*, p. 78, quoting undated letter from McLeod.

Kalawatsets to think that Smith's men were enemies of the British. From that belief it followed, he knew, that Indians of every nation would have expected the British to want the Americans killed.

There was also one decision McLeod made probably realizing that he was applying Indian concepts. He had enough experience with obtaining "satisfaction" from Indians to appreciate that, as a general rule, Indians did not determine liability for delicts by weighing such European elements as bad intentions, circumstances, malice, or the guilty mind. Consciously or unconsciously, McLeod applied the Indian principle of causation when concluding that the Americans' anti-British talk and their "harsh treatment" of the Kalawatsets "caused their untimely fate." McLeod did not elaborate on the theory, but Governor Simpson did, when explaining to Jedediah Smith why McLeod had not retaliated in kind:

> While on the spot he learnt that the Melancholy catastrophe was occasioned by some harsh treatment on the part of your people towards the Indians who visited your Camp some of whom they said had been beaten, and one of them bound hands & feet for some very light offence, which treatment they further said corroborated in their Minds a report that had preceded you from Indians that your party had been conducting themselves with hostility towards the different Tribes you passed in your way from the Bona Ventura[45] (for which it appears there were some grounds) and that as a measure of Self Preservation they determined on the destruction of your party which its injudicious conduct and unguarded situation enabled those savages to accomplish with little difficulty or danger to themselves.[46]

It would be difficult to formulate a stronger statement of the doctrine of causation. By applying that doctrine—applying general domestic and international Indian legal notions—it made perfect sense to say that the American trappers had been the cause of the Kalawatsets' attack upon them. These notions, but not European notions or any standards of conduct applied by the nineteenth-century British, made people to some degree responsible for their own destruction if,

45. The Sacramento River.

46. George Simpson to Jedediah Smith, 26 December 1828, Simpson, *Journal*, p. 303; *Travels of Jedediah Smith*, p. 137.

by their careless behavior and inattention to safety, they had been *the* "cause" of the violence committed against them.

Crosscultural difficulties must be overcome if we are to begin to imagine what Indians in the old Oregon Country would have understood about the situation and what conclusions they would have accepted. A notion not easily credited by anyone unwilling to think either as an Indian or in terms of Indian custom is that the American trappers, by their own carelessness, had only one axe, which, due to further carelessness, they had "allowed" the Kalawatsets to appropriate and to hide. Some years later John McLoughlin explicitly restated this theory to explain why McLeod's expedition had not taken vengeance in kind against the Kalawatsets. "[I]t was because Smiths people had behaved ill, in the first place," he wrote, "they had only one Axe in the party and through carelessness they allowed the Indians to steal it, and to recover which they seized on the Chief and tied him!"[47] Again, we must ask a question that has been asked before, and wonder whether McLoughlin gave any thought to the implications of what he was saying. If not, it is hard to escape the conclusion that he had been acting on Indian premises for so long that he had internalized them to such an extent as not to question—or, more likely, not to notice—his own adoption of them.

McLoughlin was saying something that would not have occurred to almost any other white person in nineteenth-century North America or nineteenth-century Great Britain. He was saying that Smith's men, by careless inattention to safety, had been a cause—if not *the* cause—of the attack that took their lives. Indeed, the argument could be extended even further. The rule that the American trappers were the responsible agents relieved the Kalawatsets of some, if not all, culpability.

The question raised at the beginning of this chapter must be left unanswered. Whether the fur men of the transboundary North American West applied rules of Indian law and did so knowingly remains too elusive to resolve. Much evidence is yet to be uncovered. We can be certain of a few matters, however. One is that the fur traders and trappers themselves did not give the question much thought. Still, there can be little doubt that when they did think about exacting vengeance from Indians for homicides, their perceptions were shaped to a discernible extent by Indian ways of thinking.

47. John McLoughlin, "Remarks on Mr. Cushing's Report," in *Letters of McLoughlin Third Series*, p. 272.

The North West Company officers knew that the Indians along the Cascades of the Columbia River expected them at least to make an effort to get back the property taken from the Stuart expedition, or future brigades would attempt to cross those portages at great risk. And Alexander Roderick McLeod knew that, even if he eschewed vengeance in kind, he had to recover the property taken from Jedediah Smith, or the trappers of the Hudson's Bay Company would have to avoid the Umpqua River region for half a decade or even more. That was why he forced its return,[48] not only from the Kalawatsets but from all the other Indians to whom the Kalawatsets had bartered it.[49]

48.
> Mr McLeod under all circumstances found that it would be unsafe and unpolitic to take any hostile steps against the Tribe but endeavoured to recover of the property which you had been pillaged and with some trouble and difficulty succeeded in getting nearly the whole of it restored.

George Simpson to Jedediah Smith, 26 December 1828, Simpson, *Journal*, p. 303.

49. McLoughlin explained the legal process:

> The plan was that the officer was, as usual, to invite the Indians to bring their furs to trade, just as if nothing had happened. Count the furs, but as the American trappers mark all their skins, keep these all separate, give them to Mr. Smith and not pay the Indians for them, telling them that they belonged to him; that they got them by murdering Smith's people.

McLoughlin, "Document," p. 48.

TWELVE

Theory of Vengeance

THE CONCLUSION of the previous chapter may not be convincing. There are other possible explanations, besides Indian law or the shortcomings of Alexander Roderick McLeod, for why the Hudson's Bay Company's retaliatory expedition seeking to avenge the attack upon Jedediah Smith did not kill Kalawatsets. Seemingly more persuasive is the argument that the expedition did not dare risk starting a war, which would not only have been expensive and perilous, but bad for trade, which would surely have been curtailed had war commenced.[1] More obvious still was the fact that the dead men were all Americans and trapping competitors of the Hudson's Bay Company. Since the company had no personal or emotional interest in avenging their deaths, it is no wonder that McLeod took no chances, went through the motions of showing the flag, and accepted every excuse the Kalawatsets gave him to avoid a fight.

These more obvious explanations are not persuasive. True, war was risky, but hopes of avoiding war did not weigh heavily in the vengeance decisions of Hudson's Bay Company officers. They simply assumed the risk of violence and counterviolence too often, visiting larger nations such as the Clatsops and Crees with death and destruction for far less than the killing of fifteen fur trappers and the conversion of thousands of dollars' worth of property. After all, John McLoughlin had been well aware of the risks when he sent McLeod down to the Umpqua River in the first place. He knew the odds were that McLeod would kill Kalawatsets, starting a war, and the possibility of war had been acceptable to him, just as it had been to

1. Douthit, "Hudson's Bay," p. 44.

George Simpson. When he gave McLeod discretion to determine what vengeance to exact, McLoughlin undoubtedly told him to keep in mind the safety of the expedition and not to take unnecessary chances. But there is no evidence that McLeod felt the brigade would have been endangered had he demanded Kalawatset blood. He did not fear the reaction of the neighboring nations. Had they taken any part, they would have joined the British against the Kalawatsets, not defended the Kalawatsets against the British.

Our best evidence is that Simpson, McLoughlin, and all other Hudson's Bay Company officers would have told McLeod that the safest policy, at least for future British trapping expeditions in the Umpqua River region, was to kill some Kalawatsets. If we credit the often-stated premises of their theory of Indian control—that failure to take vengeance in kind against manslayers or the nation of manslayers not only insured repeated insults of the same nature but encouraged neighboring nations to exploit perceived British weaknesses—it was the general sense of all the company's officers, including Simpson, McLoughlin, and McLeod, that it was more risky not to take vengeance in kind than to take it. Taking vengeance increased the probability of war or of individual retaliation by the kin of any people who were slain. Not to take vengeance ensured more attacks on trapping parties by the Kalawatsets and all other nations in the region.

That the dead men were strangers to them as well as foreigners made taking vengeance less personal for the Hudson's Bay Company's officers, but otherwise irrelevant to their scheme of values telling them that vengeance had to be taken. The attack on Smith meant that "the honour of the whites was at stake," McLoughlin told London headquarters, and that not to take vengeance "would lower us in the opinion of the Indians."[2] Once he had an idea of what had happened, McLoughlin knew McLeod would have to visit the Kalawatsets "to enquire into the cause of this horrible massacre, as the facility with which the natives had destroyed this party if allowed to pass unchecked all whites being the same kind of people in the eyes of Indians would lower us in their estimation induce other Indians to follow their example and endanger our personal security all over the Country. . . ."[3] It was well understood by "every one acquainted with

2. Fisher, *Contact and Conflict*, p. 36 (quoting McLoughlin letters of 11 July and 7 August 1828).

3. John McLoughlin [to George Simpson], 24 March 1829, *Letters of John McLoughlin*, p. 77.

the character of the Indians of the North west Coast," McLoughlin reminded Simpson, that "they can only be restrained from Committing acts of atrocity & violence by the dread of retaliation."[4]

That white trappers had been killed was bad enough. Even more serious, McLoughlin concluded, was that "this unfortunate affair is extremely injurious to us," meaning the Hudson's Bay Company, "as the success & facility with which the Natives have accomplished their object lowers Europeans in their estimation & consequently very much diminishes our security."[5]

The reason why Europeans were lowered in Indians' eyes if vengeance were not taken when affairs like the Smith attack occurred, was that Indians expected vengeance. McLoughlin explained this fact about two years later when he was criticizing the mode of vengeance taken by another company officer, while otherwise approving the fact that some vengeance had been carried out:

> Mr. Ermatingers Woman ran away with an Indian last Spring and he sent Leolo the interpreter after her, and desired him to punish the Indian by cutting the tip of his ear, which he did, and though in the civilized World such an act will appear harsh, and on that account it would be preferable that he had resorted to some other mode of punishment; still, if the Indian had not been punished it would have lowered the Whites in their estimation as among themselves they never allow such an offence to pass unpunished.[6]

McLoughlin meant that in the Indian nations with which he was in contact vengeance would have been taken against a man for running off with another man's woman. These Indians expected the fur traders to do the same. If they failed to they lost respect, not because Indians therefore thought them cowardly not to take vengeance, but because they had failed to do what was expected of them; they had failed to act as they were supposed to act.

When word of what McLeod had done to the Clallums got back to London, company headquarters was upset. Writing from North

4. Douthit, "Hudson's Bay," p. 37.

5. John McLoughlin to the Governor and Committee, 10 August 1828, Cleland, *Reckless Breed*, p. 111.

6. John McLoughlin to George Simpson, 20 March 1831, *Letters of John McLoughlin*, p. 185; John McLoughlin to George Simpson, 16 March 1831, *Letters of McLoughlin First Series*, p. 227.

America, Governor Simpson defended McLeod. If the Hudson's Bay Company were to prosper among the Indians, it had to do things the way Indians expected them to be done, he argued. "[F]rom experience," he explained, "we find, that the more lenient we are with those Savages, the more daring they become; that our forbearance is invariably ascribed to timidity, and that there will be no possibility of maintaining our ground in this country, unless we promp[t]ly resent every act of hostility they commit upon us."[7]

We may not be impressed by the theory. From our perspective, McLoughlin and Simpson seem to be excusing violence. To say that fur traders and trappers would lose Indian esteem if they failed to take vengeance as Indians expected looks like justification by rationalization, making a case that headquarters could accept, or covering up a situation that Simpson and McLoughlin had let get out of hand and did not want investigated. Of course, to an extent it was, but only to an extent. Instead of excuses, the argument that not to take vengeance for an injury inflicted by Indians—especially homicide—lowered the white men in the "opinion" of Indians was an integral part of their theory as to why vengeance had to be taken. That theory is the topic of this chapter. The question is not why they took vengeance but how they explained it, what they thought they were doing, and why they thought they had little choice but to act as they did.

On receiving the news that Samuel Black had been killed by a Shuswap at Kamloops, Chief Factor Peter Skene Ogden wrote a circular letter to the officers of the Hudson's Bay Company in New Caledonia, urging them to be on guard. "We are well aware that in this country our lives are constantly exposed," he warned, "and in regulating our treatment of Indians neither too much severity nor leniency will answer; but a medium between both is the most advisable."[8] We can imagine that the officers receiving these instructions felt they were getting precious little guidance, but what else did they think Ogden had said? What, for example, did they understand him to mean by "leniency" when telling them that "neither too much severity nor leniency will answer"? There may be no better clue to how mountain men in the transboundary West theorized vengeance than his meaning of "severity." His actions and words explain that. His definition of "leniency" is much more elusive, probably because he was reluctant to consider its implications. It seems clear, however.

7. *Simpson's 1828 Journey*, p. 76.
8. Morice, *History*, p. 181.

"Leniency" to Ogden was "severity" with good intentions. Brutal retaliation, he insisted, benefitted the Indian, not the trapper. It put the trapper to trouble and even placed him in danger. Uncompromising retaliation, according to Ogden, saved Indian lives by teaching Indians, as nothing else would, that they could not afford to commit international homicide. If they did, people of their nation would surely pay the blood price. From this perspective, severity of vengeance constituted leniency measured by the bloodshed it prevented.

Ogden's ideas of vengeance were widely shared among British and American fur men. The bourgeois at Lac Coutereille, Jean Baptiste Cabot of the North West Company, demanded that the Chippewas deliver to him for vengeance the manslayer of one of his voyageurs. The man was surrendered, and, "in order that the Ojibways might learn the proper respect for the lives of white men," Cabot "had him stabbed to death in the presence of 'a vast concourse of his people.'"[9]

After William H. Ashley was attacked by the Arikaras and driven back down the Missouri River in 1823, Benjamin O'Fallon, United States Indian agent for the Upper Missouri, warned him not to leave vengeance to the army. The military would not be severe enough. If the river were to be reopened to the fur trade, Ashley and his men had to take the vengeance:

> You have a chance, the first and I fear the last to avenge your wrongs—to revenge the death, and bury the bones & appease the spirits of your murdered comrades. A mere exhibition of soldiers—a mere military display will not be enough—The blood of *A'rickaras* must run from many vital veins or the laudable enterprise of American Citizens is at once arrested, and the fur trade of the upper Missouri is suspended for a long time—Who can tamely stand by and witness the reception, or recognize a white flag from those inhuman monsters when their brows are decorated with the fair haired scalps of our murdered Countrymen.[10]

Vengeance was the method. It was not the end. The purpose was to keep the fur trade open, to teach the Indians to respect the lives of fur trappers, and, as Ogden said, to deter future homicides.

9. O'Meara, *Savage Country*, p. 218.

10. Benjamin O'Fallon to William Ashley, 20 June 1823, in *West of Ashley*, pp. 35-36.

A few Indians dead today might mean a live mountain man tomorrow. That was the theory McLoughlin acted on time and again. In his instructions to McLeod, ordering him to avenge Jedediah Smith, McLoughlin wrote an extended explanation of the theory of vengeance with which he and others on both sides of the border justified their practice of blood for blood:

> I know many people will argue that we have no right to make war on the Natives, on the other hand if the business is drop[p]ed, will not our personal security be endangered wherever this report reaches—Again suppose that by accident a Vessel was wrecked on the Coast, to possess themselves of the property would not the Natives—seeing these Murderers escape with impunity—kill all the Crew that fell in their power & say as these [the Kalawatsets] now do—We did not take them to be the same people as you[11]—. . . is it not our duty as Christians to endeavour as much as possible to prevent the perpetration of such atrocious crimes—& is their [*sic*] any measure so likely to accomplish so effectually this object as to make these Murderers restore at least their illgotten booty now in their possession.[12]

For McLoughlin, secure in the comfort and safety of Fort Vancouver, the deterrence of vengeance was a Christian duty. Out on the trail, confronting all the perils and tribulations of leading the Snake country expeditions, the deterrence of vengeance was a necessity for Peter Skene Ogden. There were always dangers; there was always the need to make examples of Indians and not for a moment let them see a weakness. In 1826 two of Ogden's men caught three members of a Shoshone band appropriating seven horses from their detached camp. The Indians put up no resistance, surrendered the horses, and offered as compensation "some Roots they had for provisions" and "some of their arrows," but the two trappers were not appeased. Although they were alone in the wilderness and the three

11. The Indians who had guided Smith to Fort Vancouver had already told McLoughlin that the Kalawatsets would defend their actions on the grounds that the Americans were a different people from the British and they did not think the Hudson's Bay Company would resent the killings.

12. John McLoughlin to Alexander McLeod, 12 September 1828, *Travels of Jedediah Smith*, pp. 110-11; Morgan, *Jedediah Smith*, p. 276.

Indians had weapons, they began whipping them severely. "The Indians for some time endured the blows but at length becoming vexed" they resisted. In the ensuing fight, one Indian was killed and both trappers were wounded. They fled, leaving behind their horses, rifles, and blankets, booty for the two remaining Indians. Ogden was less troubled by the folly or brutality of his men than the failure of their vengeance. "[W]e have sustain'd a most shameful defeat," he lamented. "[I]t is true one Indian was kill'd [and] this according to the Indian mode is so much in our favour but they [the two surviving Indians] have gone off full impressed with the idea that both our men are dead nor will they have any difficulty in convincing their friends when they as the most convincing proofs will produce their arms Horses &c. it is most disgracefull to us." From Ogden's perspective, the Snake country would have been a safer place, for Indians as well as fur trappers, had his men killed all three Indians.[13]

About four months later the expedition had crossed the mountains west from the Snake River to the Little Applegate, where they encountered Indians who, Ogden discovered, "stand not in the least awe of Tradors and Trappers." Worse, these Indians entertained "a most contemptible opinion of all Tradors they have seen." And why not, Ogden concluded, "for from the numerous murders and thefts they have committed not one example has been made of them."[14] Examples were what Indians understood. After the expedition moved over to the Applegate River, "One of the Trappers reported that within a short distance of the Camp he met with three Indians who on seeing him strung their Bows and mad[e] preparations for sending him a few Arrows at the same time making signs for him to leave their Lands he instantly drew the cover from his Gun and was in the act of giving them a salute when they took *flight* an example must be made of them and that soon if we wish to remain in the Country without being molested."[15]

Ogden paid no heed to the fact that the Indians perceived the trappers as trespassers killing meat that would otherwise have been food for their children; he thought only of their threats and how to stop them. He needed "examples," or the expedition would have to

13. Entry for 15 October 1826, Ogden, *Second Snake Journal*, pp. 12-13. For another interpretation of this event, *see* Miller, "Ogden Discovered Indians," p. 145.
14. Entry for 9 February 1827, Ogden, *Second Snake Journal*, pp. 70-71.
15. Entry for 14 February 1827, *ibid.*, p. 78.

leave the Applegate. That is the striking fact of Ogden's theory of retaliation: he had to kill an Indian or two even if they had not yet killed a trapper. Examples were necessary because Indians expected them. That vengeance was anticipated justified anticipatory vengeance. Indeed, Ogden carried the argument about as far as it could go. Because Indians looked for vengeance, he contended, it could be anticipated that they deserved it. He wanted the Hudson's Bay Company to inaugurate a policy of what today might be called "preventive vengeance." "I am of opinion," he explained, "if on the first discovering a strange Tribe a dozen of them were shot it would be the means of preserving many lives." Perhaps "had this plan been adopted when the Snakes were first discovered they would not be so daring as they now are nor would they have murdered upwards of 40 men as they have done and the same is the case with all Indians." He even cited authority from the Old Testament. "Scripture gives us a right to retaliate in kind on those who murder and why not also if we have means of preventing them why not put our means in execution." "[T]he sooner such a plan be adopted the better," he concluded. "[W]hy allow ourselves to be butchered, [and] our property stolen by such vile wretches who are not deserving to be numbered amongst the living?"[16]

Had Ogden been asked, he would probably have said that anticipation of future homicides was not needed for preventive vengeance. It was justified by the fact he knew that Indians if not kept in awe, were always up to something and deserved vengeance merely for the worry they caused. Trapping on the Snake River just north of Idaho Falls in 1828, Ogden had a man chased into camp by Blackfoot. Four days later, he saw signs of a second Blackfoot party. "This part of the country, I verily believe, swarms with these villains at all seasons," he complained. "They certainly deserve to be punished and most severely, for the anxiety they cause us in this quarter, independent of the many murders and thefts they are guilty of."[17] After all, "we all know Indians are a treacherous blood thirsty set of beings," he wrote. "[F]or the facility of Trappers the sooner the exterminating system be introduced amongst them the better."[18]

Ogden did not borrow the idea of "preventive vengeance" from Indian law, which contained no concepts even remotely similar, ex-

16. Entry for 9 February 1827, *ibid.*, pp. 70-71.
17. Entry for 20 May 1828, Ogden, *Third Snake Journal*, p. 84.
18. Entry for 12 February 1827, Ogden, *Second Snake Journal*, p. 75.

cept for "mourning wars" or indiscriminate payback killings to avenge an international homicide. It sanctioned vengeance only after homicide was committed, and generally, in most domestic law as well as international law, did not possess coercive governmental apparatus for preventing the commission of socially objectionable acts. Instead, he justified it on the incredible dangers and hardships of life in the western mountains. Once, out in the Snake country, he encountered a party of American trappers who had lost men and property to the Snakes.

> The Americans appear and are most willing to declare war against them, and a short time since requested to know, if they did in the spring, if I would assist. To this I replied if I found myself in company with them at the time I would not stand idle. I am certainly most willing to commence, but . . . not knowing the opinion of the Concern [Hudson's Bay Company], it is rather a delicate point to decide on, but as an individual acting for myself, I will not hesitate to say I would most willingly sacrifice a year and even two to exterminate the whole Snake tribe, women and children excepted, and in doing so I am of opinion I could fully justify myself before God and man. But I full well know, those who live at a distance are of a different opinion, and the only reply I should make to them is, gentlemen, come, endure and suffer as we have done and judge for yourselves if forbearance and submission has not been carried too far, even beyond the bounds ordained by Scripture.[19]

We must not jump quickly to judgment. It is easy to read what Ogden and other mountain men said and did, and conclude they had no theory of vengeance except blind, absolute retaliation, an injury for an injury, a life for a life, or payback vengeance. That conclusion may be true, but before agreeing we should be certain the perception does not obscure a theory of vengeance that helped determine both policy and actions. It is not irrelevant to recall Morris S. Arnold's warning that with patterns of behavior there may be form hidden in apparent formlessness. Discussing the seemingly patternless decisions reached by early English cases on the law of obligations, he compares them to an "impervious black box, generating random and

19. Entry for 22 January 1828, Ogden, *Third Snake Journal*, pp. 51-52.

unreviewable results." Perhaps a better way to think about it, he suggests, "is that there can be commonly held social assumptions about a way a moral world is ordered, founded on logic and experience, that people accept in their daily dealings with each other, and this entirely apart from whether there are places to resort to for their systematic and dependable vindication. This natural law, as we may call it, counts as much for law as the product of the most sovereign decree ever could." The evidence of their thoughts that the mountain men have left us may be too sparse to find the "law" that Arnold says could be there. There is enough evidence, however, to ask whether when exacting vengeance, the fur trappers of the transboundary West shared "commonly held social assumptions about the way a moral world is ordered."[20]

On one level—perhaps we would say on the lowest level—of that moral world was the satisfaction some mountain men derived from vengeance in kind. Following the battle at the Arikara villages when William H. Ashley's fur company avenged blood and fought to open the upper Missouri to the fur trade, one trapper wrote to a friend in the East. "For myself," he reflected, "I am determined to have revenge for the loss of two young men to whom I became very much attached, and I never will descend this river until I assist in shedding the blood of some of the Ricarees."[21] One way the moral world was ordered for that mountain man was in killing Arikaras.

On a slightly different level of theory, mountain men thought of homicides by Indians as a challenge they had to meet. At the start of the most famous fight that occurred between fur trappers and Indians, the battle of Pierre's Hole near the rendezvous of 1832, William Sublette, who assumed the command of the mountain men and their Indian allies

> addressed a few words to the whites, telling them that the enemy was near, and that if at the commencement of the [trapping] season we did not shew a bold front, our prospects in the mountains would be blasted. He concluded his brief but energetic address, by remarking "and now boys, here are the Black Feet who have killed so many of your companions; . . .—and who are at this moment daring the *pale faces* to the onset. Some of us may fall; but we die in a

20. Arnold, "Ideology," p. 508.

21. Letter from one of Ashley's men to a friend in the District of Columbia, 17 June 1823, in *West of Ashley*, p. 33.

> good cause; for whose life or property will be secure if the foe be encouraged by refusing their challenge?"[22]

Sublette's assumption that failure to meet the challenge would lead to repeated Indian aggression was a given among mountain men. Governor George Simpson had spared no expense to apprehend the Shuswap manslayer of Samuel Black, he told Hudson's Bay headquarters in London, because "if he be allowed to remain at large unpunished, the impression it could have on the minds of the natives might prove dangerous to the peace of the country, and to the lives and property of the white population."[23] John McLoughlin had the same rationale for sending Alexander Roderick McLeod to force the Clatsops to return the property they had salvaged from the wreckage of the *William and Ann*. The property had been insured, so why had he bothered? "The Indians considered the property as ours," he explained. "[I]f we had not made a demand of it we would have fallen so much in Indian Estimation that whenever an opportunity offered our safety would have been endangered."[24]

Oddly, George Sutherland used somewhat the same theory when explaining why he had not taken vengeance in kind against the Gros Ventres of the Blackfoot confederacy. He was master of the Hudson's Bay Company's Edmonton House in December 1796 when four hundred of those Indians came in to trade. He wondered whether he should do business with them, "these being the nation who plundered Manchester House," another Hudson's Bay post, in 1793, and who "attacked and burnt the South Branch" in 1794, killing several people, including three company employees.[25] This was apparently the first visit the Gros Ventres had made to a Hudson's Bay house since the attacks, and Sutherland took pains to explain how he handled them.

"I thought it absolutely necessary to let them know we had not forgot that horrid affair by giving them a severe reprimand," he

22. Robert Campbell to Hugh Campbell, 18-19 July 1832, *Rocky Mountain Letters*, p. 9.
23. George Simpson to Governor and Committee, 25 November 1841, *Simpson's London Letters*, p. 54. Similarly, *see* entry for 25 September 1804, Cameron, "Extracts from Journal," p. 287.
24. John McLoughlin to Governor and Committee, 13 August 1829, *Letters of John McLoughlin*, p. 41.
25. Entries for 14 and 16 December 1787, Sutherland, *Edmonton Journal*, p. 75; Johnson, "Introduction to Edmonton," p. 75 nn. 2-3.

wrote in the post journal that would be read in York Factory and then sent to London. Collecting the principal headmen in a room at Edmonton House, he warned them "that we had not forgot their past conduct and we now had them in our powers and did not want the means of punishing them effectually." But "we would forgive them this time if they made proper acknowledgement and promise never to be even so much as impertinent to Europeans in future." That would have been remarkable behavior for any Blackfoot, but of course the Gros Ventres agreed, giving him "three horses and a few wolves skins" to prove their thoughts were good. Perhaps apprehensive that his reconciliation would be considered cowardice in London, Sutherland added, "here I solemnly declare that if they or any other tribe of Indians should again attack any of the honourable Company's settlements while I have the honour of being Inland Master, I will take such effectual revenge as will perhaps for ever deter them from committing the like [again]."[26]

What interests us is Sutherland's theory of coercion. He had done little except scold the Gros Ventres, yet he claimed he had been trying "to reduce the Indians to a sense of their duty." They had to be corrected, and he had corrected them. He knew why they had to be reduced to a sense of duty but did not explain how he had "reduced" them, except for one observation: "As it's well known to all those who understand the customs and manners of Indians that the oftener they escape with impunity the more daring they grow."[27] That was all he said. He repeated the standard theory of why vengeance had to be taken, but did not explain how he had taken it.

Men of action not given to philosophical reflection, fur traders and trappers generally did not explain all their thoughts. John Gardner was killed when the Arikaras attacked the trapping party under William H. Ashley near the great bend of the Missouri River. Writing to the young man's parents, Hugh Glass knew what had to be done: "Master Ashley is bound to stay in these parts till the traitors are rightly punished."[28] Glass did not explain why that was so, but an incontrovertible element of the general theory was that vengeance for an Indian homicide of a fur man was necessary as much to deter other nations as to chastise the nation responsible for the homicide.

26. Entry for 16 December 1797, Sutherland, *Edmonton Journal*, p. 76.

27. Entry for 16 December 1797, *ibid*.

28. Hugh Glass to the parents of John S. Gardner, [June] 1823, *West of Ashley*, p. 31.

That was the motivation for vengeance of two of the highest-ranking United States officials to react to the Arikara attack. Other nations would have an example to follow, Benjamin O'Fallon feared, unless retaliation were swift and decisive. "This unprovoked and dreadful massacre of white men, by the A'rickarar nation," he wrote the superintendent of Indian Affairs in St. Louis, "has directed the attention of all the neighboring tribes, who are suspending their opinion of us. . . . Now, say the Indians 'all will see what the white people intend to do—We will see the extent of their forbearance—We will also see (if they have any) the extent of their spirit of resentment.[']"[29] The superintendent agreed. "If this hostile Tribe are not Chastised," he wrote of the Arikaras, "it is apprehended that they will become more hostile, and other tribes will be incouraged to follow their example, and in that case, no Trader will be safe in their person or property above the influence of the Troops at Council Bluffs."[30]

Peter Skene Ogden would have understood what O'Fallon and the superintendent meant. After the three Shoshones had bested his two men, forcing them to abandon their horses, guns, and blankets when the trappers fled, Ogden saw with his own eyes the consequences of not getting the best of Indians. "In my opinion in this affray we have lost *Ground*," he told his Hudson's Bay Company superior, Chief Factor John McLoughlin, "about four hours after it took place fires were lighted in all directions by the Indians this is a signal to collect and from what we can observe the Country appears to be well stocked with Indians."[31]

Two givens fueled the belief that every homicide had to be avenged. One assumed that a nation properly abashed would be less likely to repeat offenses. "We had Saviral [several] Battils with the naison on the other side of the Mountains," Finan McDonald wrote of the second Snake country expedition sent out by the Hudson's Bay Company. "Poore Meshel Bordoe [Michael Bordeau] was kild with 5 more of the band there dath was revenge[d] as well as we

29. Benjamin O'Fallon to William Clark, 24 June 1823, *ibid.*, p. 37.

30. William Clark to John C. Calhoun, 4 July 1823, *ibid.*, p. 46. Clark's argument was also advanced by one of Ashley's commercial rivals. He wrote that "a decisive blow" by the United States Army was "indispensable for the safety of every white man on the river above Council Bluffs." Sunder, *Pilcher*, pp. 43-44 (quoting a letter from Joshua Pilcher to O'Fallon).

31. Peter Ogden to John McLoughlin, 15 October 1826, in "Appendix," in Ogden, *Second Snake Journal*, p. 138.

Could revenge it for no less than 68 of them that remane on the Planes as Pray for the wolves and those fue that askape [escaped] our Shotes they had not Britch Clout to Cover them selves We Shoe them what war was and they will not be so radey to attack People."[32]

All mountain men apparently believed that a good thrashing reformed Indians by dampening their zeal to repeat objectionable activities. They did not use this theory only as an excuse to justify vengeance after the fact. They acted on it as a guide for behavior. Sometimes trappers even reported proof that the policy worked successfully. An instance comes from Osborne Russell's account of the American rendezvous of 1837. Some Bannocks arrived at the rendezvous with horses they had taken "from a party of French trappers who were hunting Bear River" a few months earlier. While the Bannocks were away from the rendezvous hunting, "4 or 5 whites an[d] two Nez Percey Indians went to their Village" and retook the horses. When the Bannocks returned to camp and tried to recapture the horses a fight broke out, which Russell says lasted three days. It ended "when they begged us to let them go and promised to be good Indians in [the] future. We granted their request and returned to our Camp satisfied that the best way to negotiate and settle disputes with hostile Indians is with the rifle: for that is the only pen that can write a treaty which they will not forget. Two days after we left them three white trappers ignorant of what had taken place went into their village and were treated in the most friendly manner."[33]

The second given among mountain men why vengeance had to be taken against Indians for homicide was that failure to retaliate invited repeated offenses, not only by the manslayer but by members of the manslayer's nation. As just discussed, a collateral given was that it also encouraged insults from members of other nations who had no connection with the homicide, or who might even be enemies of the manslayer's nation. In 1828, a homicide occurred that has been extensively discussed in earlier chapters. Some members of the Clallum nation killed five employees of the Hudson's Bay Company who were carrying dispatches from Fort Vancouver to a post on

32. Finan McDonald to J. G. McTavish, 5 April 1824, *Minutes of Northern Department*, p. 24 n. 1.
33. Russell, *Journal*, pp. 59-60. Similarly, *see* John McLoughlin to George Simpson, 20 March 1831, *Letters of John McLoughlin*, p. 183; Donald Manson to George Simpson, 6 December 1841, Black, *Journal of a Voyage*, pp. 232-33.

the Fraser River. "[T]his is a Deed that loudly calls on us to punish the perpetrators," the chief factor on the Columbia wrote the chief factor in New Caledonia. "[I]f we do not these Barbarians will take courage and murder any one of our people when ever they have an opportunity—and Indeed not only them but all these round about when they learn at the same time we allow'd it [to] pass over with impunity."[34] The theory, Ogden explained when proposing "preventive vengeance," was that "Indians in general give us no credit for our humanity towards them, but at[t]ribute our not revenging the murders of our men to cowardice and consequently whenever an opportunity offers of murdering or stealing they allow it not to pass."[35]

The policy, which was defended by fur traders at the highest levels of the Hudson's Bay Company, might as accurately be called "preventive recidivism" as "preventive vengeance." Following the killing of Samuel Black, Hudson's Bay Company officers in New Caledonia warned Governor George Simpson that the various nations around Okanagan were becoming hostile. The news did not surprise Simpson. He knew the cause, and it stemmed from more than a failure to execute Black's manslayer. "This unfortunate state of affairs," he explained, "has arisen from an ill-judged forbearance on our part, in not punishing many cases of misconduct (such as horse thieving, pilfering from encampments, etc.), which have been committed by the natives of late years, a forbearance they ascribe to shyness or timidity, instead of the proper cause, a disinclination to have recourse to measures of severity." Simpson blamed a "laxity of discipline" for making it dangerous "even to pass through the country"—which meant, of course, that the death of Black's manslayer, or some other Shuswap in his place, was that much more urgent.[36]

A final incident is worth considering. At first glance it may not seem germane as it did not directly involve homicide, but when mountain men dealt with Indians, fear of homicide could be a factor even in cases in which homicide had not been committed. Peter Skene Ogden often made the connection, as, for example, when warning that failure to avenge destruction of property could create

34. John McLoughlin to William Connolly, 20 March 1828, Black, *Journal of a Voyage*, pp. 244-45 (quote at 245).
35. Entry for 9 February 1827, Ogden, *Second Snake Journal*, p. 75.
36. George Simpson to Governor and Committee, 25 November 1841, *Simpson's London Letters*, p. 54.

conditions of personal danger, even to the extent of encouraging homicide. When he sounded that warning, he was in unfamiliar country and had just concluded that it would be best not to retaliate against Indians who were shooting his horses at night, probably hoping that the meat would be abandoned. "[T]hey certainly evince a most malicious disposition towards us and if not checked and that soon our Scalps will soon share the fate of our Horses."[37]

Alexander Ross made the same connection, less explicitly than Ogden, but under more difficult circumstances. Ross was leader of the 1824 Hudson's Bay Company expedition to the Snake country. His brigade consisted of over forty men, plus an unknown number of women and children. For some reason that is not clear—most likely due to his own carelessness—the party found itself encamped with most of the Shoshone bands. The brigade was in the middle of the annual summer gathering when the Snakes came together to fish for salmon. Ross estimated that there were about forty-five hundred Indians encamped on the river, though few were armed with guns. Nevertheless, his men put out their beaver traps, which immediately disappeared. Ross appealed to the headmen for help in getting them back, but they paid him scant attention. The trappers had to respond, Ross believed, or they would soon lose other property. He decided that they should seize horses belonging to individual Shoshone and hold them in exchange for the traps. The object was not just to regain the equipment, but to "show them that we are not afraid of them."[38]

> On observing the daring aspect and conduct of the Indians I assembled all my people together and stated to them that I had known the character of these Indians for many years past and . . . that it appeared evident to me that they were seeking to intimidate us, and if they once thought they could succeed they would rob us, and then they might attempt something else. But before they had gone too far we must let them know that they could not encroach on our property with impunity. That united we were strong, and might teach them to respect us; whereas on the contrary, if we allowed them to take the footing they were assuming we might regret having carried our forbearance too far.[39]

37. Entry for 14 February 1827, Ogden, "Journal," in LaLande, "Journal," p. 65.
38. Ross, *Fur Hunters*, p. 270.
39. *Ibid.*

We might expect the other trappers would have rejected so wild a scheme.[40] Had matters gotten out of control, the entire Hudson's Bay Company brigade could have been obliterated. Ross's reasoning, however, persuaded his men. He later said he convinced them "of the necessity of taking a decisive step to check the insolent tone of the Indians and to pave the way for our getting away without loss or disgrace."[41] As he wrote this account some years after the event, his manner of expression takes on added interest, especially the word "disgrace." He was apparently convinced that he had to face the Shoshone down, or their "insolence" would surely become bolder and the brigade would suffer greater losses, even homicide. Despite the fact that he and his men were overwhelmingly outnumbered, it would have been a "disgrace" to have left without the traps. The strategy proved successful. The Snake horses were seized, the traps were returned, and Ross led the brigade back to the Columbia undisgraced.

40. In a less dangerous situation, Ogden could not persuade his men, also on a Snake country expedition, to retaliate against Shoshone for taking horses. Entry for 24 January 1828, *Third Snake Journal*, p. 53.

41. Ross, *Fur Hunters*, p. 271.

THIRTEEN

Conclusion

WE HAVE EXAMINED but one side of a double-sided conflict. Questions and evidence have been limited to patterns of vengeance taken by fur traders and fur trappers against Indians for Indian-committed homicides of fur traders and fur trappers. Little attention has been given to why Indians killed mountain men or to patterns of Indian vengeance against fur traders or fur trappers for killing Indians. That is a different story but—surprisingly—it may not have been a story about a different law.

The fur traders and fur trappers whom we have examined, especially those of the company organizations, the Hudson's Bay Company, the North West Company, and the American Fur Company, did not act as it might reasonably be assumed they had acted. They did not always act according to a *sui generis* code of the mountains or according to internalized norms of their own culture. It is important to recall James Ohio Pattie paying back Indians in the American Southwest and Alexander Henry the Younger sparing the life of the Chippewa who had accidently killed one of his, Henry's, men. If, when we read Chapter One, Pattie's behavior seemed unsurprising, the reason may have been in expecting the obvious. The lessons of western mythology and western fiction teach us to expect that payback would be the overarching rule of the transboundary West. Surprisingly, Alexander Henry the Younger was closer to the western norm when he weighed such factors as intent, *mens rea* or the guilty mind, malice aforethought, and reasonable doubt, determining "liability" for vengeance by common-law tests for judging "guilt." Few mountain men would have applied Henry's criterion but like Henry and unlike Pattie they exacted principled vengeance not mere payback. That is why the gravid contrast is not between Pattie and Henry, but between them and John Work ordering his men to take vengeance against the Mountain Snakes who had killed one of his trappers or, in lieu of the actual manslayers, to kill members of their "family."

Even Work's criterion was not the norm. By ordering his men to limit vengeance to the manslayers or members of their "family," Work seems to be telling them to consider the domestic law of the Mountain Snakes. In just about every other case we have seen, the fur traders and fur trappers taking vengeance against Indians for homicide applied international law, not domestic law. If unable to find the actual manslayer, they would have seen satisfied killing any Mountain Snake, and not tried to identify individuals by defining what was "family" among the Mountain Snakes.

It is not enough to acknowledge that rules governing fur traders and fur trappers when taking vengeance against Indians for homicide were principles adapted from Indian international law. Just as important is whether the mountain men understood that law and how well they applied it. These are issues for which there will always be more questions than answers. We shall never be quite confident that we understand the intricacies of international homicide, vengeance for homicide, or composition of homicide in the North American West, since we do not know as well as we should the domestic and international law of the nations against whom retaliation was exacted or to whom composition was paid. The best we can do is to concede the questions we cannot answer and not make more of the evidence than our knowledge permits. We can recognize that the fur traders and trappers of the transboundary West adapted to an Indian way of speaking about homicide, but we cannot know if they used words precisely as Indians used them, or even asked about Indian folkways.

It may have surprised us to learn that fur traders and fur trappers, when taking vengeance against Indians for homicide, adapted principles of Indian law rather than applying a *sui generis* mountain code or legal norms from their own Christian, British or American upbringing. It should not, however, be surprising that the Indian law they applied was Indian international law, not Indian domestic law. After all, international law was easily observed and easily understood. It was a law applied between nations, and members of the avenging nation could readily explain their actions to fur men, telling them that the people against whom they were taking vengeance "have killed our friend, and we must have one life to cover the dead," or whiten the path, or dry the tears. Domestic vengeance was much more difficult to comprehend, hidden not only by the reluctance of members of the nation to discuss events, but lost behind the vastly complicated rules governing liability such as the definitions of clans, bands, households, families, or soldier societies. Even if fur traders and fur trappers had recorded the details and had left us their accounts, we could not be certain that they asked the correct questions or used the proper words.

We can read in a mountain man's journal that the "son" of an Indian who had been killed was seeking vengeance for his father's death. We can only wonder whether the writer knew that the nation of the "son" was patrilineal, and, therefore, that the person whom he called the son was the person we think of as "son." More likely, the mountain man made the natural assumption for an American, Canadian, or Scotsman that sons avenge fathers, and would have been puzzled had he been told that among many of the Indian nations with whom he was in contact homicide was avenged by brothers or by sisters' sons. In those nations sons had, in most cases, no greater role to play in the exacting of the blood debt than any other member of the dead man's nation. Nineteenth-century fur traders and trappers, after all, drew their assumptions from their own culture, much as eastern governors had during colonial times when they invited headmen to have their "sons" educated at English schools. If a Catawba, Seneca, or Chickasaw headman agreed, there was a meeting of the minds, but not total understanding. The headman heard the word "son" and, on the premises of his own culture, translated it as "nephew" or "sister's son." His biological son was the concern of the boy's mother's brother.

We may be confident of some conclusions. Using Indian words did not mean that fur traders or trappers accepted Indian premises. They thought of behavior, not of custom or folk law. When the mountain men retaliated for Indian homicides, their theory of justification was not right, it was necessity. They had to exact blood for blood. If they did not, they believed that they gave Indian manslayers a license or an invitation to kill again. Told that a manslayer had not been after plunder or had not been a member of a war party but had been a nephew exercising his right and duty to avenge the death of an uncle, fur men would not have thought the homicide either legal or privileged.

We must be careful that arguments do not get mixed. Fur men

who freely adopted the vocabulary of the Indian law of blood vengeance did not conceive that private acts of homicide might be legally privileged. The point is not that they failed to distinguish, or refused to distinguish, between types or degrees of homicides committed by Indians. They did that all the time. They usually did not seek blind, payback vengeance simply because the manslayer was an Indian. But they quite often applied rules that seemed rational to them, rules of culpability based on intent or circumstances (such as accident or self-defense), not causation.

A typical case, occurring in the 1810s, involved Manuel Lisa, the leading St. Louis fur trader during the years just after the United States purchased the Louisiana Territory. Lisa also served briefly as United States Indian agent, and later complained that "scandalous reports circulated against me" for his conduct in office. One of these reports charged that he "had prevented the Omahas from avenging upon the Sioux the murder of Pedro Antonio." Admitting the fact, he pleaded the circumstances of the situation:

> Antonio, a Spaniard in my service, was killed nine miles from my establishment. His comrades fled and gave me intelligence. I took one hundred and ninety-two warriors of the Omaha tribe and went to the spot. Those who did the mischief had fled. The Omahas, impatient for blood, were eager to follow. I stopped them with my own presents and my own influence, and I take honor to myself for having done it. The body of Antonio was not mutilated; it was covered with a blanket and his face with a hat; his comrades might have been killed—they were not hurt. The death of Antonio, then, was a case of simple murder, and not an act of national hostility on the part of the Sioux. For one guilty act, must I turn loose two hundred warriors upon the innocent? Forget all moral principle, and turn barbarian myself because in a country called *savage*?[1]

Lisa termed the killing of Antonio "murder," the common-law term for culpable homicide, yet did not judge it by common-law principles. He weighed culpability by Indian or Sioux standards. Although they did kill Antonio, the Sioux apparently had not intended to kill a non-Indian, and regretted the action. They had not treated him in death as they would have a national enemy. The face

1. Manuel Lisa to William Clark, 2 July 1817, in Douglas, *Manuel Lisa*, p. 97.

had not been disfigured. The head had not been cut off. Parts of the body were not stuffed into the mouth. The Sioux had actually shown respect, covering the body with a blanket and putting Antonio's hat over his face so that the eyes would not be pecked by birds. Lisa knew what he was doing. He may have avoided turning "barbarous" or "savage," but he did so by judging Sioux intentions by their own rules of behavior. Like other fur traders and trappers, however, he was not crediting Indians with notions of "right" or "duty" or "privileged act." If mountain men knew they were using Indian values, and some did, they thought those values explained behavior—why people they considered "savages" reacted in certain ways to homicide—not how folk custom required people to act.

We should also be cautious about weighing the "harshness" or "justice" of practices we do not fully understand and will never accept. In the twentieth century we may think the principles of vengeance harsh, yet we should still acknowledge that mountain men thought them necessary. Though we need not credit their sincerity, we should attempt to measure it. There were a few fur men, even a Hudson's Bay Company officer, for whom the practice of retaliation was too harsh. Although that officer would aid in the capture of Indian manslayers, he would not kill them.[2] Most mountain men, however, believed that vengeance in kind for Indian homicide was no more harsh than necessity required. If they had been asked their test for determining necessity, they would have said it was as much vengeance as was needed to deter Indian violence. By that yardstick, some fur traders claimed, their program of vengeance was proven successful. Certainly John McLoughlin thought so. The measure of vengeance he had meted out, he claimed in 1843, had prepared the way for the settlement of Oregon by either the British or the Americans: "Having by our system of management, and protracted intercourse, subdued the ferocity of the Indian tribes, converted their former hostility against the whites into feelings of respect and attachment, introduced order, and a respect for property, and moral obligation which did not before exist among them, . . . The British or American Government have only to send an Officer with a Commission in his pocket, to have their authority acknowledged and maintained."[3]

2. *E.g.*, as previously quoted, John Tod of the Hudson's Bay Company. *See* Tod, "Scotch Boy," p. 196.

3. Douthit, "Hudson's Bay," p. 53.

Of course, much of what McLoughlin said was nonsense. Still, if we can believe Robert "Doc" Newell, there was a grain of substance in his boast. Newell was one of the best-known American mountain men of his day, an independent trapper who had led at least one company of his countrymen across the Oregon country at a time when the Hudson's Bay Company still considered it a private fief. He became an Indian agent under the United States government, and in a report written in 1849, when Oregon had been troubled by a number of Indian wars, he recalled that conditions had been less dangerous under McLoughlin's management. "[B]ut few occasions had we to raise arms against the Indians considering all the circumstances," he wrote of American trapping brigades, "and ten years ago that number of men [he does not say what number] could go the length and breadth of the Territory in safety with proper management."[4]

It was Newell, an American fur trapper who had fought his share of Indians, who took the trouble to remind us that fur traders and trappers went into the mountains neither to fight nor to make war. "The trapper's first policy," he wrote, "is to get furs, to trade and induce the Indians to work, trap, hunt, etc. and on as reasonable terms as possible." By following three rules, he thought, the mountain men were, according to their own lights, fair to Indians. "Their policy was . . . never to justify themselves when wrong, or to take undue advantage or to let a crime go unpunished if possible. But at all times when quarter was asked, the same was given."[5]

Newell was writing of individual American mountain men, but he could also have been speaking for fur men working for companies on both sides of the border. Alexander Simpson, an officer with Hudson's Bay, described that company's policy also in terms of three rules:

> Mildness and conciliation in the intercourse of its officers and servants with Indians of every tribe; and absence of interference in the quarrels of individuals, in the internal disputes of tribes, and in the wars which they may wage with one another, and an invariable rule of avenging the murder by Indians of any of its servants, blood for blood, without trial of any kind, are the three and only *principles* followed out by the Hudson's Bay Company in its transactions with

4. Newell, "Report on Indians," p. 153.
5. *Ibid.*, pp. 152-53.

> the numerous inhabitants of the extensive territory under its control; and its sole *aim* is to derive the greatest possible revenue from that territory.[6]

If Newell, the American free trapper, and Simpson, the Hudson's Bay Company officer, were saying that the same rules of conduct toward Indians were followed on both sides of the border, there are two questions for future historians to pursue. One is whether the conduct of British fur men toward Indians, once touted as more humane, more mild, and more successful than American Indian policy, was really different from the conduct of American fur men. Except for the likelihood that British policy was more harsh, there was little substantive difference, at least in the important matter of retaliating against Indians for homicide. If anything, the Hudson's Bay Company was more effective at exacting vengeance than were individual mountain men, more certain to pursue vengeance, and, at times, more brutal.

The second question follows from the first: Were British and American principles of vengeance for homicide much the same because they were derived from Indian law? We must be careful with this question. A century and a half after the era of beaver trapping, the answer should not be determined by the fashions of the times. Many scholars during the last decade of the twentieth century, their reflexes programmed to the stimulus of political correctness, need only be told that the principles of vengeance were much the same on both sides of the border to know that the connecting link is racism, not principle.

Perhaps the question of whether British and American principles of vengeance were much the same because they derived from Indian law is more jurisprudential than historical. That may be why this book puts greater emphasis on what those principles were, how they worked, and how they related to Indian rules than on speculation about origins. Still, the cases we have seen and the words that have been quoted from fur traders and trappers show that there is much evidence on which to base sound historical inference. There are, to be sure, various ways to evaluate that evidence. One we have already used is Morris Arnold's suggestion that seemingly formless actions may be given shape, meaning, and pattern if we find that the people taking those actions, such as the mountain men exacting

6. Simpson, *Simpson*, p. 418.

vengeance in kind, shared "commonly held social assumptions about the way a moral world is ordered."[7] If we look at the moral world of the fur traders and trappers, however, we still will have to answer a question. It is not the obvious question. From whom were those moral assumptions derived? There is a more pertinent question. Whose world in nineteenth-century North America was based on a morality of vengeance?

7. *See* text at ch. 12, n. 20 *supra*.

Acknowledgments

LEAVE FROM TEACHING RESPONSIBILITIES at New York University School of Law was provided by the Filomen D'Agostino Greenberg and Max E. Greenberg Faculty Research Fund at New York University School of Law, and by John Sexton, dean of the School of Law. Research was made both easier and more pleasant by the professional competence of the staff of the Huntington Library, most particularly Virginia Renner and Jill Cogen. Martin Ridge made a contribution by telling me how to pronounce "Arikara." As always, the librarians at New York University School of Law were just as professional. Jay Shuman mastered Canadian relations, Carol Alpert solved the problem of deadlines, Gretchen Feltes generously kept after nondeliveries, Elizabeth Evans was always online, and Ronald Brown wondered how to pronounce "Shuswaps." It does not seem likely, but perhaps in some inexplicable fashion this study profited by being read and discussed by the premier group of American legal historians, members of the New York University School of Law Colloquium in Legal History: R. B. Bernstein, Gerald Giannattosio, Elizabeth Wiltshire, Michael Millender, William LaPiana, and William E. Nelson. There is, however, no question that it benefitted from the cite and substance checking done by Barbara Wilcie Kern of East Ninth Street.

This publication would not have been polished to its final luster without advice from two colleagues. Gordon Morris Bakken of the California State University, Fullerton, read the manuscript through all its chapters and concluded that it was not too long. William R. Swagerty of the University of Idaho also read the manuscript with a critical eye, and insisted that it could be improved.

Extended parts of these chapters were previously published as four articles and benefitted from the careful, professional expertise of their editors. The articles were "Principles of Vengeance: Fur Trappers, Indians, and Retaliation for Homicide in the Trans-boundary North American West," *Western Historical Quarterly* 24 (February 1993): 21-43; "Certainty of Vengeance: The Hudson's Bay Company and Retaliation in Kind Against Indian Offenders in New Caledonia," *Montana: The Magazine of Western History* 43 (Winter 1993): 4-17; "Crosscultural Vengeance: Sources of Legal Principles in the Formulation of Mountain Men Vengeance Against Indians in the Old Oregon Country," in *Fretskrift Till Jacob W. F. Sunberg*, ed. Erik Nerep and Wiweka Wainling-Nerep (Stockholm: Författarns och Juristfölaget JF AB, 1993), 255-66; "Restraints of Vengeance: Retaliation-in-Kind and the Use of Indian Law in the Old Oregon Country," *Oregon Historical Quarterly* 95 (Spring 1994): 48-85.

Finally, special thanks are due to Tara Jane Walsh. It was she who found in the archives of the Fordham Law School a copy of the long-lost and forgotten talk that Franklin Pierce gave to the Daughters of Chief Piscataqua. That speech proves what has long been suspected, that it was in 1856 that Pierce first announced his plan for crosscultural compensation in all cases of payback vengeance, but only if it were Native Americans who were paid back and New Hampshire natives who were compensated.

Washington Square, Greenwich Village

Short Titles

Arnold, "Ideology"
Morris S. Arnold, "Towards an Ideology of the Early English Law of Obligations." *Law and History Review* 5 (Fall 1987): 505-21.

Ball, "Across the Continent"
John Ball, "Journal," in "Across the Continent Seventy Years Ago." Kate N. B. Powers, ed. *Quarterly of the Oregon Historical Society* 3 (March 1902): 82-106.

Bancroft, *History*
Hubert Howe Bancroft, *History of the Northwest Coast, 1800–1846.* 28 vols. San Francisco: A. L. Bancroft, 1886.

Barrett, "McKenzie, McDonald, Ross"
Lynn Murray Barrett, "McKenzie, McDonald, and Ross in Snake River Country." Master's thesis, University of California, 1925.

"Beaver's Law in Elephant Country"
John Phillip Reid, "The Beaver's Law in the Elephant's Country: An Excursion into Transboundary Legal History." *Western Legal History* 4 (Summer-Fall 1991): 149-201.

Before Lewis and Clark
Before Lewis and Clark: Documents Illustrating the History of the Missouri, 1785–1804. Abraham Philneas Nasatir, ed. 2 vols. St. Louis: St. Louis Historical Documents Foundation, 1952.

Begg, *British Columbia*
Alexander Begg, *History of British Columbia From its Earliest Discovery to the Present Time.* Toronto: William Briggs, 1894.

Benedict, *Patterns of Culture*
Ruth Benedict, *Patterns of Culture.* New York: Houghton Mifflin, 1934.

Better Kind of Hatchet
John Phillip Reid, *A Better Kind of Hatchet: Law, Trade, and Diplomacy in the Cherokee Nation during the Early Years of European Contact*. University Park: Pennsylvania State University Press, 1976.

Black, *Journal of a Voyage*
[Samuel Black,] *A Journal of a Voyage from Rocky Mountain Portage in Peace River to the Sources of Finlays Branch and North West Ward in Summer 1824*. Vol. 18. E. E. Rich, ed. London: Hudson's Bay Record Society, 1955.

Bradbury, *Travels*
John Bradbury, *Travels in the Interior of America, in the Years 1809, 1810, and 1811*. Lincoln: University of Nebraska Press, 1986.

Brown, *Strangers in Blood*
Jennifer S. H. Brown, *Strangers in Blood: Fur Trade Company Families in Indian Country*. Vancouver: University of British Columbia Press, 1980.

Brown, *Three Years*
David L. Brown, *Three Years in the Rocky Mountains*: One hundred copies separately printed from *The Daily and Weekly Atlas*, Cincinnati, Ohio, September 1845, for the friends of Edward Eberstadt & Sons, Christmas 1950.

Bruner, "Mandan"
Edward M. Bruner, "Mandan," in *Perspectives in American Indian Culture Change*, 187-277.

Cameron, "Extracts from Journal"
Duncan Cameron, "Extracts from the Journal of D. Cameron, Esq North West Company While in the Nipigon Department 1804–1805," in Masson, *Les Bourgeois*, 2:267-300.

Campbell, *Journals*
Two Journals of Robert Campbell (Chief Factor Hudson's Bay Company) 1808 to 1853. Limited ed. Seattle: Shorey Bookstore, 1958.

Carey, *General History*
Charles H. Carey, *General History of Oregon Prior to 1861*. 2 vols. Portland, Ore.: Metropolitan Press, 1935.

Carter, "Ewing Young"
Harvey L. Carter, "Ewing Young," in *Mountain Men* 2:397-401.

Chance, *Influences of HBC*
David H. Chance, *Influences of the Hudson's Bay Company on the Native Cultures of the Colvile District*. Moscow, Idaho: Published as Northwest Anthropological Research Notes, vol. 7, no. 1, pt. 2, 1973.

Chardon's Journal
Chardon's Journal at Fort Clark 1834–1839: Descriptive of Life on the Upper Missouri; of a Fur Trader's Experiences Among the Mandans, Gros Ventres, and Their Neighbors; of the Ravages of the Small-Pox Epidemic of 1837. Annie Heloise Abel, ed. Reprint. Freeport, N.Y.: Books for Libraries Press, 1970.

"Charles McKenzie's Narratives"
"Charles McKenzie's Narratives," in *Early Fur Trade on the Northern Plains*, 228-96.

Christopher and Hafen, "William F. May"
Adrienne T. Christopher and LeRoy R. Hafen, "William May," in *Mountain Men* 4: 207-16.

Cleland, *Reckless Breed*
Robert Glass Cleland, *This Reckless Breed of Men: The Trappers and Fur Traders of the Southwest.* New York: Alfred A. Knopf, 1963.

Cline, *Ogden*
Gloria Griffen Cline, *Peter Skene Ogden and the Hudson's Bay Company*. Norman: University of Oklahoma Press, 1974.

Coats and Gosnell, *James Douglas*
Robert Hamilton Coats and R. E. Gosnell, *Sir James Douglas*. Toronto: Morang, 1908.

Cocking, "Journal"
"Journal of Matthew Cocking, from York Factory to the Blackfeet Country, 1772–73." Lawrence J. Burpee, ed. *Proceedings and Transactions of the Royal Society of Canada—Third Series—Vol. II—Meeting of May, 1908: Transactions, Section II* (1908): 89-121.

Cole, *Exile in Wilderness*
Jean Murray Cole, *Exile in the Wilderness: The Biography of Chief Factor Archibald McDonald 1790–1853*. Don Mills, ed. Ontario: Burns & MacEachern, 1979.

Cox, *Columbia River*
Ross Cox, *The Columbia River: Or Scenes and Adventures During a Residence of Six Years on the Western Side of the Rocky Mountains among various Tribes of Indians hitherto Unknown; together with "A Journey Across the American Continent*. Edgar I. Stewart and Jane R. Stewart, eds. Norman: University of Oklahoma Press, 1957.

Cumberland Journals—Second Series
Cumberland House Journals and Inland Journal 1775–82: Second Series, 1779–82. E. E. Rich, ed. London: Hudson's Bay Record Society, 1952.

Dale, *Ashley-Smith Explorations*
Harrison Clifford Dale, *The Ashley-Smith Explorations and the Discovery of a Central Route to the Pacific 1822–1829*. Cleveland, Ohio: Arthur H. Clark, 1918.

Douglas, *Manuel Lisa*
Walter B. Douglas, *Manuel Lisa*. Abraham P. Nasatir, ed. New York: Argosy-Antiquarian, 1964.

Douthit, "Hudson's Bay"
Nathan Douthit, "The Hudson's Bay Company and the Indians of Southern Oregon," *Oregon Historical Quarterly* 93 (Spring 1992): 25-64.

Dunn, *Oregon Territory*
John Dunn, *History of the Oregon Territory and British North-American Fur Trade; with an Account of the Habits and Customs of the Principal Native Tribes on the Northern Continent*. 2d ed. London: Edwards & Hughes, 1846.

Early Fur Trade on the Northern Plains
Early Fur Trade on the Northern Plains: Canadian Traders Among the Mandan and Hidatsa Indians, 1738–1818—The Narratives of John Macdonell, David Thompson, Francois-Antoine Larocque, and Charles McKenzie. W. Raymond Wood and Thomas D. Thiessen, eds. Norman: University of Oklahoma Press, 1985.

Eberstadt, *Robert Campbell*
Charles Eberstadt, ed. *The Rocky Mountain Letters of Robert Campbell*. New Haven: Yale University Press, 1955.

Elliott, "Fur Trade to 1811"
T. C. Elliott, "The Fur Trade in the Columbia River Basin Prior to 1811," *Washington Historical Quarterly* 4 (January 1915): 3-10.

Ermatinger, *Hudson's Bay Territories*
Edward Ermatinger, *The Hudson's Bay Territories: A Series of Letters on the Important Question*. Toronto: Maclear, Thomas, 1853.

Evans-Pritchard, "Nuer"
E. E. Evans-Pritchard, "The Nuer of the Southern Sudan," in M. Fortes and E. E. Evans Pritchard, *African Political Systems*. London: Oxford University Press, 1940.

Ferris, *Life in Mountains*
Warren Angus Ferris, *Life in the Rocky Mountains 1830–1835*. Herbert S. Auerback, arr. J. Cecil Alter, annot. Salt Lake City: Rocky Mountain Book Shop, 1940.

Fidler, *Cumberland Journal*
Peter Fidler, *Cumberland Journal*. Hudson's Bay Company MS. B. 49/a/27b.

Fidler, *Second Chesterfield Journal*
Peter Fidler, *Journal of Peter Fidler 1801–1802*, in *Saskatchewan Journals*, 293-321.

Fisher, *Contact and Conflict*
Robin Fisher, *Contact and Conflict: Indian-European Relations in British Columbia, 1774–1890*. Vancouver: University of British Columbia Press, 1977.

Fleming, "Mackenzie"
R. Harvey Fleming, "Alexander Mackenzie," in *Minutes of Northern Department*, 447.

Fleming, "McLeod"
R. Harvey Fleming, "McLeod," in *Minutes of Northern Department*, 449.

Foster, "Kamloops Outlaws"
Hamar Foster, "The Kamloops Outlaws and Commissions of Assize in Nineteenth-Century British Columbia," in *Essays in the History of Canadian Law*. David H. Flaherty, ed. Toronto: Osgood Society, University of Toronto Press, 1983. 2:308-64.

Franchère, *Journal of Voyage*
Gabriel Franchère, *Journal of a Voyage on the North West Coast of North America during the Years 1811, 1812, 1813 and 1814*. W. Kaye Lamb, ed. Wessie Tipping Lamb, trans. Toronto: Champlain Society, 1969.

Francis, Jones, and Smith, *Origins*
R. Douglas Francis, Richard Jones, and Donald B. Smith, *Origins: Canadian History to Confederation*. Toronto: Holt, Rinehart & Winston of Canada, 1988.

French, "Wasco-Wishram"
David French, "Wasco-Wishram," in *Perspectives*, 337-430.

Gale, *Missouri Journal*
The Missouri Expedition 1818–1820: The Journal of Surgeon John Gale With Related Documents. Roger L. Nichols, ed. Norman: University of Oklahoma Press, 1969.

Garry, "Diary"
"Diary of Nicholas Garry, Deputy-Governor of the Hudson's Bay Company from 1822–1835. A detailed narrative of his travels in the Northwest Territories of British North America in 1821." *Proceedings and Transactions of the Royal Society of Canada—Second Series—Vol. VII—Meeting of May, 1900: Transactions, Section II* (1900): 73-204.

Gearing, *Priests and Warriors*
Fred Gearing, *Priests and Warriors: Social Structures for Cherokee Politics in the 18th Century*. Manasha, Wisc. *American Anthropologist* vol. 64, no. 5, pt. 2 (Memoir 93), October 1962.

Gough, "Introduction to Henry"
Barry M. Gough, Introduction, in Henry, *Journal One*, xv-lxxi.

Grinnell, *Blackfoot Lodge Tales*
George Bird Grinnell, *Blackfoot Lodge Tales: The Story of a Prairie People*. Lincoln: University of Nebraska Press, 1962.

Hafen, "Etienne Provost"
LeRoy R. Hafen, "Etienne Provost," in *Mountain Men* 6: 371-85.

Hafen, "James Ohio Pattie"
Ann W. Hafen, "James Ohio Pattie," in *Mountain Men* 4: 231-50.

Haines, "Hugh Glass"
Aubrey L. Haines, "Hugh Glass," in *Mountain Men* 6: 161-71.

Haines, "Johnson Gardner"
Aubrey L. Haines, "Johnson Gardner," in *Mountain Men* 2: 157-59.

Handbook
Handbook Of North American Indians. William C. Sturtevant, ed. 9 vols. of projected 20. Washington, D.C.: Smithsonian Institution, 1978–. Vol. 2: *Great Basin*. Warren L. D'Azavedo, ed.

Hargrave Correspondence
The Hargrave Correspondence 1821–1843. G. P. De T. Glazebrook, ed. Toronto: Champlain Society, 1938.

Henry, *Journal One*
The Journal of Alexander Henry the Younger 1799–1814 Volume I: Red River and the Journey to the Missouri. Barry M. Gough, ed. Toronto: Champlain Society, 1988.

Henry, *Journal Two*
The Journal of Alexander Henry the Younger 1799–1814—Volume II: The Saskatchewan and Columbia Rivers. Barry M. Gough, ed. Toronto: Champlain Society, 1992.

Hobsbawm, *Bandits*
E. J. Hobsbawm, *Bandits*. 2d ed. Harmondsworth, England: Penguin Books, 1985.

Holmgren, "Fort Dunvegan"
Eric J. Holmgren, "Fort Dunvegan and the Fur Trade on the Upper Peace River," in *Rendezvous: Selected Papers of the Fourth North American Fur Trade Conference, 1981*. Thomas C. Buckley, ed. St. Paul, Minn.: North American Fur Trade Conference, 1984, 175-84.

Howay, Sage, and Angus, *British Columbia*
F. W. Howay, W. N. Sage, and H. F. Angus, *British Columbia and the United States: The North Pacific Slope From Fur Trade to Aviation*. H. F. Angus, ed. Toronto: Ryerson Press, 1942.

Johansen, "McLoughlin and the Indians"
Dorothy O. Johansen, "McLoughlin and the Indians," *The Beaver* (June 1946): 10-13.

Johnson, "Introduction to Edmonton"
Alice M. Johnson, Introduction and footnotes, in *Saskatchewan Journals*.

Journal of Henry
Alexander Henry, *Journal*, in *New Light on the Early History of the Greater Northwest: The Manuscript Journals of Alexander Henry Fur Trader of the Northwest Company and of David Thompson Official Geographer and Explorer of the Same Company 1799–1814*. Elliott Coues, ed. Vol. 2. New York: Francis P. Harper, 1897, 747-916.

Journal of John Work
The Journal of John Work: A chief-trader of the Hudson's Bay Co. during his Expedition from Vancouver to the Flatheads and Blackfeet of the Pacific Northwest, William S. Lewis and Paul C. Phillips, eds. Cleveland: Arthur H. Clark, 1923.

LaLande, "Journal"
Jeff LaLande, *First Over the Siskiyous: Peter Skene Ogden's 1827 Journey through the Oregon-California Borderlands*. Portland: Oregon Historical Society Press, 1987.

Lamb, "Introduction to McLoughlin"
W. Kaye Lamb, Introduction, in *Letters of John McLoughlin*, xi-cxxviii.

Law for the Elephant
John Phillip Reid, *Law for the Elephant: Property and Social Behavior on the Overland Trail*. San Marino, Calif.: Huntington Library, 1980.

Law of Blood
John Phillip Reid, *A Law of Blood: The Primitive Law of the Cherokee Nation*. New York: New York University Press, 1970.

Lecompte, "David Crow"
Janet Lecompte, "David Crow," in *Mountain Men* 6: 139-41.

Leonard, *Narrative*
Adventures of Zenas Leonard Fur Trader. John C. Ewers, ed. Norman: University of Oklahoma Press, 1959.

Letters of John McLoughlin
Letters of Dr. John McLoughlin Written at Fort Vancouver 1829–1832. Burt Brown Barker, ed. Portland, Ore.: Binfords & Mort, 1948.

Letters of McLoughlin First Series
The Letters of John McLoughlin From Fort Vancouver to the Governor and Committee: First Series, 1825–38. E. E. Rich, ed. Toronto: Champlain Society, 1941.

Letters of McLoughlin Second Series
The Letters of John McLoughlin From Fort Vancouver to the Governor and Committee: Second Series, 1839–44. E. E. Rich, ed. Toronto: Champlain Society, 1943.

Letters of McLoughlin Third Series
The Letters of John McLoughlin From Fort Vancouver to the Governor and Committee: Third Series, 1844–46. E. E. Rich, ed. Toronto: Champlain Society, 1944.

Longmoor, *Second Hudson Journal*
Robert Longmoor, *A Journal of the most remarkable Transactions & Occurrences at Hudsons House from 12th September 1780 to 22nd May 1781*, in *Cumberland Journals—Second Series*, 161-93.

Lowie, *Crow Indians*
Robert H. Lowie, *The Crow Indians*. New York: Rinehart, 1956.

Luttig, *Journal*
John C. Luttig, *Journal of a Fur-Trading Expedition on the Upper Missouri 1812–1813*. Stella M. Drumm, ed. New York: Argosy-Antiquarian, 1964.

McDonald, "Autobiographical Notes"
John McDonald of Garth, "Autobiographical Notes 1791–1816," in Masson, *Les Bourgeois*, 2:1-59.

McDonald, *Letters of Ermatinger*
Lois Halliday McDonald, *Fur Trade Letters of Francis Ermatinger Written to his brother Edward during his service with the Hudson's Bay Company 1818–1853*. Glendale, Calif.: Arthur H. Clark, 1980.

McDonald, *Peace River*
Archibald McDonald, *Peace River: A Canoe Voyage from Hudson's Bay to Pacific by the late Sir George Simpson (Governor, Hon. Hudson's Bay Company) in 1828 Journal of the late Chief Factor, Archibald McDonald (Hon. Hudson's Bay Company), who accompanied him*. Malcolm McLeod, ed. Ottawa: J. Durie, 1872.

McLean, *Notes of Service*
John McLean's Notes of a Twenty-Five Year's Service in the Hudson's Bay Territory. W. S. Wallace, ed. Toronto: Champlain Society, 1932.

McLeod, "Alexandria Diary"
Archibald Norman McLeod, "The Diary," in *Five Fur Traders of the Northwest Being the Narrative of Peter Pond and the Diaries of John Macdonnell, Archibald N. McLeod, Hugh Faries, and Thomas Connor*. Charles M. Gates, ed. St. Paul: Minnesota Historical Society, 1965, 125-85.

McLeod, *Journal Southern Expedition*
Alex R. McLeod's Journal Southern Expedition, in *Travels of Jedediah Smith*, 111-35.

McLeod, *Umpqua Journal*
Alexander Roderick McLeod, *Journal of a hunting Expedition to the Southward of the Umpqua under the command of A. R. McLeod C.T. September 1826*, in Ogden, *Second Snake Journal*, 175-226.

McLoughlin, "Document"
"Copy of a Document Found among the Private Papers of the Late Dr. John McLoughlin," *Transactions of the Eighth Annual Re-Union of the Oregon Pioneer Association for 1880* (1881): 46-55.

MacKay, *Honourable Company*
Douglas MacKay, *The Honourable Company: A History of the Hudson's Bay Company*. New York: Tudor Publishing, 1938.

MacLean, *Canadian Savage Folk*
John MacLean, *Canadian Savage Folk: The Native Tribes of Canada*. Toronto: William Briggs, 1896.

Mandelbaum, *Plains Cree*
David G. Mandelbaum, *The Plains Cree: An Ethnographic, Historical, and Comparative Study*. New York: Anthropological Papers of the American Museum of Natural History, no. 37, pt. 2 (1940): 155-316.

Masson, *Les Bourgeois*
L. R. Masson, *Les Bourgeois de la Compagnie du Nord-Ouest: Récits de Voyages, Lettres et Rapports Inédits Relatifs au Nord-Ouest Canadien. Première Série*. Quebec: Générale A. Coté, 1889; Deuxième Série, 1890.

Mattison, "Joshua Pilcher"
Ray H. Mattison, "Joshua Pilcher," in *Mountain Men* 4: 251-60.

Merk, "Introductions"
Frederick Merk, "Introductions to the Revised Edition: The Strategy of Monopoly," and "Introduction to the First Edition," in Simpson, *Journal*, xi-lxii.

Meyer and Thistle, "Saskatchewan Rendezvous"
David Meyer and Paul S.Thistle, "Saskatchewan River Rendezvous Centers and Trading Posts: Continuity in Cree Social Geography," *Ethnohistory* 42 (Summer 1995): 403-44.

Miller, "Ogden Discovered Indians"
David E. Miller, "Peter Skene Ogden Discovered Indians," in *Essays on the American West*, no. 3. Thomas G. Alexander, ed. Provo, Utah: Brigham Young University Press, 1974, 137-66.

Minutes of Northern Department
Minutes of Council Northern Department of Rupert Land, 1821–31. R. Harvey Fleming, ed. Toronto: Champlain Society, 1940.

Morgan, *Jedediah Smith*
Dale Morgan, *Jedediah Smith and the Opening of the West*. Lincoln: University of Nebraska Press, 1969.

Morice, *History*
A. G. Morice, *Primitive Tribes and Pioneer Traders: The History of the Northern Interior of British Columbia*. 3d ed. Toronto: William Briggs, 1905.

Morton, *Canadian West*
Arthur S. Morton, *A History of the Canadian West to 1870–71 Being a History of Rupert's Land (the Hudson's Bay Company's Territory) and of the North-West Territory (including the Pacific Slope)*. 2d ed. Lewis G. Thomas, ed. Toronto: University of Toronto Press, 1973.

Morton, "Jurisdiction Act"
A.S. Morton, "The Canada Jurisdiction Act (1803) and the North-West," *Proceedings and Transactions of the Royal Society of Canada—Third Series—Vol. XXXII—Meeting of May 1938: Transactions Section II* (1938): 121-37.

Mountain Men
The Mountain Men and the Fur Trade of the Far West: Biographical Sketches of the Participants by Scholars of the Subject and with Introductions by the Editor. LeRoy R. Hafen, ed. Vols. 1-10. Glendale, Calif.: Arthur H. Clark, 1965–72.

Murphy, "Northern Shoshone"
Robert F. Murphy and Yolanda Murphy, "Northern Shoshone and Bannock," in *Handbook* 2:284-307.

Newell, "Report on Indians"
Robert Newell, " A Report on the Indians of Sub-Agency First District South of the Columbia, August 10th, 1849," in *Robert Newell's Memoranda: Travles in the Teritory of Missourie; Travle to the Kayuse War; together with a Report on the Indians South of the Columbia River*. Dorothy O. Johansen, ed. Portland, Ore.: Champoeg Press, 1959, 144-59.

Nidever, *Life and Adventures*
The Life and Adventures of George Nidever [1802–1883]. William Henry Ellison, ed. Berkeley: University of California Press, 1937.

Nunis, "Alexander Roderick McLeod"
Doyce B. Nunis, Jr., "Alexander Roderick McLeod," in *Mountain Men* 6: 279-97.

Nunis, "Introduction to McLeod"
Doyce B. Nunis, Jr., Introduction to *The Hudson's Bay Company's First Fur Brigade to the Sacramento Valley: Alexander McLeod's 1829 Hunt*. Doyce B. Nunis, ed. Fair Oaks, Calif.: Sacramento Book Collectors Club, 1968, 1-30.

Nunis, "Michel Laframboise"
Doyce B. Nunis, Jr., "Michel Laframboise," in *Mountain Men* 5: 145-70.

Ogden, *First Snake Journals*
Peter Skene Ogden's Snake Country Journals 1824–25 and 1825–26. E. E. Rich and A. M. Johnson, eds. London: Hudson's Bay Record Society, 1950.

Ogden, *Fourth Snake Journal*
Peter Skene Ogden, *Snake Country Journal 1828–1829*, in *Peter Skene Ogden's Snake Country Journals 1827–28 and 1828–29*. Glyndwr Williams, ed. London: Hudson's Bay Record Society, 1971, 95-166.

Ogden, *Second Snake Journal*
Peter Skene Ogden's Snake Country Journal 1826–27. K. G. Davies and A. M. Johnson, eds. London: Hudson's Bay Record Society, 1961.

Ogden, *Third Snake Journal*

Peter Skene Ogden, *Snake Country Journal 1827–1828*, in *Peter Skene Ogden's Snake Country Journals 1827–28 and 1828–29*. Glyndwr Williams, ed. London: Hudson's Bay Record Society, 1971, 1-94.

[Ogden,] *Traits of Indian Life*

[Peter Skene Ogden,] *Traits of American-Indian Life and Character*. San Francisco, Calif.: Grabhorn Press, 1933 [Rare American Series no. 9]. Reprint. New York: Dover Publications, 1995.

O'Meara, *Savage Country*

Walter O'Meara, *The Savage Country*. Boston: Houghton Mifflin, 1960.

Patterson, "Introduction of Journal"

R.M. Patterson, Introduction and Appendix, in *A Journal of a Voyage From Rocky Mountain Portage in Peace River to the Sources of Finlays Branch and North West Ward in Summer 1824*. E. E. Rich, ed. London: Hudson's Bay Record Society, 1955, xiii-c; 215-46.

Personal Narrative of Pattie

The Personal Narrative of James O. Pattie of Kentucky. Timothy Flint, ed. Chicago: Lakeside Press, 1930.

Perspectives

Perspectives in American Indian Culture Change. Edward H. Spicer, ed. Chicago: University of Chicago Press, 1961.

Pinkerton, *Hudson's Bay*

Robert E. Pinkerton, *Hudson's Bay Company*. New York: Henry Holt, 1931.

Pollard, "Smith Massacre"

Lancaster Pollard, ed. "Site of the Smith Massacre on July 14, 1828," *Oregon Historical Quarterly* 45 (1944): 133-37.

"Principles of Vengeance"

John Phillip Reid, "Principles of Vengeance: Fur Trappers, Indians, and Retaliation for Homicide in the Transboundary North American West," *Western Historical Quarterly* 24 (February 1993): 21-43.

Ray, *Cultural Relations in Plateau*

Verne F. Ray, *Cultural Relations in the Plateau of Northwestern America*. Los Angeles: Southwest Museum, 1939.

Rich, *Fur Trade and Northwest*

E. E. Rich, *The Fur Trade and the Northwest to 1857*. Toronto: McClelland & Stewart, 1967.

Rich, "James Douglas"
E. E. Rich, "James Douglas," in *Letters of McLoughlin, Third Series*, 311-12.

Rocky Mountain Letters
The Rocky Mountain Letters of Robert Campbell. Charles Eberstadt, ed. New Haven: Printed for Frederick W. Bernicke, Christmas 1955.

Ronda, *Astoria*
James P. Ronda, *Astoria & Empire*. Lincoln: University of Nebraska Press, 1990.

Ronda, *Lewis and Clark*
James P. Ronda, *Lewis and Clark Among the Indians*. Lincoln: University of Nebraska Press, 1984.

Ross, *Adventures*
Alexander Ross, *Adventures of the First Settlers on the Oregon or Columbia River: Being a Narrative of the Expedition Fitted out by John Jacob Astor, to Establish the "Pacific Fur Company;" With an Account of Some Indian Tribes on the Coast of the Pacific*. London: Smith, Elder, 1849.

Ross, *First Settlers*
Alexander Ross, *Adventures of the First Settlers on the Oregon or Columbia River: Being a Narrative of the Expedition Fitted out by John Jacob Astor, to Establish the "Pacific Fur Company"* (1849), in *Early Western Travels 1748–1846*. Vol. 7. Reuben Gold Thwaites, ed. Cleveland, Ohio: Arthur H. Clark, 1904.

Ross, *Fur Hunters*
Alexander Ross, *The Fur Hunters of the Far West*. Kenneth A. Spaulding, ed. Norman: University of Oklahoma Press, 1956.

Ruby and Brown, *Chinook*
Robert H. Ruby and John A. Brown, *The Chinook Indians: Traders of the Lower Columbia River*. Norman: University of Oklahoma Press, 1976.

Russell, *Journal*
Osborne Russell, *Journal of a Trapper: Edited from the Original Manuscript in the William Robertson Coe Collection of Western Americana in the Yale University Library*. Aubrey L. Haines, ed. Portland: Oregon Historical Society, 1955.

Ruxton, *Life in West*
George Frederick Ruxton, *Life in the Far West*. LeRoy R. Hafen, ed. Norman: University of Oklahoma Press, 1951.

Sapir, "Social Organization of Coast"
Edward Sapir, "The Social Organization of the West Coast Tribes," *Proceedings and Transactions of the Royal Society of Canada—Third Series—Vol. IX. Meeting of May 1915: Transactions Section II* (1915): 355-74.

Saskatchewan Journals
Saskatchewan Journals and Correspondence: Edmonton House 1795–1800; Chesterfield House 1800–1802. Alice M. Johnson, ed. London: Hudson's Bay Record Society, 1967.

Schilz, "Indian Middleman"
Thomas F. Schilz, "Indian Middlemen in the Northern Plains Fur Trade," *Montana: The Magazine of Western History* 40 (Winter 1990): 2-13.

Secoy, *Changing Military Patterns*
Frank Raymond Secoy, *Changing Military Patterns of the Great Plains Indians*. Lincoln: University of Nebraska Press, 1992.

Shapiro, "Kinship"
Judith Shapiro, "Kinship," in *Handbook* 2:620-29.

Simpson, *Journal*
George Simpson's Journal Entitled Remarks Connected with the Fur Trade in the Course of a Voyage from York Factory to Fort George and Back to York Factory 1824–25, in *Fur Trade and Empire: George Simpson's Journal Entitled Remarks Connected with the Fur Trade in the Course of a Voyage from York Factory to Fort George and Back to York Factory 1824–25*. Frederick Merk, ed. Rev. ed. Cambridge, Mass.: Harvard University Press, 1968, 3-360.

Simpson's 1828 Journey
Part of Dispatch from George Simpson Esqr Governor of Ruperts Land to the Governor & Committee of the Hudson's Bay Company London: March 1, 1829. Continued and Completed March 24 and June 5, 1829. E. E. Rich, ed. Toronto: Champlain Society, 1947.

Simpson's London Letters
London Correspondence Inward from Sir George Simpson 1841–42. Glyndwr Williams, ed. London: Hudson's Bay Record Society, 1973.

Simpson, *Simpson*
Alexander Simpson, *The Life and Travels of Thomas Simpson, The Arctic Discoverer*. London: Richard Bentley, 1845.

Skinner, *Adventurers of Oregon*
Constance L. Skinner, *Adventurers of Oregon: A Chronicle of the Fur Trade*. New Haven: Yale University Press, 1920.

South Carolina Council Journal
Manuscript. South Carolina State Archives.

Spier, "Kinship Systems"
Leslie Spier, "The Distribution of Kinship Systems in North America," in *University of Washington Publications in Anthropology*, vol. 1, no. 2. Seattle: University of Washington Press, 1925, 69-88.

Spier and Sapir, "Wishram Ethnography"
Leslie Spier and Edward Sapir, "Wishram Ethnography," *University of Washington Publications in Anthropology* vol. 3, no. 3. Seattle: University of Washington Press, 1930, 151-300.

Stern, *Chiefs and Traders*
Theodore Stern, *Chiefs & Chief Traders: Indian Relations at Fort Nez Perces, 1818–1855*. Corvallis: Oregon State University Press, 1993.

Steward, "Shoshonean"
Julian H. Steward, "The Great Basin Shoshonean Indians," in Roger C. Owen, James J. F. Deetz, and Anthony Fisher, *The North American Indians: A Sourcebook*. New York: Macmillan, 1967, 241-59.

Stuart, "Narratives"
Robert Stuart, "Narratives," in *The Discovery of the Oregon Trail: Robert Stuart's Narratives of his Overland Trip Eastward from Astoria in 1812–13. From the Original Manuscripts in the Collection of William Robertson Coe, Esq*. Philip Ashton Rollins, ed. New York: Charles Scribner's Sons, 1935.

Sunder, *Pilcher*
John E. Sunder, *Joshua Pilcher, Fur Trader and Indian Agent*. Norman: University of Oklahoma Press, 1968.

Sutherland, *Edmonton Journal*
George Sutherland, *A Journal of Transactions at Edmonton House*, in *Saskatchewan Journals*, 63-97.

Swagerty, "Marriage and Settlement Patterns"
William R. Swagerty, "Marriage and Settlement Patterns of Rocky Mountain Trappers and Traders," *Western Historical Quarterly* 11 (April 1980): 159-80.

Swagerty, "View from Bottom"
William R. Swagerty, "A View from the Bottom Up: The Work Force of the American Fur Company on the Upper Missouri in the 1830s," *Montana: The Magazine of Western History* 43 (Winter 1993): 18-33.

Tanner, *Narrative*

A Narrative of the Captivity and Adventures of John Tanner, (U.S. Interpreter at the Saut de Ste Marie,) During Thirty Year Residence Among the Indians in the Interior of North America. Edwin James, ed. New York: G. H. & C. Carvill, 1830. Reprint. Minneapolis, Minn.: Ross & Haines, 1956.

Teit, "Middle Columbia Salish"

James H. Teit, "The Middle Columbia Salish." Franz Boas, ed. *University of Washington Publications in Anthropology* vol. 2, no. 4. Seattle: University of Washington Press, 1928, 83-128.

Thompson, *Narrative*

David Thompson's Narrative of his Explorations in Western America 1784–1812. J. B. Tyrrell, ed. Toronto: Champlain Society, 1916.

Thompson, *Travels*

David Thompson, *Travels in Western North America, 1784–1812*. Victor G. Hopwood, ed. Toronto: Macmillan of Canada, 1971.

Tod, "Scotch Boy"

John Tod, "Career of a Scotch Boy Who Became Hon. John Tod," *British Columbia Historical Quarterly* 18 (1954): 134-238.

Tomison, *Hudson Journal*

William Tomison, *A Journal of the most remarkable Transactions and Occurrences from York Fort to Cumberland House and from thence to Hudson House from 28th July 1779 to 29th January 1780*, in *Cumberland Journals*, 59-86.

Tout, "Ethnology"

Charles Hill Tout, "Report on the Ethnology of the Okanaken of British Columbia and Interior Division of the Salish Stock," *Journal of the Royal Anthropological Institute of Great Britain and Ireland* 41 (1911): 130-61.

Travels of Jedediah Smith

The Travels of Jedediah Smith: A Documentary Outline including the Journal of the Great American Pathfinder. Maurice S. Sullivan, ed. Santa Ana, Calif.: Fine Arts Press, 1934.

Truteau, "Journal"

J. B. Truteau, "Journal," in *Before Lewis and Clark*, 259-311.

Van Kirk, *Many Tender Ties*

Sylvia Van Kirk, *Many Tender Ties: Women in Fur-Trade Society, 1670–1870*. Norman: University of Oklahoma Press, 1980.

Vestal, *Joe Meek*
Stanley Vestal, *Joe Meek the Merry Mountain Man: A Biography*. Lincoln: University of Nebraska Press, 1963.

Washburn, "Symbol and Aesthetics"
Wilcomb E. Washburn, "*Symbol*, *Utility*, and *Aesthetics* in the Indian Fur Trade," *Minnesota History* 40 (Winter 1966): 198-202.

Watson, "Hudson's Bay Explorers"
Robert Watson, "Hudson's Bay Company Explorers: Chief Factor Samuel Black," *The Beaver* (June 1928): 10-12.

Weber, *Californios v. Smith*
David J. Weber, *The Californios versus Jedediah Smith 1826–1827: A New Cache of Documents*. Spokane, Wash.: Arthur H. Clark, 1990.

Wentzel, "Letters"
W. F. Wentzel, "Letters to the Hon. Roderic McKenzie 1807–1824," in Masson, *Les Bourgeois* 1:67-153.

West of Ashley
The West of William H. Ashley: The International Struggle for the Fur Trade of the Missouri, the Rocky Mountains, and the Columbia, with Explorations Beyond the Continental Divide, Recorded in the Diaries and Letters of William H. Ashley and his Contemporaries 1822–1838. Dale L. Morgan, ed. Denver, Colo.: Old West Publishing, 1964.

White, *Middle Ground*
Richard White, *The Middle Ground: Indians, Empires, and Republics in the Great Lakes Region, 1650–1815*. New York: Cambridge University Press, 1991.

White, "What Chigabe Knew"
Richard White, "What Chigabe Knew: Indians, Household Government, and the State," *William and Mary Quarterly* 52 (January 1995): 151-56.

Work, *California Journal*
Fur Brigade to the Bonaventura: John Work's California Expedition 1832–1833 for the Hudson's Bay Company. Alice Bay Maloney, ed. San Francisco: California Historical Society, 1945.

Wyeth, *Correspondence and Journals*
The Correspondence and Journals of Nathaniel J. Wyeth 1831–6. F. G. Young, ed. Sources of the History of Oregon 1: pts. 3-6. Eugene: Oregon University Press, 1899.

Index

Index prepared by Barbara Wilcie Kern with the assistance of R. B. Bernstein